IBSEN'S HOUSES

Henrik Ibsen's plays came at a pivotal moment in late nineteenth-century European modernity. They engaged his public through a strategic use of metaphors of house and home, which resonated with experiences of displacement, philosophical homelessness, and exile. The most famous of these metaphors – embodied by the titles of his plays *A Doll's House*, *Pillars of Society*, and *The Master Builder* – have entered into mainstream Western thought in ways that mask the full force of the reversals Ibsen performed on notions of architectural space. Analyzing literary and performance-related reception materials from Ibsen's lifetime, Mark Sandberg concentrates on the interior dramas of the playwright's prose-play cycle, drawing also on his selected poems. Sandberg's close readings of texts and cultural commentary present the immediate context of the plays, provide new perspectives on them for international readers, and reveal how Ibsen became a master of the modern uncanny.

MARK B. SANDBERG holds the position of Professor, jointly appointed in the Department of Scandinavian and the Department of Film and Media at the University of California, Berkeley. He is currently President of the Ibsen Society of America and a member of the International Ibsen Committee, and is also a past President of the Society for the Advancement of Scandinavian Study. His research focuses on late nineteenth- and early twentieth-century visual culture, including work in theater history, early cinema, paracinematic media and entertainment, and Scandinavian cultural history. He is the author of *Living Pictures, Missing Persons: Mannequins, Museums, and Modernity* (2003) and numerous articles on international silent film, the plays of Henrik Ibsen, and other topics in Scandinavian literary and cultural history.

IBSEN'S HOUSES
Architectural Metaphor and the Modern Uncanny

MARK B. SANDBERG

University of California, Berkeley

CAMBRIDGE
UNIVERSITY PRESS

University Printing House, Cambridge CB2 8BS, United Kingdom

One Liberty Plaza, 20th Floor, New York, NY 10006, USA

477 Williamstown Road, Port Melbourne, VIC 3207, Australia

314–321, 3rd Floor, Plot 3, Splendor Forum, Jasola District Centre, New Delhi-110025, India

79 Anson Road, #06-04/06, Singapore 079906

Cambridge University Press is part of the University of Cambridge.

It furthers the University's mission by disseminating knowledge in the pursuit of education, learning and research at the highest international levels of excellence.

www.cambridge.org
Information on this title: www.cambridge.org/9781108458108

© Mark B. Sandberg 2015

This publication is in copyright. Subject to statutory exception and to the provisions of relevant collective licensing agreements, no reproduction of any part may take place without the written permission of Cambridge University Press.

First published 2015
First paperback edition 2018

A catalogue record for this publication is available from the British Library

Library of Congress Cataloging in Publication data
Sandberg, Mark B., 1958–
Ibsen's houses : architectural metaphor and the modern uncanny / Mark B. Sandberg, University of California, Berkeley.
pages cm
Includes bibliographical references and index.
ISBN 978-1-107-03392-4 (hardback)
1. Ibsen, Henrik, 1828–1906 – Criticism and interpretation. 2. Space (Architecture) in literature. 3. Metaphor in literature. I. Title.
PT8895.S27 2015
839.822′6–dc23
2014050257

ISBN 978-1-107-03392-4 Hardback
ISBN 978-1-108-45810-8 Paperback

Cambridge University Press has no responsibility for the persistence or accuracy of URLs for external or third-party internet websites referred to in this publication, and does not guarantee that any content on such websites is, or will remain, accurate or appropriate.

Contents

List of figures	*page* vi
Acknowledgments	viii
Note on the text	x
Introduction	1
1 Ibsen's uncanny	18
Ibsen's unhomely	20
The lure of *hygge*	25
Christmas *hygge*	35
"The master of *uhygge*"	44
2 Façades unmasked	56
The model home	60
Doll housing	68
3 Home and house	85
True homes	87
Mere homes	103
Marginal occupants	115
The resilience of home	122
4 The tenacity of architecture	130
Ownership disputes	134
Brand's church	146
Renovation and razing	153
An architecture of forgetting	168
Conclusion	176
Notes	191
Bibliography	215
Index	223

Figures

1 The tarantella disrupts the *hyggelig* Christmas scene in Act Two of *A Doll House*. Production: Christiania Theater, prem. January 20, 1880. Source: Illustration from *Ny Illustreret Tidende* 7 (8 February 1880), p. 60. Owner: National Library of Norway. Artist: Olaf Jørgensen. 33
2 Agnes giving away the last scrap of children's clothing in *Brand*, Act Four. Production: Nya Teatern (Stockholm), prem. March 24, 1885. Source: *Ny Illustrerad Tidning* 15 (April 11, 1885), p. 124. Owner: National Library of Norway. Artist: Vicke Andrén. 43
3 Studio photograph of August Lindberg as Osvald and Hedvig Winterhjelm as Mrs. Alving in *Ghosts*. Production: August Lindberg Scandinavian touring production, August 1883–May 1884. Owner: Theater Collection, National Library of Norway. Photographer: Unknown. 48
4 Hedvig's body is carried out from the attic in the final scene of *The Wild Duck*. Production: Christiania Theater, prem. January 11, 1885. Source: *Ny Illustreret Tidende* 12 (5 April 1885), p. 109. Owner: National Library of Norway. Artist: A. Jensen. 52
5 Set photograph from a later production of *The Wild Duck*. Production: National Theater (Oslo), prem. March 16, 1904. Source: Norwegian Folk Museum. Photographer: Anders Beer Wilse. 53
6 Act Two of *Pillars of Society*. Production: Royal Theater (Copenhagen), prem. November 18, 1877. Source: *Illustreret Tidende* 19 (November 25, 1877), p. 82. Owner: National Library of Norway. Artist: Knud Gamborg. 63
7 *Dukkestue* used in the Norwegian Folk Museum's display of "The Doll's House 1879" interior in the *Wessels gate 15* exhibit. Dollhouse created by a watchmaker in Kristiansand in the 1860s. Dimensions: H 53.5" × W 34.5" × D 15". Source: Norwegian Folk Museum. Photographer: Anne-Lise Reinsfelt. 73

List of figures

8 Swedish *dockskåp* from the 1860s–70s, from the display of dollhouses at the Nordic Museum. Dimensions: H 50" × W 44" × D 14.5". Source: Nordic Museum (Stockholm). Photographer: Peter Segemark. 75

9 Set design from the final act of *An Enemy of the People*. Production: National Theater (Oslo), prem. September 2, 1899. Source: Norwegian Folk Museum. Photographer: Anders Beer Wilse, 1906. 92

10 From Act Four of *The Wild Duck*. Production: Royal Theater (Copenhagen), prem. February 22, 1885. Source: *Illustreret Tidende* 26 (March 1, 1885), p. 286; Owner: The Royal Library (Copenhagen). Artist: Tom Petersen. 99

11 From Act Two of *Little Eyolf*. Production: Christiania Theater, prem. January 15, 1895. Source: *Tyrihans* 4 (January 25, 1895), p. 38. Owner: National Library of Norway. Artist: Unknown. 106

12 Betty Hennings as Nora, newly dressed as a traveler in Act Three. Production: Royal Theater (Copenhagen), prem. December 22, 1879. Source: *Ude og Hjemme* 3.119 (January 11, 1880), p. 160. Owner: National Library of Norway. Artist: Erik Henningsen. 120

13 Betty Hennings posed in a studio actress portrait as Hilde Wangel in hiking clothes, as described in Act Two of *The Master Builder*. Production: Royal Theater (Copenhagen), prem. March 8, 1893. Owner: Theater Collection, National Library of Norway. (Photo is likely not original to the Daniel George Nyblin studio, whose photo frame surrounds the image.) 121

14 The Pillar of Shame erected for Corfitz Ulfeldt (1664/1728). Located at The National Museum of Denmark (Copenhagen). Author photo. 173

15 Close-up of the base of the Pillar of Shame. Author photo. 174

16 Henry Provensal, *La Maison de Solness le Constructeur* (1902) (RF 2005 6) Paris, Musée d"Orsay, acquired in 2005. Oil on canvas, 110 cm × 91.5 cm. Courtesy of Musée D'Orsay, Paris. 187

Acknowledgments

It has been a privilege in working on this book to have such an interesting ongoing conversation with so many insightful colleagues, talented researchers, and skilled librarians working within the field of Ibsen studies. I have received significant support from the Centre for Ibsen Studies in Oslo from the very beginning research phase of this project, and my thanks go to those who hosted me there during on-site visits (especially Frode Helland and Astrid Sæther) and to the center's friendly and knowledgable librarians, Mária Faskerti and Randi Meyer, who gave me access to their substantial resources while I was there and fielded my follow-up questions about materials from abroad. Parallel to the life-span of this project, there was also a really remarkable expansion of resources for Ibsen studies overall, surely one of the most impressive in any author-based field of research. A new critical edition of Ibsen's complete works appeared both in print and online; the Ibsen Centre's extensive online bibliography of secondary literature continued to be developed; and under the capable guidance of Jens-Morten Hansen at the National Library in Oslo, the Ibsen website project (http://ibsen.nb.no) has developed into what now is surely one of the most ambitious repertoire, manuscript, and reception resources for the study of any world author. All of this has been an embarrassment of riches for researchers, and when I say that this project would not have been possible in the way I have done it without this rapidly developing and remarkable infrastructure, it is not the least bit hyperbolic. New kinds of intellectual overview and synthesis have been made possible by these powerful research tools, and my thanks go out to all of those in Norway who have worked so diligently to bring these initiatives to completion.

In addition to these material and digital resources, personal conversations were of course crucial to the development of my thinking as well. I am especially grateful to those who read this manuscript at different stages and commented so carefully on it, including Karin Sanders, Joan Templeton, Lisbeth P. Wærp, and Linda Rugg. Anonymous reviewers have also provided valuable feedback, as have many other colleagues who have given their reactions to various presentations and intermediate written versions of this material along the way, including Narve Fulsås and others. Thanks go also to my Berkeley colleagues Karin Sanders and Anne Nesbet for cheerleading at a particularly difficult and crucial time. I am also grateful for the input of my Berkeley students to ongoing conversations about Ibsen in my classrooms, at both the undergraduate and graduate levels.

In researching the images for this book, I received special help on the Scandinavian history of dollhouses from Erika Ravne Scott, curator of the toy collection at the Norwegian Folk Museum, and from Ulf Hamilton at the Nordic Museum in Stockholm. It was a pleasure to be working with such knowledgable museum professionals again in connection with this book, as I had done earlier on other projects. Trine Næss at the National Library in Oslo took the time to discuss the particulars of relevant pictures in its Ibsen-related theater collection and was a valuable source of information.

Portions of this manuscript rework and expand materials previously published elsewhere, though in substantially different form. These articles include "The Architecture of Forgetting," *Ibsen Studies* 7.1 (2007), 4–21; "Doll Housing," in Sanda Tomescu (ed.), *Henrik Ibsen*, special issue of *Studia Universitatis Babes-Bolyai, Philologia* (Cluj, Romania; November 2006), 53–60; and "Ibsen and the Mimetic Home of Modernity," *Ibsen Studies* 2 (Spring 2001), 32–58.

My thanks go also to my sons, remarkable individuals all, who have grown into adulthood along with this book. All along the way, they have enriched my thinking about house and home and provided me with good reasons to argue back from experience against Ibsen's deep skepticism of domestic life, while still appreciating the need for new forms of living to develop with each generation. And finally, my deepest appreciation goes to Betts for her patience, good humor, and compassion; our own common adventure in "home making" has given me the leverage I needed to work on this topic.

Preliminary note to text

There are two authoritative editions of Ibsen's writings, the *Samlede Verker* edition (the so-called *Hundreårsutgave*, or Centenary Edition), published in 1928–57, and the more recent comprehensive *Henrik Ibsens Skrifter* (Henrik Ibsen's Writings), published by Aschehoug in collaboration with the University of Oslo in 2005–10. The latter is used here as the default source for cited material from Ibsen's plays, poems, and letters and is the platform used for my translations into English as well. Since the references to *Henrik Ibsens Skrifter* are frequent, they will be abbreviated as "*HIS*" with volume and page number in both the notes and the bibliography. Moreover, since each volume comes in two parts, one for text and one for commentary, that information will be indicated as well (e.g., as 7.1 or 7.2). The earlier *Hundreårsutgave* edition of Ibsen's works has not been made obsolete by the new critical edition, however, and individual volumes will occasionally be cited here in shortened references, especially for information about play drafts and for textual and historical commentary at appropriate junctures.

Because of space considerations, it is not possible to provide full original citation material in Norwegian, the other Scandinavian languages, and German throughout the main text. However, since the argument here often revolves around nuance of usage and repeated patterns of discourse and metaphor, there are many moments where original terminology is essential and has been provided in brackets or in footnotes as a courtesy to those familiar with those languages. This seems especially important when the primary-source material might be less familiar. I have tried to keep interruptions of this sort to a minimum to facilitate reading flow, but I see some original language as necessary to the project.

Introduction

In the fall of 1877, just after Ibsen had published his contemporary prose drama *Pillars of Society*, his fellow Norwegian writer Arne Garborg wrote this critical response in a weekly periodical:

> He has torn down (been "negative") without building up ... Anyone can tear down, even if not as successfully as Ibsen has; but to build up, which is needed much more – there are few who can do that, Ibsen included. It is a bad sign when a young nation not even close to finishing its social edifice [*Samfundsbyggverket*] gets razers before builders, as we seem to have done with this Ibsen.[1]

Garborg's nationalist critique was essentially this: Ibsen cannot build something lasting for Norway because he can only pose questions and express doubts; he cannot come up with the constructive answers that distinguish truly great authors. By invoking this commonplace metaphor equating building with positive action (i.e., "builders of the nation"), Garborg taps into a long-standing discourse of architectural thought that enables his criticism of Ibsen's negativity. Ibsen, he implies, is a Master Razer, not a Master Builder. According to this seemingly inherently persuasive metaphorical system, consensus and positive social engagement (especially of the nationalist variety) resemble a construction project, while doubts and critiques are like demolition.

Granted, when Garborg gets past his initial complaint and actually reviews *Pillars of Society* in this article, he wonders if this new play might be different: "It is as if Ibsen were tired of all the tearing down now and wanted to try building instead." In historical retrospect, those who know Ibsen's work might be surprised to find that in 1877, before writing any of the prose plays in which he would most famously devastate the "social edifice," he had already developed a reputation among his Norwegian compatriots as a "razer." One might be equally amused by Garborg's obliviousness at this early point of just how severe Ibsen's socio-architectural skepticism would become in the following plays. Even with the full benefits of historical hindsight, however, one might nevertheless find Garborg to be justified in his eventual conclusion about this particular play – namely, that when Ibsen backs away from his usual demolition project, he generally has less interesting ideas to offer, no matter how one feels about the targets of his relentless dismantling. If *Pillars of Society* was an attempt to build, Garborg suggests, its solutions were too tame and routine. In Garborg's view, what Ibsen was best at – unfortunately – was pure destruction.

Critiques of this sort only intensified after the publication of Ibsen's next two plays, in which the central architectural metaphor of *Pillars of Society* – society as an edifice – continues prominently. *A Doll House* (1879) and *Ghosts* (1881) both elicited similar critiques across the Nordic region, as this Swedish response to *Ghosts* makes clear: "Many complain that the representatives of the new ideas tear everything down without managing to put anything in its place, and Ibsen especially has been the object of this kind of reproach."[2] A German review from 1908 joked that the North had produced two dynamite specialists, Alfred Nobel and Henrik Ibsen.[3] Another Swede dubbed Ibsen's writing "Nordic nihilism" because of his relentless and exclusive pursuit of questions intended to pull back "the covering of habit and everyday language from the abyss that they hide."[4] Similarly, a particularly prescient Swedish review of Ibsen's *Rosmersholm* (1886) described reader anticipation in this way, inadvertently predicting the later central metaphor of *The Master Builder* (1892): "Each of his new works in recent years has been anticipated in our country with a certain anxious trembling. What new crack in our social building [*samhällsbygnad*] will he reveal this time?"[5] Again and again, Ibsen's contemporaries spoke the language of architectural metaphor in their defense of society's *foundations*, its *edifice*, and its *homes*.

Ibsen himself, it should be noted, framed the discussion that way by relying consistently on building imagery in his writing. One can start with the overtly architectural titles of several of the plays: *Pillars of Society*, *A Doll House*, and *The Master Builder* are only the most obvious examples. A persistent and foregrounded attention to the peculiar properties of built structures pervades his other prose plays as well, even if not advertised so directly in their titles: the Rosenvold villa and its accompanying memorial building project in *Ghosts* spring to mind, as does the theatrical attic space in *The Wild Duck* (1884). One might add to the list of unusual imagined structures a hybrid modern-Gothic haunted house (*Rosmersholm*); a starkly territorial house and garden (*The Lady from the Sea*, 1888); an overly mortgaged, accidentally occupied villa (*Hedda Gabler*, 1890); a two-story house with strictly segregated living space (*John Gabriel Borkman*, 1896); and a ramshackle hunting shack that is claimed to be a castle (*When We Dead Awaken*, 1899). Ibsen's use of architectural tropes precedes his prose plays as well: the early play *Brand* (1866) devotes considerable attention to figurations of home and to the main character's church-building project, and *Peer Gynt* (1867) can be seen as one long evaluation of the resonances of "home" and "abroad," ranging from the idealized cottage where the faithful Solveig waits to the asylum in Egypt where Peer is crowned king of the lunatics.

In all of these plays, Ibsen foregrounds the qualities of built structures beyond what is minimally necessary for any drama to "take place," which is to provide a physical set. In a limited sense, of course, the realization of written dramas on stage is always architectural, concerned as it is with the interaction of bodies in articulated space and with the representation of built environments. Ibsen's architectural imagination exceeds the rudimentary requirements of theater, however; his dramas call attention to themselves both meta-theatrically and meta-architecturally. One finds the same insistent attention to architecture in many of his poems as well, which bear titles such as "Building Plans," "A Church," and "The School House" and explore pervasive themes about national edifices, burned houses, ruins, suddenly estranged interiors, and lost homelands.

Significantly, when Ibsen composed his only (fragmentary) attempt at autobiography in the early 1880s, he narrated his earliest memories as a dawning phenomenological interaction with the buildings of his hometown, Skien, Norway. His entry into consciousness was strikingly framed on all sides by built structures; after describing the spatial relationships of all of the buildings surrounding his first home near the marketplace in Skien, Ibsen wrote: "This perspective was thus the first view of the world that presented itself to my eyes. Architecture everywhere [*Altsammen arkitektur*]; nothing green; no open rural landscape."[6] The date of this composition is significant, coming as it did just after his most celebrated theatrical critique of architecture's confining qualities, the 1879 *A Doll House*, had taken Europe by storm. He was also in the midst of composing *Ghosts*, which carries out its own relentless destruction of an elaborate building project. "Architecture everywhere" could well serve as the guiding compositional principle throughout Ibsen's career – this particular "Nordic nihilist" remained in the grip of an unusually lively architectural imagination throughout his life. For most of his career, despite his notorious desire to "gladly put a torpedo under the Ark" as he expressed it in his most revolutionary poem,[7] it is probably more accurate to say that his work remained poised on the threshold to the void; no matter how powerful the critique of the structured interior and all that it represents, he never abandoned his fundamental socio-architectural questions, even in the seeming negation thereof. Late in his life, he famously identified strongly with the metaphor of the master builder when he told the Norwegian painter Erik Werenskiold in 1895 that he was not only interested in architecture but that it was in fact his profession.[8]

This book examines the architectural imagery and accompanying thought structures in the discourse generated by Ibsen and his immediate commentators during his lifetime, with a special emphasis on discussion within the three Scandinavian countries. It seeks to investigate the expression of a persistent interest in architecture in that increasingly influential public discussion. Ibsen's position at the cusp of modernity is one fruitful area in which to seek explanations, since architecture's durational qualities make it a powerful symbol of intransigent tradition. The shifting attitudes toward family, sexuality, and gender are another, since theatrical figuration of the home can concentrate these issues with a spatial and material immediacy. Ibsen's voluntary separation from his Norwegian homeland for the twenty-seven years he lived in Italy and Germany between 1864 and 1891 is yet another explanatory rubric, since his double vision of "home" from his memories of Norway and his life in continental Europe endows his architectural imagination with the extra cultural and political resonances of a lost homeland as well.

Ibsen's attraction to the figuration of built structures should be seen as part of a more general "thickening" of architectural metaphor in late nineteenth-century Western culture and literature. He was not the only writer with a particular interest in houses; one might equally turn to any number of other writers for whom built structure was anything but a simple and transparent setting for action: E. T. A. Hoffmann, Edgar Allan Poe, Nathaniel Hawthorne, Honoré de Balzac, Charles Dickens, Henry James, George Bernard Shaw, and August Strindberg spring immediately to mind as examples of writers for whom architecture takes on special emphasis and agency. The variety of that list, however, ranging as it does from Gothic haunted houses to Victorian hearths to proto-modernist ruins, is the best argument for a sustained and careful study of individual cases and authorships, with Ibsen's drama landing in the heart of the question as one of the most sustained career explorations of architectural metaphor.

Take, for instance, the sense of paradox conveyed in Ibsen's poem "A Church" (1865), a poem that the influential Danish critic Georg Brandes unfortunately singled out as "flawed and expendible" in his review of Ibsen's poetry collection in 1871.[9] While the three simple five-line stanzas might leave something to be desired from a purely aesthetic standpoint, the poem nevertheless communicates an interesting architectural idea about the simultaneity of constructive and deconstructive forces (my English translation is intentionally literal here):

> The king built
> all the day long.
> When night fell,
> the troll came and undid it
> with pike and pole.
>
> Thus rose the church
> to the top of the spire;
> but the king's work
> and the troll's prying
> produced a double style.
>
> Everyday people moved in
> trusting, even so;
> because the day's accomplishments,
> taken with those of the night,
> are of course those of a full day.[10]

The final stanza, which depends on a double meaning in the Norwegian, requires a bit of linguistic explanation. The word *døgn* (the "full day" of the final line) denotes any twenty-four-hour period, the combination of day and night, but *Døgn-folk* (translated here as "everyday people") conveys the notion of people who live day to day, not looking beyond the immediate context. The dictionary definition of *Døgn-folk* in the *Riksmålsordbok* underscores this sense: "people who merely live in and have a sense for the small events of the here-and-now and daily life."[11] Although one can imagine ways in which another writer might turn this lack of concern for the future into a more positive image, in Ibsen's hands it is no better than neutral in valence.[12] The point of the double meaning seems to be that people living for the present moment, *døgn-folk* who are unconcerned with the past or the future, would be unbothered by the "double style" of a church that was built by a king during the day and taken apart again by a troll at night, because the day and night together make up both parts of the twenty-four-hour *døgn*.[13] *Døgn*-people get a *døgn*-church.

Still, the *døgn*-church is clearly the more interesting part of this little poetic joke, made at the expense of the oblivious people worshipping there. The reader is allowed to see what the short-sighted crowd does not: that the church was created by a process of simultaneous construction and demolition, that the earnest, productive work of the king and the mischievous poking and prodding of the troll have both contributed to the church's eventual character and style. By extrapolating more generally from the poem, one can discern a claim that artistic creation requires a balance of both kingly and trollish forces. This is the point made by Nina S. Alnæs in her reading of the poem's folkloric content:

> The dark, the troll, or the demonic forces are thus closely tied to creative powers in existence. Even when the king builds a sacred house to the glory of God, evil powers mix themselves in and want to exert influence in their own way, to place their mark on the results ... The troll's "prodding" has given the building a "double style," a disharmony. But in this lies a virtue as well; the result becomes more exciting. An Ibsenian aesthetic therefore lies concealed in this little poem.[14]

Like the troll, Ibsen was not averse to "working the night shift" in his writing projects; one might say that he was most interested in poking around with spikes and poles to test the integrity of the ideas and social structures around him. In this sense, Garborg and others were justified in seeing him as the Master Razer, the writer with a gift for tearing down. But the poem helps remind us as well that Ibsen was equally meticulous with structure and form "by day," also working like the king in the poem to build finely crafted, carefully constructed dramatic works.

His contemporaries repeatedly recognized these building skills as well; even the most vociferous critics of his so-called nihilistic world view often begrudgingly acknowledged the aesthetic achievements of his dramatic constructions. Indeed, the basic vocabulary of dramatic criticism at the time was itself inescapably architectural, emphasizing especially the "construction" and "design" of dramatic compositions. Though Ibsen's debt to the Scribian "well-made" or "well-wrought play" (*la pièce bien faite*) is often noted, it is perhaps worth emphasizing anew that the very formulation of that term reveals the assumed equivalence of play*wright* and builder in the late nineteenth century.

Manifestations of this assumption are frequent in assessments by Ibsen's contemporaries. One conservative reviewer of *Rosmersholm* wrote in 1886: "A dramatic work can be well built [*fint bygget*], and its knots well tied, without necessarily containing life's best thoughts."[15] The depiction of Ibsen's playwriting as an architectural pursuit was especially irresistible after the publication of *The Master Builder* in 1892, since that play's metaphoric world seemed quite clearly to equate the pursuits of a dramatist with those of an architect. A revival of *The Wild Duck* at the Christiania

Theater the following year elicited a reaction of both pain and admiration for Ibsen's unpleasant "building": "And every time one sees it, its clammy cheerlessness [*klamme Uhygge*] will engulf one more oppressively – to such a degree that at times it almost feels like a physical pain, – at the same time that one's admiration will grow for the artistic perfection with which the dramatic building [*den dramatiske Bygning*] is raised."[16] A commentary on *Little Eyolf* (1894) one year later continues the image:

> As one might expect, the great dramatist's most recent work is a new triumph for his unquestioned mastery. Here once again there is conjured up one of these monumental dramatic buildings [*dramatiske Bygværker*], whose pure architectonic perfection and strict symmetrical beauty would be enough to secure for them the entire world's enduring admiration.[17]

The dramatic world evoked in Ibsen's following play, *John Gabriel Borkman*, was also likened to a building, but one with a particularly sterile and cold design:

> Every stone in the building is in place; it rises before our eyes with the firm lines of a model building. There are no towers shooting to the skies, no golden wing reflecting the glowing sun, there is no bay window for tender words, no halls open to light and warmth. The building stands there, strong, heavy, in iron and stone – one of the modern buildings that society builds with dutiful care for its unhappy [members].[18]

The ease with which critics adopted this metaphoric register equating dramas and buildings, society and edifice, world view and architectural plan suggests that both Ibsen and his contemporary interlocutors were fluent in a discourse of architectural imagery. The basic metaphoric system was not in question for either side, no matter how intense the disagreement over ideas and philosophical content.

Interestingly, Ibsen's reputation for architectonic writing persists to this day, though after more than a century of modern drama and postmodern performance, the recognition of his plays' meticulous construction does not always count as a concession to his genius. Today, Ibsen is more likely to appear in dramatic criticism as the all-too-predictable play builder who relied dutifully on the same basic blueprint for most of his prose dramas: the retrospective, analytic, interior conversation drama. He is often placed in contrast to later, more formally experimental and versatile playwrights not locked quite so tightly into the model of "great reckonings in little rooms," to borrow a phrase from Bert O. States.[19] Ibsen's architectural sensibility has in this sense retrospectively become both his strength and his liability; his authorship represents one of the most thorough explorations of the architectural aspects of drama and society precisely because he masters the discourse so completely. But perhaps because we no longer inhabit this late nineteenth-century metaphoric system as fully native speakers, the stakes of the discussion are no longer so immediately apparent.

It is precisely this notion that Ibsen's particular form of architectural imagination might be dated, however, that creates the most productive argument for treating it as a richly historical phenomenon. "Dated" is intriguing for historians; it is a pejorative term only when framed by perspectives that demand constant novelty. One goal of this study is to blow some life into this notion of "Ibsen the architect," to show the complexity of his explorations, not only to allow his work to resonate more obviously with concerns today (exile, mobility, homelessness, etc.) but also to measure the distance between his situation and that of the current day. The temporal and cultural gaps, that is, can provide critical leverage and a sense of historical alterity that can bring today's tacit assumptions about house and home more clearly into view.

With this in mind, the present study charts the terrain of a nineteenth-century Ibsenian discourse in which architectural metaphors framed debates about modernization, individual liberty, and free thought. The fact that Ibsen framed these debates so consistently in terms of foundations, pillars, windows, façades, and slammed doors demonstrates the historical existence of a consensus point of departure: for all parties in the debate, society was assumed to be like a building. The burning question was what to do about it: Preserve it? Renovate it? Raze it to the ground? The method I pursue is an analysis of Ibsen's provocative use of architectural metaphor on the one hand and of the discourses of response that formed both consensus and eccentric reception positions on the other. The focus will be on selected prose plays (1877–99), with supplementary attention given to selected poems from Ibsen's only published collection (*Digte*, 1871) and to the dramatic poem *Brand* (1866).

The chapters are organized conceptually around thematic issues rather than thorough sequential readings of individual plays. This approach incurs some obvious costs; the integrity and specific dramatic arguments of individual works are necessarily put under pressure when one disperses material across a thematic argument, as I do. But the advantage of this approach is that a more synthetic critical assessment becomes possible, one whose insights will hopefully compensate for the violation of individual textual boundaries. Moreover, since my interest is in a discourse that in itself tended to see Ibsen's plays as a cumulative argument, frequently referencing earlier motifs and metaphors when reading his latest drama, it seems useful to approach analysis of the plays in the same way.

Guiding the discussion of metaphor will be several key concepts that have come out of the rich research on the topic in the field of linguistics over the past thirty years, which found an influential early articulation in the work of George Lakoff and Mark Johnson, especially the book *Metaphors We Live By*. In that pioneering work on conceptual metaphor from 1980, Lakoff and Johnson use as one of their more famous examples the metaphor "Theories (and arguments) are buildings." They note the frequency with which reference to an argument's foundations, structure, and strength or shakiness deploy metaphoric terminology that normally passes below the threshold of awareness but implictly posits a particular likeness between theories and buildings.[20] As they point out, a systematic approach to conceptual metaphor can help make one aware of the ways in which metaphoric relations both "highlight" and "hide" characteristics of the domains being compared, a dynamic that Zoltán Kövecses has summarized as "partial metaphorical utilization."[21]

Seen through this framework, the Ibsenian version of the society-as-building metaphor could be said to use society as a "target domain" and building as a "source domain." The source domain tends to be rich in a variety of concrete, embodied experiences and lived knowledge, from which only a certain partial subset is activated for the metaphoric comparison. The target domain is a more abstract concept that gains in legibility through the comparison. From this simple observation about partiality proceeds a series of productive analytic questions that guide my thinking in this study, all of which highlight the cultural motivations for making the comparison between society and building in the particular way that Ibsen and his commentators do.

For instance, the idea of "metaphoric entailment,"[22] as Kövecses describes it, would in the Ibsenian example involve the particular range of architectural experience available to his cultural interlocutors. On the one hand, the richness of the experience in this source domain would by definition necessarily have exceeded the particular qualities of "Ibsen's houses," since all metaphoric relationships are partial. On the other hand, the architectural experience of his Scandinavian interlocutors is nevertheless still culturally bounded; while his readers and viewers in late nineteenth-century Scandinavia would possibly have had historically and culturally specific experiences living in rural cottages, farmhouses, urban apartments, or villas, they would have had less familiarity with suburban tract housing, piazzas, skyscrapers, row houses, or any number of other possible architectural experiences of other times and places. The word "building" is thus at once more culturally extensive than Ibsen's particular imagining of it, yet importantly still culturally bounded in some ways.

Thinking systematically about metaphor also reveals a range of other possibilities for each of the compared terms. For example, if society is a building, what else is a building? I have already suggested that for many of Ibsen's commentators, his plays were also buildings. One can imagine other conventional metaphors in which a body is a building (with a foundation of good nutrition) or perhaps more specifically a mind (and its well-structured thought). Or to turn the analysis around, if society can be a building, what else can society plausibly be? It seems likely that many will recognize immediately that society can be a body (healthy or sick), or a machine (with its institutions as well-oiled parts), or a plant (when it grows and thrives). To put it in terms of systematic conceptual metaphor, each target domain can have other sources, and each source other targets.

Reminding oneself of the range of possible metaphoric relationships aids in understanding the full historical and cultural contingency of the society-as-building metaphor, but there is more this framework can contribute to the present discussion. The idea of utilization can also help one pose questions about exactly which aspects of buildings are activated in the "Ibsenian house" and which are neglected. As is shown throughout this study, the cultural discussion of Ibsen's plays that emphasizes architectural metaphor concentrates especially on façades, doors, floors, supporting pillars, and walls, but it is less interested in windows, roofs, stories, corridors, kitchens, bedrooms, cellars, or other possible features of the house. Lakoff and Johnson claim that some of this partiality in the "used" and "unused" part of the metaphor's source domain is simply a function of convention, but they imply that creative activation of neglected parts of a source domain, as often happens in literary use of metaphor, would be special cases worth investigation.[23]

The close rhetorical reading of Ibsen's prose plays and of his commentators reactions in what follows pursues the claim that Ibsen took the highly conventional metaphor of society-as-building and transformed its meaning in ways that called consensus values into question. Throughout Ibsen's writing, habitual ways of regarding house and home were undermined (proving the point that avoiding architectural metaphors of my own is difficult when making an argument) by a meticulous and deliberate investigation of the metaphors of "home" that tested their limits, extended their meanings, reversed their connotations, and delegitimized their cultural authority.

Ibsen accomplishes this in a way that has ensured his continued relevance across time and place. When Ibsen's characters discuss "home," there is an elasticity to the term that allows for projection of specific cultural meaning. Different readers and audiences read and hear that word differently, even today in cultures across the globe whose source domain of architectural experience is quite different from Ibsen's original context. Even in Ibsen's day, when he wrote about his home Norwegian culture from the distance of Italy or Germany, his metaphoric source domain had likely become wider than that of many of his readers or viewers, as he and his family had constantly shifted domiciles throughout his time abroad, as Astrid Sæther has observed in her biography of Suzannah Ibsen.[24] Through the ambiguities of the metaphorical relationship, its partial activation of source domain, and its extendability, Ibsen created a literature of home that functioned effectively in its original cultural-historical context but has also continued its resonance well beyond nineteenth-century Scandinavia. Key to his housing practice, in other words, are metaphor's essential ambiguities and transformational possibilities.

The themes that guide the following chapters are, in order, the concepts of hominess and the uncanny, the trope of unveiled façades, the conceptual relation between house and home, and the durational aspects of architecture. Chapter 1 begins with the ways that theories of the uncanny can be made relevant to Ibsen's works. The approach follows the critical lead of work that places emphasis on the "unhomely" aspects of the uncanny. It traces Ibsen's insistence on unsettling notions of domestic comfort, drawing on both textual and reception examples. Chapter 2 examines the rhetoric involved in unmasking façades, focusing primarily on *Pillars of Society* and *A Doll House*. In each case, I argue that the attention paid to the façade as a deceptive surface actually protects notions of a deeper authenticity that are revealed in the unmasking. Chapter 3 concerns Ibsen's strategic exploitation of the distinction between "house" and "home." Most central here is Ibsen's cumulative denigration of domesticity as an inferior, inherently deceptive form of existence. His assessment thereof shifts valence throughout his career, but the interest in unmasking domestic façades is constant. The fourth chapter deals with the perceived tenacity of architecture and the problems its persistence and duration pose for progressive thinking. Here, the discussion begins with *Ghosts* and *Rosmersholm* but also engages with other figurations of razing and renovation developed in *Brand* as alternative architectural relationships to the past. Taken together, these four main themes convey the predominant features of what we might call Ibsen's "architectural unease."

A critical articulation of that stance can be used to make sense of the response to Ibsen's plays by his contemporary commentators. Ibsen provoked a level of public discussion that was unprecedented, especially for a Norwegian author. At the height of Ibsen's prose-play production, both the publication and performances of his plays were reviewed immediately in multiple newspapers in Norway, throughout the Nordic countries, and in Europe as well. The quite general public furor and debate in response to plays such as *A Doll House* have been well documented in scholarship,[25] but it is equally important to emphasize that from that breakthrough play forward, the publication of almost every Ibsen text set off a similar flurry of reading, private discussions, and reviews, some of these appearing within a day or two of publication. The regular appearance of a new Ibsen play in the early winter of every second year through the 1880s and 90s created a surge of interest and anticipation each time, an experience of remarkable simultaneity that was instrumental in coalescing the literary cultures of the Nordic region. By the time *The Wild Duck* was published, there was even a public debate in Norwegian newspapers about the ways in which theater criticism had devolved into lightning journalism; the publication of an Ibsen play had become both a literary and a news event, with the lines between the two now uncomfortably blurred.[26] Judging from the tight clustering of printed reviews and the offhand comments therein about the anticipation and reactions of the reading public, it is clear that in the wake of each publication, the Nordic public turned a kind of collective attention to Ibsen and formed a more or less simultaneous reception community. As Ibsen's fame grew, the borders of that community expanded beyond the North as well.

The sense of an attentive public is especially clear from reviews of the first stage performances of Ibsen's plays as well, which at the height of his fame would often occur within just a few weeks of their publication and near-simultaneous translation into the other Nordic languages. For the purposes of the present study, the early experience of Ibsen's plays on stage is directly relevant to the development of a shared discourse of architectural metaphor. First, theater in performance is an inescapably architectural medium: phenomenological elements of lighting, scenography, and bodies in space all contribute to the resonance of "home" (the impression of belonging and inhabitation conveyed by the actors), and the connotations of existence outside the depicted world of the set serve as a constant contrast to the built world inside it. The Ibsen prose plays are meticulous in their construction of the offstage world through verbal reference, so an element of world building is always at work in this highly metonymic use of realistic stage space.²⁷ Members of the audience share that architectural space and, especially in the realistic theater, spectatorship can be understood as a mode of strongly vicarious inhabitation. For all of these reasons, considering the impact of plays in performance on Ibsen's contemporaries and the ways those audience impressions entered into the discourse of house and home that was generated by Ibsen's plays is essential to this project.

The reception of stage performance is also important conceptually speaking since metaphor as a cognitive structure often depends on bodily experience for its persuasive meaning, as was mentioned earlier. Since the rich lived experience with a source domain is so important to understanding how metaphor works, a consideration of theatrical metaphor demands that not all of the discussion remain on the textual level. Granted, it is not always possible to find good visual evidence of early Ibsen performances in Scandinavia (only a few sketches and set photographs survive from the period examined here), in part because photographic techniques of the time required exposure times too long to document performances as they were happening. Similarly, the genre of Scandinavian theater criticism at the time paid much more attention to recounting plot developments and evaluating acting performances than it did to scenographic description and analysis, so it was generally not the most architectural theater discourse I might have liked to have seen documented for a topic of this sort. These reviews, however, often did contain descriptions of audience behavior and general ambience in the theater, and reading between the lines one can sometimes discern reactions that would have come primarily from the stage and its visual, acoustic, and spatial effects. To the degree that it is possible to reconstruct through surviving visual evidence and critics' reports of audience reaction to the early Scandinavian productions of Ibsen's plays, that material will be included in the present study when it helps advance the argument about the nature of this shared architectural discourse.

It would be a mistake, however, to imagine for that historical period the kind of split between stage and page that sometimes exists in current academic theater studies. Ibsen himself was keen on characterizing his plays as books, and the line between readers and audience members was less important then than it is now. One finds frequent offhand comments by Scandinavian drama critics, for instance, about the theater audience's thorough familiarity with the play in question by the time they entered the theater, despite the short lag time between publication and performance in the Nordic countries. One reviewer of the premiere of *The Master Builder* in Copenhagen estimated that ninety-nine of one hundred audience members had already read the play by the time they saw the performance three months after its initial publication.[28] That same reporter notes that the character Hilde Wangel's catchphrase "harps in the air" (*Harper i Luften*) had entered into Copenhagen street slang well before the play appeared on stage, simply from public awareness of Ibsen's new play. The many similar comments give a collective sense of a dynamic, simultaneous literary and theatrical reception and discussion. This audience experience had a suprisingly durative aspect as well, since many Ibsen productions (*A Doll House* in particular) stayed in repertory performance for many years after their premiere dates. In a similar fashion, many of his plays were continually republished in new editions during his lifetime, so the reception of his plays achieved a sense of simultaneity and overlap as his fame grew. The plays continued their constant input to a dramatic-architectural discourse throughout the span of their publication and performance history, and not just at the initial moment of publication or premiere.

In this rich discourse of public reaction to both the publication and performance of Ibsen's plays, it is noteworthy how often the discussions relied on "foundational" architectural metaphors. The particular nature of Ibsen's provocation, that is, seemed to "hit home" in both a literal and metaphorical sense for readers and audience members, often putting pressure on their most basic shared assumptions. When Nora slammed the door on Torvald, it was not just the fate of two characters that hung in the balance; it seemed as if comfort, security, and familial warmth were all at stake, and the public response was at some level almost instinctively defensive. As one Swedish writer put it in response to *Rosmersholm* in 1887: "But his works have consistently awakened interest and discomfort. Especially since *A Doll House* one has with respect to his works felt compelled to defend one's own house and home. It has been *us* he has attacked – our customs, our views, our society."[29] Indeed, throughout his career, Ibsen can be seen as reversing the semantic field of some of the most intuitive, commonly accepted architectural notions: he shifted "coziness" from connotations of warmth and security to those of temptation away from the artistic calling; "home" from connotations of shelter and refuge to those of confinement and claustrophobia; "memorial" from veneration and commemoration to deceptive distortion; and "foundation" from a sense of secure grounding to that of unimaginative, static inflexibility. These were all notions that had been left mostly unchallenged by previous writers, especially in Norway, so that when Ibsen began his relentless counterintuitive revision of society's consensus metaphors, the protest and discomfort were almost immediate and reflexive.

Some reviewers commented directly on the discussion dynamic surrounding the play, such as this description of the Copenhagen public after the premiere performance of *A Doll House*: "And what did people say? Quite a bit! Between acts there was a lot of conversation; after the ending it was hardly possible to get out of the theater, given the way everyone was asking and answering questions, and the tearooms nearby were packed with groups conversing and discussing for a long time."[30] But even this kind of direct description leaves the content of these many discussions unspoken, tantalizingly out of reach; this same reporter continues on to say: "But I do not have the time or the ability or the right to expose the private circle to the public [*at føre den private Kreds ud for Offentligheden*], and I will only emphasize a few remarks."[31] It is the sum of these conversations in the "private circles" of the tearooms, the cafés, the clubs, the kitchens, the drawing rooms, and especially the bedrooms that would together comprise a more complete discourse of reaction to Ibsen's plays.

Although it is routine in Ibsen scholarship to refer to the *existence* of intense semipublic or private discussions surrounding the plays, this is by definition difficult to document and evaluate because the vast majority of these discussions were oral and ephemeral. From the oblique references to a more popular discourse that exist in reviews and lectures that reference the public discussion, it is probably safe to say that much of this discussion revolved around analysis of characters' motivation: Why would Nora leave her husband, and why would Mrs. Alving stay? Would readers and viewers behave in a similar fashion? One finds traces of this sort of popular discussion in Swedish feminist Sophie Adlersparre's public lecture on *Ghosts* in 1882, when she describes the opinions of those writing letters to the editors in Sweden about precisely this kind of character motivation, and she joins herself to those voices by pursuing the same.[32] This level of discourse probably comes closer to those private discussions than would an official review of a play.

It is likely that this kind of evaluation of character behavior dominated (as it often does now as well) public discussion of Ibsen's plays. The architectural discussion of Ibsen's plays during his lifetime was admittedly a specialty discourse, albeit one of the most interesting of the time. My primary evidence for reconstituting a portion of the architectural discourse generated by Ibsen's plays is the discussion that took place in the public forum of newspapers, magazines, and journals. This is a fairly professionalized level of response that conveys only part of the picture. And there are blind spots for both gender and class in this kind of discourse, since most of the journalists who had access to these public platforms were male and bourgeois. To be sure, there were occasional published articles by women (ranging from the liberal Norwegian writer Amalie Skram to more conservative, religious writers),[33] and left-leaning newspapers such as *Dagbladet* and *Social-Demokraten* eventually became quite regular in their reviews of Ibsen's plays; nevertheless, there is little question that most printed commentary came predominantly from a particular segment of society. One can triangulate from a normative response to more hidden responses, giving special critical attention to what these journalists report about public attitudes and comments. Likewise, offhand comments by reviewers in their plot summaries and assessments of dramatic character often provide inadvertent evidence of the tenor of the discourse. But there is no getting around the fact that when a reviewer writes that "all" of Christiania (Oslo) or Copenhagen was abuzz in discussion of Ibsen's latest play, one should picture a more limited circle of the culturally initiated.

For these reasons, I attempt throughout this study to subject the surviving, baseline discourse to the pressure of interpretive, critical analysis. The goals of my discourse sample are *not* merely descriptive; my approach differs from more traditional reception studies in that it does not seek to reconstitute an entire horizon of discourse or an accurate reproduction of the complete range of response. Instead, it samples different literary and theatrical circles, countries, and languages, always looking for the deployment of certain key critical terms or concepts. For practical reasons, it remains limited to about the first twenty years of reaction to the plays and centers mostly on the Scandinavian cultural context, since there is ample indication there that published newspaper accounts were part of a mutual, ongoing conversation.

Still, one might argue, this leaves a key component of the discussion in the "private circle" untouched, namely, the reaction of those for whom the stakes were in some sense the highest: women in the domestic sphere. Just as Ibsen's preparatory notes for *A Doll House* described "an exclusively masculine society, with laws written by men,"[34] the architectural debates of the late nineteenth-century literary criticism clearly convey preoccupations with structure and foundational social norms that tend to slant in masculine directions. It may be that the appeal of speaking in architectural metaphor lay precisely in its distance from the physical and social realities of women's daily lives – think of Gina Ekdal's bluntly literalist deflation of figurative speech in *The Wild Duck*[35] – and in this sense, the pervasiveness of a metaphoric discourse among male critics and journalists may be further evidence of a certain protective insulation and distance. There are, in other words, certain forms of privilege that allow the participants in this discourse, Ibsen included, to conduct the late nineteenth-century debate about house and home at a certain level of abstraction and remove from women's lived domestic experience. The fact remains, however, that these public arguments about the "social edifice" are the ones that have left the most retrievable forms of historical documentation. They are worth examining in detail in spite of the male bias, if only as a first step toward understanding the ways in which architectural thinking performed a more general social function in the late nineteenth century.

It is also possible to follow a trail of intertexts, as theater scholar Margareta Wirmark has done in tracing the reception dynamic that led outward from Ibsen's dramas into women's playwriting, literature, and politics throughout Scandinavia.[36] Rebecca Cameron has done similar work on Ibsen's influence on female playwrights in Britain.[37] Key to Wirmark's approach is developing the idea of "Nora's sisters" as a way of depicting the network of literary and dramatic production by women that came in response to Ibsen's *A Doll House* and other plays.[38] The production of intertexts among subsequent writers lies beyond the scope of the present study, however; instead, it will concentrate on a more detailed treatment of Ibsen's architectural provocations and their immediate published critical responses. Taken together, these two sides of a public conversation help map the contours of a historical discourse in which architectural metaphor served as a particularly potent node of figural energy. With both conservatives and revolutionaries alike resorting to talk of buildings, foundations, pillars, walls, façades, edifices, hearth, and home, it becomes clear in retrospect that the architectural imagination of the late nineteenth century is a key to understanding some of modernity's most central conflicts. Ibsen's recurring return to the architectural locates his writing at the nexus of these concerns.

CHAPTER I

Ibsen's uncanny

Ibsen's reputation as a master of social-realist dramas obscures a dynamic central to his authorship: he is also a master of the uncanny. This assessment will not strike all readers as immediately convincing, so the discussion in this chapter will lay both the theoretical and historical groundwork for that claim. The particular inflection of the uncanny put forward here will provide a framework for several of the later chapters, so it is important to make clear from the start the aspects of the voluminous literature on this subject that are most relevant. Direct applications of the uncanny to Ibsen's work have been fewer still, so my approach will also need some justification and explanation.

A survey of critical thinking on the uncanny by Nicholas Royle provides a glimpse into the wide range of topics now accepted as engaging with the phenomenon in some way. These include a "crisis of the proper," a "crisis of the natural," "a commingling of the familiar and the unfamiliar," a "strangeness of framing and borders, an experience of liminality," fears of dismemberment or loss of body parts, or the sudden perception of aspects of the self as foreign, to name just a few. These experiences of the uncanny, all of which are essentially varieties of decentering and uncertainty, are typically prompted by encounters with "curious coincidences," various kinds of "mechanical or automatic life," tokens of death, or remnants of the past experienced out of proper place and time.[1] In twentieth-century philosophy, the notion of the uncanny as "unsettling" experience has been especially productive and resonant for various thinking about the alienation of the subject, and Royle traces the precedents for his study through Marx, Nietzsche, Freud, Heidegger, and Wittgenstein.[2] Because the uncanny almost always involves the commingling of opposites and the dissolution of borders, it has proven to be an enormously elastic concept with wide resonance in critical theory.

As Royle points out, however, Freud's 1919 essay "Das Unheimliche" remains the touchstone articulation for theories of the uncanny, and that psychoanalytic exploration of the term has given the critical literature a certain structuring point of departure.[3] For Freud, it is the blurring of distinctions between the "familiar" and the "unfamiliar" that is most interesting, since that provides him with a powerful way to think about the process of repression. His argument proceeds etymologically from the fact that in German, the word *heimlich* has two strands of meaning, indicating on the one hand something that is secret and on the other something that is familiar. Although one can conceive of a way in which the two meanings might have overlapped at some point (something secret is kept private, "within the family," so "familiar" in that sense), in modern usage a tension exists between resonances pointing simultaneously toward "strange" secrets and "habitual" familiarity.

It is this layering of the root term that Freud finds so productive in his investigation of *das Unheimliche*, usually translated into English as "the uncanny." For him, something *unheimlich* is not merely the familiar made strange, but the revelation of a fundamental link between the two: the uncanny is a reappearance of something formerly familiar that has been made strange through the process of repression. It is a border phenomenon in which the usual distinctions between life and death, present and past, and the familiar and the strange fall away. Freud was especially intrigued by the idea that familiarity and estrangement might be joined at some common, primitive level, and that the rational division between the two might be more tenuously suspect than is often assumed: "Thus *heimlich* is a word the meaning of which develops in the direction of ambivalence, until it finally coincides with its opposite, *unheimlich*."[4]

The English translation of *das Unheimliche* as "the uncanny" slights one significant aspect of Freud's argument, namely the centrality of "home" to the concept. The word *heimlich* in German is not only used to denote a general sense of familiarity but also more specifically resonates with notions of domestic comfort, security, peace, and protection. Among the dictionary entries Freud cites in his essay are several that might be used synonymously with the English word "cozy."[5] To experience something as *unheimlich* is to lose the equivalent of that quiet interior and the protected domestic sphere, as well as to lose one's center in more extended senses. One finds oneself unsheltered and unprotected. Things become un*familiar*, which is another way of saying outside the family. If the sensation of *heimlichkeit* is one of cozy comfort and ease, then that of *unheimlichkeit* is one of unease. The fact that we might also use the term un*settled* is further indication that issues of domestication and possession are important to the resonance of the term.

An alternative trend in Anglo-American criticism has been to use the awkward neologism "unhomely" to translate *unheimlich* to preserve the root notion of a displaced home. The move away from the use of "uncanny" as the preferred term is not trivial; implicit in the choice to translate *unheimlich* as "unhomely" is a paradigm shift that supplements the psychoanalytic with sociocultural models of explanation. Preserving the stakes of home in the experience of *das Unheimliche*, that is, makes it useful in new ways for experiences of historically modern and postmodern forms of belonging and estrangement. One of the most productive treatments of the uncanny from this angle has been that of Anthony Vidler in his book *The Architectural Uncanny: Essays in the Modern Unhomely*. Vidler emphasizes the connection between modernity, architecture, and the unhomely by tracing a trajectory of displacement from home that begins in late eighteenth-century Romantic theorists and continues through postmodernism. Vidler's shift in emphasis in translating *unheimlich* as "unhomely" produces a more socially inflected argument that follows a series of permutations beginning with Gothic "alien presences" in the secure bourgeois home of the early nineteenth century, leading through the "economic and social estrangement" experienced on a larger scale in the urbanization of modern cities, and arriving at the no-man's land of twentieth-century battlefields and the intellectual and philosophical aftermath in our current day.[6] The tendency to see the "modern" uncanny as distinct from other kinds is a trend that can also be seen in publications following Vidler's.[7]

In what forms does "home" appear in such a trajectory? We can view it as an object of compensatory desire; as nostalgia for history and origin; and as a belief, against mounting evidence to the contrary, in the possibility of secure dwelling. If, as Vidler claims, "estrangement and unhomeliness have emerged as the intellectual watchwords of our century,"[8] then a fundamental homelessness has moved into the position of "given" in modern existence. Even so, one never quite loses the vestigial gestures toward lost origin when one continues to speak of being *dis*-placed or home-*less*, since both terms preserve the priority of grounded location as the unmarked case. But the crucial possibility introduced by modernity and its later permutations is precisely to think of *belonging* as the constructed effect and of *home* as the deceptive façade rather than as a secure emotional anchor.

Ibsen's unhomely

Those with a passing familiarity with Ibsen would probably not turn to him first in pursuit of uncanny literary motifs and themes; more obvious when thinking of the most common manifestations of the uncanny (e.g., the depiction of doubles, eerie repetition, mechanical life, unsettling copies, the living dead) would be to look to writers such as Edgar Allan Poe or E. T. A. Hoffmann, as Freud and others have done. It is most natural to think of the Gothic-Romantic period as the proper literary-historical home of the uncanny. This is not to say that Gothic motifs are absent from Ibsen's work – he too includes at least vestigial forms of Gothic imagery. One has only to think of the uncanny doubles and haunting presence of the dead Captain Alving in *Ghosts*, the mysterious white horses of *Rosmersholm*, the demonic "helpers" and "servants" from *The Master Builder*, and the living-dead characters from both *John Gabriel Borkman* and *When We Dead Awaken* to see that there is inviting material for a Freudian analysis (after all, Freud himself found plenty to work with in his renowned essay on *Rosmersholm*).[9] The work of Unni Langås is a rare example of a successful application of a psychoanalytically inflected model of the uncanny to Ibsen,[10] but no extensive body of research uses that approach.

An emphasis on the "homely" and "unhomely" aspects of the uncanny, however, could be an especially promising application of theories of the modern uncanny to Ibsen's works, since his position at the cusp of modernity makes him especially interested in depicting the displacement and persistence of traditional structures and attitudes. One of the key tenets of positivist modernity, that is to say, was the confidence in the power of the new to overcome once and for all the remnants of the past. This clean-break mentality had as a collateral effect the endowment of the uncanny with a new imaginative power, especially its atemporality and violation of proper sequence; without the operative assumption that the past could be left behind, there would be no acute discomfort at its unruly return. Expanding on this idea, Vidler seizes especially on the train of thought proceeding from the quotation to which Freud gives such pride of place: "*Unheimlich* is the name for everything that ought to have remained secret and hidden but has come to light."[11] As Vidler puts it, "Indeed the entire argument of 'The Uncanny' was to devolve around this apparently simple statement,"[12] not only for the way it opens obviously onto a Freudian theory of repression but also because of the social attitude concealed in the phrase "ought to," which is quintessentially modern and progressive in its assumptions.

One is reminded of the most powerful moment of insight in Ibsen's *Ghosts*, Mrs. Alving's oft-quoted lines that extend the implications of her own experience into a more general sociocultural claim:

> But I almost think we are all ghosts [*gengangere*], Pastor Manders. It is not only that which we have inherited from our mother and father that repeats in us. It is all sorts of old, lifeless opinions and all kinds of old, lifeless beliefs and such. It is not alive in us, but it is stuck inside us even so and we can't get rid of it. I just have to pick up a newspaper and read in it, and it is as if I see ghosts slip in between the lines. There must be ghosts all over the country. They must be as thick as sand, I think. And we are all so pitifully afraid of the light, every one of us.[13]

This is a peculiarly modern sort of Gothic imagery – ghosts, to be sure, but inflected with the logic of modern progressivism. Dead doctrines and useless beliefs *ought to* stay buried once they have been identified and debunked, implies Mrs. Alving, *and yet* they keep on returning, swarming thickly around the present, even among the most enlightened members of society. The ghostly ideas of tradition in Ibsen's play are *unheimlich* not because they are frightening and eerie, but because their powerful return contradicts and takes by surprise the modern confidence in the inevitability of rational progress. They are vestigial in a way that only makes sense from a modern, evolutionary perspective.

Jo Collins and John Jervis have underlined this point about the modern inflection of the uncanny in the introduction to their anthology of articles on the subject:

> As reflection and rationality become central cultural values, so the threats posed to them by recalcitrant experiences, seemingly emanating from "inside" (the "unconscious") as much as "outside," become all the more troubling. Thus we need to consider the possibility that the uncanny may be a fundamental, constitutive aspect of our experience of the modern.[14]

If, as Martin Jay has asserted, the uncanny was also "the master trope" of the 1990s in critical theory,[15] it may be that in late modernity there is something inherently appealing in the idea that powerful experiences of the uncanny are still possible, since it is proof that the world has not yet been completely flattened and mixed. There are still boundaries that carry a charge, encounters with "vestiges" in which we can be ambushed by the uncanny's unsettling effects. The postmodern worry, as Collins and Jervis articulate it, is that "if everything becomes potentially uncanny, nothing is experienced *as* uncanny, or as *sufficiently* uncanny."[16] This is the reason for the attraction of the term in critical theory at the millenial moment, as well as its appeal as a retrospective historical phenomenon: "More generally, the uncanny troubles the serene confidence of any explanatory or interpretive framework through which we seek to capture it, whether in everyday life, literary reflection or cultural theory." They further state that "this uncertainty is both unsettling, even potentially terrifying, yet also intriguing, fascinating."[17]

The problem of a residual past is writ large on all of Ibsen's prose plays. The action typically begins in an apparently confident present and ends with the triumphant return of past forces (*Pillars of Society* and *A Doll House* are the exceptions in this latter respect). The secrets that destabilize the present sometimes take the shape of crucial bits of hidden information (a forgery, an unknown family tie, a political cover-up, a love affair), or sometimes that of a character returning unexpectedly from the past (Brendel in *Rosmersholm*, the Stranger in *The Lady from the Sea*, Hilde in *The Master Builder*). But the logic of Ibsen's analytic-dramatic model, especially from *Ghosts* forward, is fundamentally *unheimlich* in its temporality. The present, that is, *ought to* be able to banish the effects of the past (as Georg Lukács, citing Marx, would have it, we all ought to manage a "cheerful parting from the past"[18]) and yet is nevertheless defeated in the face of its return.

The same might be said of the relationship between each Ibsen play as well, especially when seen through the lens of Ibsen's unhomely; how else to explain the constant return to scenarios that seem to have been definitively put to rest in previous plays? Although Nora seemingly empties out the rhetoric of the dollhouse quite definitively and appears to leave it behind for good, the following play *Ghosts* "rewinds" to a similar point of decision and then depicts the alternative fate of the wife who stayed. (Noteworthy here is Ibsen's insistent depiction of *Ghosts* as a necessity, as something he simply *had* to write.[19]) Or after having shown the utter futility of Mrs. Alving's building projects in *Ghosts* in 1881, why repeat the depiction of another lifelong construction project riddled by self-deception in *The Master Builder* ten years later? Or having unmasked the motives of the capitalist who falsely claims to be building for the happiness of others in *Pillars of Society* in 1877, why does Ibsen return to the same theme in both *The Master Builder* and *John Gabriel Borkman* in the 1890s?

Does the rhetoric of unmasking not last? Does it actually not "settle" anything, at least anything that cannot immediately be unsettled again? If one simply regards the coherence of Ibsen's twelve-play prose cycle as an effect of repeated character motifs, themes, and ideas, one remains on familiar critical terrain; after all, all writers repeat their favorite questions across works, to some extent. But there is something about Ibsen yoking his thematic repetitions to architectural metaphors that creates a particularly strong sense of unnerving return, since demolition after demolition has no apparent lasting effect. There is always another home to empty of its rhetoric; there is always another edifice to raze. As Ibsen's contemporaries imaginatively entered each new home at the start of each play – or as the audience members saw each new setting unveiled as the curtain rose – the potential existed for an unsettling recognition in the repeated rewind to yet another intact architectural structure. (One can imagine some thinking, "Are we back here in the bourgeois interior *again*? I thought Ibsen took care of that in the last play," or conversely, more conservative readers and viewers being relieved to see the previously devastated social structure reasserting itself from play to play in different architectural configurations and imagining, "Maybe *this* one will withstand the storm.") Even after each thoroughly convincing deconstruction (the slam of the door, the burning of the orphanage, the fall from the tower), something about the architectural – something *fundamental* – returns in a way that is precisely and in a technical sense of the term, uncanny.

A sociocultural inflection of the *unheimlich* also helps explain the ongoing contradiction of Ibsen writing about small-town Norway while living in cosmopolitan settings abroad. After all, isn't the opening of consciousness that comes with experience of the wide world just as irreversible in its effects as an unmasking? It falls fully within the logic of modern positivism, as a legacy of Enlightenment thinking, to assume that a wider perspective is naturally superior to a narrow one, and that shifts in consciousness are leaps *forward* that are temporally layered in some irreversible way. Instead, Ibsen's prose dramas, written mostly as exilic literature in a continental urban setting, return both to the small-town milieu on the verge of full modernization and to the small-scale domestic interior for his dramatic experiments about the cusp of modernity.

As Helge Rønning puts it in his Frankfurt-school approach to the plays, Ibsen and his fellow Scandinavian writers experienced the potency of continental modernity during their lengthy sojourns in the European capitals during this period, but without necessarily adopting those perspectives whole-cloth: "Through their long periods of residence abroad, they experienced [modern] development in two phases at the same time. They had a double perspective on development."[20] Because we are speaking here of "development," the perspective is not merely overlapping, but temporally layered, and also in this sense the experience of these exile writers is "unhomely." That which "ought to" be superseded by urban, continental modernity nevertheless persists in their writing as a residual provincial setting.

Rønning's main argument is intended to strengthen the links between Ibsen's dramatic work and dominant sociocultural models of modernity; he writes, "Ibsen is thus not first and foremost a Norwegian author, but a European dramatist who was incidentally born in Norway, and who for that reason wrote in Norwegian."²¹ This is a useful correction to the national claims on Ibsen; Rønning's critical position carves out some space for thinking anew the paradoxes of Ibsen's cultural and national affiliations. It is also important, however, to emphasize that the urbanity that marks much of modern literature appears only indirectly in Ibsen, mainly as a reported, off-stage effect. Rønning accounts for Ibsen's lack of direct representation of modern life in terms of medium, claiming that while novels use the city as a physical setting for their action, dramas of the same period use it more as a reported "symbol for everything entailed by modern life."²² Thus, there is no real sense of the street in any Ibsen play and few hints of a crowd (*Pillars of Society* and *An Enemy of the People* being the most prominent exceptions). No "botanizing on the asphalt," as Walter Benjamin would put it,²³ no depictions of *flâneurs*. Instead, the effects of modernity seem to be experienced from a distance by Ibsen's characters, as outside attitudes and reported actions in the small towns and middle-class living rooms of his plays. Just as Ibsen himself recalled provincial Norwegian life from afar, his characters react to *reports* of European modernity more than they experience it themselves. One might characterize Ibsen's dominant mode as "modernity elsewhere," or perhaps "modernity encroaching."

The depicted discrepancies between the small world "up here," as many of Ibsen's characters express it, and the cosmopolitan life "out/down there" that can be found in the centers of European culture lend themselves to an emphasis on the modern unhomely as a result of their foregrounded sense of overlap and uneven progress that maps temporal differences (the sense of lagging behind) onto the spatial relationship of center and periphery. Even if it is not important that Ibsen's settings be clearly locatable to Norway per se, it is nevertheless important to see the ways in which Ibsen's small towns are the functional equivalent of the cozy living room on the verge of invasion by modernization and urbanization.

The lure of *hygge*

A more detailed discussion of the "modern unhomely" in Ibsen's plays and their immediate reception context will help cast light on one of the central architectural issues of Ibsenian discourse: his attack on the notion of domestic comfort and security. The terms at stake in Danish and Norwegian are *hyggelig* and *uhyggelig*, words that run like a red thread through both Ibsen's plays and their contemporary reception. I argue that although it is possible to find this issue amply attested in the texts of the plays themselves, a full appreciation of Ibsen's strategic undermining of consensus domestic ideals cannot be fully appreciated without reading the plays as embedded in a physical and cultural context of performance and reception.

My choice of these particular Dano-Norwegian terms for examination is prompted by the fact that they can function as rough equivalents for the terms *heimlich* and *unheimlich*, which, as I have argued, are central to thinking about the uncanny within a social framework. When Freud's essay was translated into Danish in 1998, for example, it was entitled "Det Uhyggelige."[24] The Dano-Norwegian terms provide a considerable advantage over the English term "uncanny," since they suggest the root notion of domestic comfort and discomfort more directly.

Some semantic explanation is necessary here: a well-staged domestic interior can be *hyggelig*, as can a sympathetic person or a cheerful, cozy, or pleasant situation. The opposite term, *uhyggelig*, might conversely be translated into English as "unpleasant," "uncomfortable," "eerie," "disturbing," or "scary." The terms do not perform all of the etymological work of *heimlich* and *unheimlich* – the word "home" is not literally at their root in the way it is in German, nor is there any competing sense of secrecy attached to the word *hyggelig*. One would have to turn to other Dano-Norwegian cognates for the German word *heimlich* to recover those resonances, either with the word *hemmelig* (secret) or *hjemlig* (homey). In other words, *hyggelig* by itself does not single-handedly do the work of *heimlich* and all of its rich associations. *Uhyggelig* converges more closely with *unheimlich* and would be the term used to describe those same eerie or unsettling experiences of coincidence, *déja vu*, or an unexpected likeness or unpleasant reminder of the past (although it can also be used more generally to mean "gloomy" or "dismal"). But to get the full resonance of *unheimlich* in Danish or Norwegian, one would still have to resort to *uhjemlig*, a term as awkward and invented in Dano-Norwegian as "unhomely" is in English.

Both *hyggelig* and *uhyggelig*, however, center on the central concept of interest here, that of "ease" and "unease," or "comfort" and "discomfort." The intention in the remainder of this chapter is not to prove a strict correspondence between Ibsenian *uhygge* and the way Freud uses the German term *unheimlich*; it is not important to argue that Ibsen "qualifies" as a proper devotee of the uncanny, nor will it be particularly interesting to see the Freudian uncanny vindicated yet again as an explanatory rubric. Instead, the interest lies in the ways that Ibsen, as a rough contemporary of Freud, made use of the corresponding distinctions in his available linguistic and metaphoric system to similarly unsettle the assumed priority of domestic comfort and security. Like Freud, I am interested in the deployment of the terms *hyggelig* and *uhyggelig* on the ground in a discourse community; unlike Freud's essay, here the relevant language sample will not come from a dictionary's summary, but from Ibsen's writing and that of his cultural interlocutors. The Freudian model (and Vidler's sociocultural, architectural extension thereof) will simply provide a productive set of questions and issues that can guide the selection of evidence relevant to this topic.

Take, for example, a back-and-forth discussion by Scandinavian intellectuals about the publication of Ibsen's play *Ghosts* in 1881. Arne Garborg's stance toward the work was even more critical than that of his earlier reaction to Ibsen's "razing" mentality in his review of *Pillars of Society*; he found this new play outright destructive on moral grounds, stating most famously: "It is as if Ibsen took pleasure in saying the worst things he could imagine, and saying them in the most extreme way that he could," and "when Ibsen has gone so far as to call it a 'family drama', – then there is an unpleasant [*uhyggelig*] derision in the term." His conclusion? "The overall impression the book conveys is decidedly unpleasant [*uhyggelig*]."[25] In this review, I would say that Garborg uses the critical term in an uncareful way, simply expressing disgust at the unpleasant, uneasy feel of the play. As this quote shows, the term *uhyggelig* is not always used in a more technical sense as a synonym for the uncanny.

The great Danish critic of the Scandinavian Modern Breakthrough, Georg Brandes, however, came closer to that more specific meaning two weeks later in his review of the published version of the play, a critique that in many ways seems to be a direct response to Garborg's. Paraphrasing Mrs. Alving's observations in the play, Brandes wrote:

> That is to say: not only do the parents and forefathers of every single individual repeat themselves in him, their product, and not only do dispositions and situations return in uncanny ways [*paa uhyggelig Vis*], but the prejudices, opinions, and delusions of long-dead generations repeat themselves [*gaa igjen*] in the inner life of the present generation, which is the former's half involuntary, half lazy and cowardly heir.[26]

It is clear from this passage that Brandes was interested in a more specific use of the term *uhyggelig*, one that denoted the return of vestigial structures and opinions out of proper time and place.

Attention to this kind of language use at the time in question is important, since determining the range of the semantic field is actually Freud's method as well: to look at the convergence and divergence of the terms *heimlich* and *unheimlich* by seeing how they had been used. My aim is not purely descriptive, however. Instead, I am interested in the ways in which *hygge*, which had become entrenched as a mostly transparent and unassailable cultural value in mid-to-late nineteenth-century Scandinavia, became a point of contestation toward the turn of the century, with some writers coming to the defense of the idea, others shifting the meanings slightly, and others subjecting it to sustained irony and attack.

To my knowledge, there has been no thorough cultural-semantic history of *hygge*, but one can easily imagine the preconditions that would be necessary for its ascendancy as a cultural value: a strong middle class, sufficient economic prosperity to make comfort widely affordable, and a cultural motivation for drawing strong emotional boundaries around the home and family. These early-to-mid nineteenth-century cultural developments in Denmark occured somewhat later in Norway, and it was the ascendancy of these cultural values that attracted Ibsen's sustained critique. It would be radically overstating the case, however, to say Ibsen's attack on *hygge* in the 1880s and 90s was successful in any widespread cultural sense because still today, a powerful cultural norm in Scandinavia invests special energy in creating an intimate social space of comfort, warmth, and cheer. It is part of a repertoire of hospitality widely accepted as a baseline cultural attitude and is motivated as much by climate (the production of cheer and comfort in the dark winter months) as it is by culture. Instead, the point here would be to note that in the late nineteenth century and beyond, with Ibsen's help, it became possible as a dissenting view to raise philosophical and intellectual objections to *hygge*, attacking a concept that in commonsense terms would otherwise seem unassailable, especially since the metaphors of *hygge* and home are so tightly connected to an embodied sense of comfort.

The possibility of an alternative position gained traction throughout the period ranging from the realistic literature of the Scandinavian Modern Breakthrough to the writings of culturally radical architects and designers in early Scandinavian Modernism of the 1920s and 30s. Increasingly, modernists of various sorts challenged previously accepted ideals of comfort, good cheer, and intimacy among friends and family on the grounds that comfort can lead to self-satisfaction and that the domestic nest can contribute to middle-class materialism and an essential social conservatism. *Hygge* is, in other words, alien to world views based on notions of risk, progressive development, avant-garde art, and individual freedom. One twentieth-century Danish writer recalls his own youthful radical feelings this way: "Good art does not have *hygge* as its goal."[27] Indeed, the dominant strain of Scandinavian cultural radicalism, beginning with the Modern Breakthrough writers of the 1870s, might well be classified under the rubric "*Hygge* and its Discontents."

As one of the first, most prominent such discontents, Ibsen employed a strategy of strategic reversal. Given Ibsen's reputation as a "gloomy" playwright, it might seem strange to turn to his plays looking for *hygge*. It was not the case, however, that "Ibsen the pessimist" was constitutionally unable to convey that kind of warmth and family intimacy, because many of his scenes could be described in exactly that way. That is to say, many *opening* scenes, for Ibsen's central strategy was to create a kind of ambush for readers and spectators who were all too ready to attach themselves to and identify with scenes of comfortable domestic happiness, and to judge from many of the responses to his plays, many of his contemporaries were the perfect victims. Today, the overall trajectories of his now-canonical plays are so well known that it might be hard to recover a full sense of that original dynamic of reversal; readers and viewers now know too much about the shocks awaiting them in the endings. At the time, however, Ibsen's contemporaries were initially not so thoroughly prepared for his relentless deconstruction of family happiness. A look at several of Ibsen's opening scenarios back to back, together with reactions thereto, will make clear the importance for Ibsen of building up a certain kind of expectation before beginning his work of demolition.

Of the twelve prose plays Ibsen wrote between 1877 and 1899, ten of them begin indoors, the exceptions being *The Lady from the Sea* and *When We Dead Awaken*. Of these ten plays, four take place in a single room, three move between different indoor locations, and three (*The Master Builder*, *Little Eyolf*, and *John Gabriel Borkman*) follow a trajectory from inside to outside, which one might say is also the general overall trajectory from the early to the late plays. The economic level of the depicted interiors ranges from modest to well-to-do, but almost all of them are conceived of as presenting an inviting initial impression. The Helmer household of *A Doll House* is described in the stage directions as "A comfortably [*hyggeligt*] and tastefully, but not expensively furnished room."[28] The Ekdal dwelling in *The Wild Duck* is described like this: "The studio is modestly but comfortably [*hyggeligt*] arranged and furnished."[29] Again: "The living room at Rosmersholm: spacious, old-fashioned, and comfortable [*hyggelig*]."[30] Interiors in several of the other plays are also described as *smuk* (attractive), *rummelig* (spacious), or *smagfuldt* (tasteful).[31]

If we might generalize for the sake of an overview, it seems safe to say that the typical point of departure for Ibsen's prose plays is a *hyggelig*, physically appealing interior. None of the plays begins in squalor, as they would be likely to do in continental forms of naturalist drama by Zola or Hauptmann, for example. To be sure, there might be signs of economic pressure in some of them, a fraying around the edges usually conveyed by the word *tarvelig*, an elastic term that can range in dictionary meaning from "wretched" to "modest." When that word appears in Ibsen's stage directions, however, it is always accompanied by a mitigating term such as *hyggelig* or *net* (nice/tidy). We might thus think of the opening gesture in most of Ibsen's plays as an essentially constructive one of a literal *mise-en-scène*; by way of his stage directions, he calls into existence a basically attractive interior and gives himself a positive architectural value to work against as the play develops.

Many of Ibsen's dramatic characters go out of their way to show their attachment to this ideal of a comfortable home. In *Pillars of Society*, Karsten Bernick says, "Of course, the family is the core of society. A good home, honorable and faithful friends, a small, tightly knit circle, where no disturbing elements cast their shadows."[32] Nora Helmer warns in *A Doll House* that if her husband were to find out about her loan, "our beautiful happy home would no longer be what it is now."[33] Even in *Ghosts*, hardly a cheerful play, Osvald tells Mrs. Alving, "But I think it is so pleasant [*hyggeligt*], mother. Just think – for me, having come home, to sit at my mother's own table, in mother's room, and to eat mother's delicious food."[34] In the next play, *An Enemy of the People*, the initial distinction between the Stockman brothers revolves precisely around the issue of *hygge*: Dr. Stockman's house is filled with guests and the free-handed hospitality of a spontaneous toddy party, while Peter Stockman is described as a frugal devotee of weak tea and sandwiches. Peter the town mayor is, in other words, a domestic ascetic; as Thomas later tells his guests, "We have to remember that Peter is single, poor man. He doesn't have a home where he can be comfortable [*hygge sig*]; only business, business. And then there's all that damned thin, weak tea that he guzzles down."[35]

In the next several plays, Ibsen depicts *hygge* more equivocally from the start. In *The Wild Duck*, it becomes clear that the pleasures and comfort of the Ekdal home, like those of the wild duck's attic nest, are a kind of necessary life-lie. *Hygge* in this play is a product of twilight and shadow – in Relling's terms, a compensation for those too weak to live in the stark light of truth. As he tells Gregers, "The people in this house are not turned toward the sun [*her bor ikke solvente folk her i huset*]."[36] Similarly, in *Rosmersholm*, the flowers with which Rebecca West has filled the home are praised because "they lull one into a pleasant state [*de bedøver så dejligt*]"; literally, "they tranquilize (or anaesthetize) so wonderfully."[37] In both plays, *hygge* is clearly marked as an atmospheric effect that disguises unpalatable facts.

Hygge also comes to be marked as a naive, even impossible position. In *Rosmersholm*, it becomes clear that *hygge* depends on the suppression of individual differences and opinions – it is a false form of family unity. Ibsen insists on this in a conversation between Rosmer and Kroll:

ROSMER: Don't you think we have it nice and comfortable [*hyggelig*] here?
KROLL: Yes, now it is really nice and comfortable [*hyggeligt*] – and peaceful. Yes, now you have really gotten a home, Rosmer. And I have lost mine.[38]

In this scene, Kroll is alarmed that modern, political positions have made their way into his family life. By imagining difference of opinion as the end of home and *hygge*, Kroll conveys the weakness in his position: not far from his ideal intimacy of identical opinions is the dynamic of enforcement that protects such unity. By giving the defense of *hygge* to a conservative character such as Kroll, Ibsen reveals his growing difficulties in the plays following *The Wild Duck* in seeing anything but reactionary conservatism in the concept.

When one looks at the contemporary reception of the plays mentioned to this point, it is striking to see how quickly audiences identified with these *hyggelige* rooms. In some cases, the degree of attachment verged on misreading, especially with the later plays in which the value of domestic comfort is clearly made more equivocal from the start. It is as if the readers and audience members could not help themselves, so strong was the wish to believe in the authenticity of such scenes of family cheer. This is quite understandable, since *hygge* is more palpable on the realistic stage, where the living room confronts the spectator as a real and emotionally inviting visual environment – it is hard to resist in purely phenomenological terms. A cheerfully lit and comfortably arranged space prompts a visceral physical identification and connection with atmosphere and affect. The many "dollhouse" living rooms presented to audiences when the curtain rose on the premiere performances of that play in both Copenhagen and Christiania were consistently described in reviews as *hyggelige*, and also as "beautiful," "lively," "warm," and "cozy."[39] The very tone of these reactions is interesting: reviewers evaluated the Helmers' living room the way one might compliment the house of a host when invited for dinner.

Take this early response to a first reading of *A Doll House*, for example, one that appeared in print in Denmark a mere two days after the publication of the play in 1879:

> If one had in real life entered into this kind of "doll home" [*Dukkehjem*] where the self-assured, proper, refined, and handsome lawyer Helmer is

hovered over by his lively, bubbly, constantly singing young wife, where the children – the "doll children" – cry out joyfully in their midst, while the whole house is preparing for Christmas Eve, one would have instinctively judged this to be a model home [*et Mønsterhjem*].⁴⁰

The word "instinctively" (*uvilkaarlig*) is the most interesting one here, because it conveys the sense that viewers easily fell into a habitual reaction at the sight of this happy home, jumping to conclusions about the happy character of the lives lived therein. Ibsen intentionally set the stage for that reaction in the early scenes of the play, and this reader responded precisely in the imagined ways.

The *hyggelig* effect was even stronger when *A Doll House* was performed, as might be expected given the immediate and positive physical cues in the setting. One paradigmatic reaction to the premiere performance of *A Doll House* in Copenhagen shows how difficult this was to resist, especially when the performance itself took place on Christmas Eve, as this one did:

> In the first act we cast our glance into an apparently happy home, in which we see husband, wife, and children in the happiest of moods preparing themselves for the beloved Christmas Eve, and one instinctively wishes to be included in their Christmas and takes quiet pleasure in the fact that as a member of the honored audience one has in a way invited oneself along [*som Medlem af det ærede Publikum paa en Made er som selvindbuden*]. One is delighted and takes pleasure in it.⁴¹

Clearly, this spectator was more than willing to be taken in by the holiday *hygge* at the beginning of the play, perhaps conflating the mood just outside the theater with that of the first act of the play. It would have been a *hygge*-saturated cultural context at the holiday time of the play's premiere, one that would have made it difficult to watch the otherwise reliable signs of Christmas cheer – the tree, the decorations, the young children – in Act One of the play *without* activating the reflexive cultural responses. As another Danish reviewer put it, "This pleasant home [*Dette hyggelige Hjem*], these turtle doves, this rather aesthetic relationship are all things we are very familiar with."⁴²

A well-known illustration of the play's tarantella scene from the original Christiania Theater production (hand-drawn to capture action that would elude the cameras of the day) shows the scene in which Nora is rehearsing her dance (Figure 1). The illustration is a rare surviving visual depiction of that production (there is a a similar extant illustration of the staging of the dance in the earlier Copenhagen world premiere, as well as studio actor portraits from that production), and this picture from the Christiania

Figure 1: The tarantella disrupts the *hyggelig* Christmas scene in Act Two of *A Doll House* (note the Christmas tree in the background). Production: Christiania Theater, prem. January 20, 1880.

Theater is often used to convey a sense of the scale and proportions of the set. Unlike the Danish illustration, this one also preserves the Christmas tree in the back of the set and gives some sense of the holiday cheer that Norwegian audiences responded to in the beginning of the play.

It is understandable that *A Doll House*, a play that conflated real and fictional Christmas settings because of the timing of its first performances in late December, would elicit strong affective connections to the opening sight of a cheery domestic setting. What is more interesting, however, is the pattern of reaction to Ibsen's subsequent plays that similarly grasps at the straw of the initial pleasant atmosphere of the homes. August Lindberg's touring 1883 Scandinavian production of *Ghosts*, surely the most *uhyggelig* of Ibsen's plays in overall effect, nevertheless began by conveying the impression of a pleasant interior to one viewer, at least when it was performed in Helsingborg: "The furniture was stylish. We saw a pleasant [*hyggelig*] room with Nordic comfort."[43] The degree to which the recognition of familiar cultural qualities of *hygge* played an important subliminal role in the initial visual impressions taken in by Nordic audiences can be measured through a counterexample, a production of *Ghosts* in Rome in 1898 that elicited this response from a Norwegian commentator living abroad:

> Chamberlain Alving's living room had pieces of furniture from a second-rate boarding house. They were surely at one point purchased from some drab store. Everything that we in the North understand about *hygge* in the home, the Latin race knows nothing about, even though their living rooms are filled with both luxury and comfort. It was cold in Chamberlain Alving's salon, and one did not see the smallest bit that could indicate that there was culture here.[44]

The main point of this memoir by the respected Norwegian author Peter Egge is to make amusing observations about the cultural differences between Scandinavia and Europe that he encountered in his various travels in the south, but most interesting in the present context is the fact that his encounter with this Italian production clashes with expectations already established for *Ghosts* through performances in the Nordic region: that the Alving home should initially appear *hyggelig*, not oppressive and gloomy. It also points to the idea that this elusive sense of Nordic domestic comfort and style is a cultural value that does not transplant easily.

Reactions to *The Wild Duck* were complicated by the insistently multi-vocal aspects of that play, which famously cannot easily be read as a "statement" on any one position or idea. Perhaps for that very reason, however, it was common for reviewers to fasten their attention on an aspect of the play or a character that they thought they understood. One Norwegian reviewer, for example, managed this positive, sentimental response to the family scenes of Act Two:

> The opinion of some individuals who find the Ekdal home to be *uhyggeligt*, taken purely from a distance, will not find resonance with anyone other than those who are used to being unusually comfortable. At any rate it will be hard to draw a conclusion of *uhygge* from the studio [depicted] at the Christiania Theater, which on the contrary seems quite homey [*hjemlig*] and has something of the poetry expressed by the well-known [poem] "High under the Roof, where the Swallows [sic] Dwell." And the beautiful family scene in Act Two, where Hjalmar goes to and fro playing his flute – how that spreads *hygge* throughout the room! One almost wishes that Old Ekdal will forsake his toddy and come in and take his cozy [*lune*] place by the stove, and that Gregers will not show up and cast his strong shadow over the bright image.[45]

For those familiar with the pitiless force of *The Wild Duck*'s ending and its reputation in the Ibsen repertoire, this contemporary evaluation of the play's opening scenes will likely come as a surprise, and it must be said that this reading of the play is an especially "willful" one, although in a very interesting way. The commentator "H. H." simply wishes away the unpleasant parts of the play by locking his attention onto the early scenes of family happiness. Away with Old Ekdal's alcoholism, away with Gregers's momentous arrival into the home, so the cozy family scenes can be enjoyed more fully! The reviewer amplifies his sentimental response by linking the atmosphere of the Ekdal home to "High under the Roof, where the Swallow Dwells," which is actually not a title but the opening line from the early Hans Christian Andersen poem "The Student" (1829).[46] There, the impression of *hygge* comes from a romanticized student poverty, which this reviewer sees duplicated here in the poor but happy photographer's studio. It is hard to imagine coming to that conclusion from a careful reading of the text, with its ironies and ambiguities and inexorable cruelty, but that seems precisely the point; the seemingly anomalous reaction here was surely facilitated by a powerful physical reaction to the visual and phenomenological qualities of the play in performance.

I want to emphasize here that this kind of positive response to the initial atmosphere of Ibsen's prose plays is evidence that Ibsen's strategy of setting up his readers and audience members worked somewhat too effectively. Viewers like "H. H." bought completely into the scenes, identified with the family life depicted on the stage, and imagined inhabiting the appealing homes shown there, to the point that they simply ignored the play's outcome. It is as if a *hyggelig* scene had the power to conjure up an alternative play – a "familiar" one, in the etymological sense – that competes with the actual one. Although Ibsen probably did not imagine a viewer as stubborn in his attachment to domestic bliss as "H. H.," it is important to see that he did want to evoke this positive attachment to architectural space as a point of departure, even if he did not expect viewers to go on with an imaginative inhabitation of the houses he thought he was demolishing.

Christmas *hygge*

I have argued earlier that it is important to think contextually about the effect on a viewer of walking from the Christmas atmosphere of a Copenhagen street a few days before Christmas into a theater performance of *A Doll House*, which used the same tokens of holiday *hygge* to deconstructive ends. Once one has become alert to the way *A Doll House* landed in this particularly *hyggelig* time of year, as, in Carl Thrane's witty remark, "an unusual sort of Christmas gift" (*en Julegave af ualmindelig Art*),[47] the reception of Ibsen's remaining prose plays gains extra resonance. Except for *Pillars of Society*, which was published in October 1877, the ten plays following *A Doll House* were all published in November or early December, just in time for the Christmas book-buying season in Denmark and Norway. This was a conscious marketing strategy for Ibsen; for many years, his writing schedule was built around this crucial timing. His longtime British translator and advocate, Edmund Gosse, shared his amusement in 1891 about the writing schedule that had become as regular as a Christmas comet:

> During each period of four-and-twenty months Ibsen is the least accessible of European authors. Then, early in December of the alternate year, the mephitic vapour begins to rise from the well of Cassotis, the journalism of Scandinavia shudders in prophetic paragraphs, the chasm of the Gyldendalske Boghandel is shaken, and suddenly, about a week before Christmas, the Pythian utterance, in four acts, and in prose, is communicated to Germany and Italy, to Hungary and France, to the parts of Massachusetts about Boston. The whole proceeding has the regularity of an astronomical phenomenon.[48]

This publication strategy had two consequences, each slightly at odds with the other: every two years Ibsen's plays were put into circulation within the advantageous economic context of Christmas gift giving and reading, and they were presented at a time of year that was particularly devoted to the production of *hygge*.

Since the plays were often intended to undermine precisely the consensus cultural values enshrined by holiday celebrations, this made for sometimes jarring contrasts. Just after the publication of *Ghosts*, Ibsen addressed this issue directly in a response to a Christmas *skål* (toast) given in his honor at the Scandinavian Club in Rome. The Norwegian scholar Francis Bull conveys the gist of Ibsen's speech that day: "Christmas, which otherwise brought joy and peace, brought him battle as a rule, because his books were published at that time; but then it is true that in his view battle was a joy, and peace just a moment of rest before taking it up again."[49] One only has to imagine a provocative play like *Ghosts* making its debut on the Christmas market to understand the particular vehemence of the negative reaction. One outraged reader built an entire review on this point, namely, what horrors one might expect to see on the *next* Christmas table – perhaps a drama about the wholesale murder of old people who have become too burdensome to society: "A Christmas play of that sort could be recommended to many elderly people as edifying, if sobering, Christmas reading." That reviewer's comments end with, "The book does not belong on the Christmas table of any Christian home,"[50] a line often quoted as typical of the vituperative public criticism of *Ghosts* but rarely noted for its emphasis on the Christmas context and connection with other similar statements.

Ghosts in particular seems to have elicited such comments about the disparities between Ibsen and Christmastime. Another Norwegian critic noted that "it was that kind of 'slice of reality' that Henrik Ibsen gave us as a Christmas gift," complaining further that Ibsen's muse inappropriately gave birth to a monstrosity just before Christmas.[51] A Swedish review made the point even more vividly:

> There are two strange Christmas presents that have been released into the literary Christmas market: Ibsen's *Ghosts* and Kielland's *Else*. Amidst the atmosphere of Christmas peace and Christmas joy [*julfrid och julglädje*] that tends to flow through the individual's heart, family life, yes, all of society at this holiday time, these books will sound a strange, discordant tone, like marshal trumpets in a psalm; they tell of strife, friction, and misery. It is a tone of suffering, unhappiness, and torment that forces its way into circles in which just for a moment one would like to listen to a mild symphony of peace, calm, prosperity, and happiness.[52]

Even Sophie Adlersparre, cited earlier for her sympathetic lecture on *Ghosts*, deployed the gift metaphor in the culmination of her remarks, albeit repurposing the metaphor to more positive ends: "The skald has in actuality with this, his Christmas present, not invited us to something *pleasant*, but in many respects to a repulsive *task*; not to *enjoyment*, but instead to *suffering*; not to *a lesson for the moment*, but instead a *purpose for life*. And for that reason, we convey to him our thanks."[53] In essence, Adlersparre defends Ibsen's unwanted Christmas gift as educational but implicitly admits that the timing may be difficult for many.

A literal way of recovering the emotional context of Ibsen's Christmas publication schedule is to scan a historical Scandinavian newspaper page in which a book review of an Ibsen play appeared in mid-to-late December in the years 1879–99. Alongside in-depth discussion of the play, its characterizations, and its provocative philosophies and world view, one is likely to find sentimental Christmas short stories, Christmas poems, holiday advertisements, and the like. The newspaper layout itself, in other words, reproduces the discordant tone of the plays in their seasonal context and provides a visualization of the strange cultural adjacency that governed their initial publication.

Not all of Ibsen's plays were produced on stage as quickly as *A Doll House*, so it was most frequently the printed publication thereof that performed the Christmas sabotage. Moreover, the collision of expectations was strongest with the earliest of Ibsen's prose plays, through the mid-1880s, before the public had become accustomed to the regularity of tone and timing in Ibsen's onslaught. Only gradually did the sometimes hostile reading public accustom itself to expect Ibsen's inappropriate Christmas presents, perhaps growing to regard them like the real-life holiday gifts of a tactless, impossible relative. By the time *The Lady from the Sea* came out in 1888, the Christiania writer and journalist Alfred Sinding-Larsen had come to expect the worst:

> Over Ibsen's two most recent works – *The Wild Duck* in 1884 and *Rosmersholm* in 1886 – there hovered a dark, chilly grey, oppressive winter mood, and since they both were published precisely in the depressing darkness before Christmas, they had that same coloring and did not contribute any spirit of light and warmth to that season.[54]

Here Ibsen's usual playwriting strategy is equated with the forces of natural gloom (*Mørketid*) pressing in on the home around Christmastime in the Northern climate, against which the festive, light-saturated holiday normally functions as the cultural defense. *The Lady from the Sea*, with its more conciliatory ending, seemed to Sinding-Larsen to change the dynamic, although we see in retrospect that the milder effects would be temporary (after all, Ibsen would publish *Hedda Gabler* during the Christmas season two years later on December 16, 1890, gifting the Nordic region with one of its most famous literary suicides). By 1896, the gloomy tone of Ibsen's plays was apparently no longer even worth much comment; a review of *John Gabriel Borkman* that was also published on Christmas Eve that year makes no mention of the seasonal disparity at all, even though that devastatingly bleak wintry drama would have again provided a maximum of contrast.[55]

Ibsen's assault on *hygge* through its association with Christmas was more than a coincidence of marketing strategy and holiday calendar, as important as that timing was for an author who for years had felt insecure about his finances. It was a substantial, aggressive intellectual tactic as well, a way of striking out at the home at its most *hyggelig* moment. Lest there be any doubt about this, a close examination of a section from one of Ibsen's most important poems ("On the Heights [*Paa Vidderne*]," written in late 1859 and published in early 1860, republished in 1871[56]) provides a pointed example of the way Ibsen used Christmas to undermine the values of homey *hygge*. In this poem, the poetic "I" describes the process of detachment from domestic life in favor of a wilder, freer life as a hunter on a mountain plateau, where another hunter he meets there teaches him the ways of steely indifference and detachment from society. The poem has usually been read as a personal artistic manifesto of sorts, following the lead of Georg Brandes's early review,[57] or more recently as a conflict between ethics and idealist aesthetics, as Toril Moi has suggested.[58] I would add to this range of interpretations a particular emphasis on the narrator's rejection of home per se, as a way of getting at the complex of ideas that attaches to domesticity in Ibsen's thinking.

Chief among them in this poem are the comforts of fur covers and mothers singing children to sleep with cats curled up at the foot of the bed – in short, warmth and cozy security. The narrator's hunter-mentor scorns such pleasures and teaches resistance to the soft temptations of the home. This culminates on Christmas Eve as the narrator looks down on the valley below and is momentarily seized by a longing for an imperfectly remembered coziness as he hears the church bells ring (here in my literal translation):

> They ushered in solemn Christmastime
> with the old familiar bells.
> There is a light behind my neighbor's gate,
> from my mother's cottage proceeds a glow
> that strangely charms and entices me.
>
> Home, with all its impoverished life,
> became a saga of rich images!
> Up here lay the mountain plateau, vast and rigid,
> down there I had a mother and wife –
> it is no surprise that I would yearn for them.[59]

The setting down below when viewed from the heights is not just literally "familiar," but "homey": the adjective describing the "familiar" bells in Norwegian is precisely that, *hjemlig*. Their sound entices the narrator to ignore the harsh memories of scarcity and need that actually marked his childhood experience "on the ground" and to imagine instead on this Christmas Eve an idealized home of comfort and ease.

At this moment, his strange companion breaks the spell with a scornful, dismissive remark: "it seems to me that my young friend is moved, – / oh of course, the homey cottage!"[60] With the help of this sudden deflation, the poem's narrator quickly recovers his hardened composure:

> Once again I stood there with arm of steel,
> and felt that I was the strong one;
> the breeze of the mountains cooled my breast,
> which never again will stir up in warmth
> for a blinking Christmas beacon![61]

The poem then takes a horrifying turn as the beckoning light from the narrator's homey cottage reveals itself to be a conflagration. As the narrator watches, the light and the curling smoke transform themselves from typical signs of the *hygge* of cottage life into something quite *uhyggelig*: the total destruction of the narrator's childhood home and the certain death of his mother. But as the narrator cries out in sorrow, the other hunter remonstrates: "But the hunter comforted him: 'Why the fuss? / After all, it's just the old house burning up, / with the Christmas beer and the cat!'"[62] With an awful, unsettling turn of perspective, the mentor urges his pupil to step back and look at the scene precisely *as* a scene, framing it with his hands in a certain way "to get the perspective right [*til vinding for perspektivet*]."[63] Seen through a frame, from that angle, and with enough distance, his childhood nest becomes just an "old house." Of course, it is more than that: since the narrator's mother perishes in the flames, his last connection to childhood is destroyed, and the entire complex of Christmas *hygge* that was initially called up by that scene is overturned with one stroke. Quickly the narrator comes to see the scene in the same way as his hunter companion; as the angels carry his mother's soul up to the "Christmas-Eve joy in the heavens [*til julekvelds-glæde i himlen*]," the narrator is able to appreciate the aesthetics of her journey: "but it can't be denied that there *was* quite an effect / in the double lighting of the night sky!"[64]

The poem's complexity derives from the splitting of the hunter position into two voices, a hardened mentor and a wavering apprentice. Without that split, the poem would present a simple contrast between low and high, between home and abroad, between family ties and individual freedom. Instead, there are hints of past vulnerability in the mysterious hunter: "tears play in his laughter, / his lip speaks when it is silent."[65]

A further mitigation of the poem's apparent polemic is conveyed by the fact that the training of the poem's narrator in the ways of callous independence is implied to be a theft of his will. Enticed on both sides, the narrator wavers for most of the poem between home and independence without landing clearly with both feet in either camp. The fifth section of the poem is a dialogic argument in which every imagined comfort of home is trumped with a superior correlative up in the solitude of the mountain heights. The effect of this back and forth is not so much to prove the superiority of a free, isolated existence – though that is ostensibly where the narrator arrives by the end of the poem – but instead to carve out an observer position in between. This, I would argue, is the position Ibsen himself takes up with respect to *hjemlig hygge* in this poem, interestingly enough just after he himself had married.[66] His overriding impulse is the rejection of comfort as a cage and a trap, but competing with it is a hesitation about the isolation from human contact that a completely ascetic rejection of *hygge* would entail. In the poem, the narrator's resolve never to fall for that temptation again seems overly strident, as if to cover up a more persistent ambiguity.

The burning up of that "old house" will not be the only instance of total loss by fire in Ibsen's works, as I discuss in more detail in a later chapter. Here, however, the main point is this: throughout his career, Ibsen consistently shuttled back and forth between the *heimlich* and the *unheimlich* to catch readers and viewers flat-footed entertaining the wrong assumption. The transformational dynamic at work in the fire scene in "On the Heights," when the *hjemlig* slides into the *uhjemlig*, the *hyggelig* into the *uhyggelig*, is only one early example. A more prominent, even perverse treatment of homey comfort can be found in Ibsen's *Brand*, his breakthrough dramatic poem of 1866, written six years after the publication of "On the Heights." In many ways, the pastor Brand is an extension of the isolated hunter from the earlier poem, but the *uhyggelig* home plays an even stronger role here, perhaps because Ibsen's own departure from Norway in 1864 had intervened. It is likely that his new experiences abroad and concomitant widening of perspective approximated the experiences of the hunter on the mountain plateau depicted in the earlier poem. The shift in perspective allowed the traveling Ibsen to frame his experience of origin "just so," transforming it into something more aesthetic and distant, so when he returned to the theme in *Brand*, the issues had intensified.

First, there is the itinerant preacher Brand's relationship to his childhood home, which he has forsaken even more resolutely than the hunter in the earlier poem. When he meets Ejnar on the road in the beginning of the play, he says that although he is close to his home village, he will only pass through and beyond it. Further, he claims, "Like the rabbit under the forest spruce, / I have my house sometimes here, sometimes there,"[67] signaling a complete lack of attachment to the idea of home. This creates a link with the two gypsy characters in the poem: the madwoman Gerd and the old woman at the end of the fourth act: "we shall travel, we shall wander, / house and home are for you others."[68] Toril Moi calls Gerd and Brand "symbolic siblings" for this reason.[69]

As Brand nears his actual childhood place of origin, though, his confidence falters:

> here, as I approach home,
> I see myself as a stranger, –
> Awaken bound, shaved, and tamed
> Like Samson in the lap of the harlot.[70]

Home is a threat, signaled from the start as a force that robs Brand of vitality, resolve, and transcendent vision, and to follow the metaphor, the equivalent of Samson's hair is Brand's freedom of movement and position away from home. In the second act of the play, it is easy to see why. When Brand encounters his mother, she appears as a grotesque and grasping figure who conveys a distinctly *uhyggelig* idea of home:

> What ice-cold childhood memory,
> What puff of wind from home and fjord
> drops frost all around this woman, –
> drops frost still worse inside me – –?
> God of mercy! It is my mother![71]

The moment of recognition depicted here follows a textbook definition of the uncanny – the strange, threatening and icy figure approaching him turns out to be the most familiar (and familial) figure possible, his mother. His mother's house lay in the shadow under the glacier, a frozen, dark place where years of toil and hoarding of wealth never created any warmth or emotional connection. When Brand sets up his own family home with Agnes, he unwittingly repeats his mother's choice by selecting a similar location in the shadow of a cliff. The home is protected in one sense, since the falling rock and ice land out beyond the domestic structure, but it is depicted as a costly form of security in real emotional terms.

It is the gloom and the shadow of the spot that proves fatal for Brand's infant son and creates his central ethical dilemma: to stand firm and risk his child or to choose family over his sense of transcendent calling. When he chooses his "mission," his child dies. Significantly, Ibsen once again uses Christmas Eve as the setting for sorrow, depicted at the start of Act Four. Here, too, we see Ibsen's transformational dynamic at work on the traditional Christmas signifier, as the happy holiday recalled from the previous year has turned ghastly and funereal. This Christmas Eve interior finds Agnes sorrowing in the shadows, with Brand lighting a single, faltering candle upon entering. Desperate for some shred of comfort, she lights the Christmas candles, but they simply cast more light out onto the cemetery where the child lies buried. Agnes concludes bitterly that the "God of Christmas [*Julens Gud*]" is busy listening to the celebrations of the rich and has abandoned them completely.[72] When he requires her to give her last remembrance of her dead boy, a small piece of clothing, to the traveling beggar woman on this Christmas Eve (Figure 2), it is as if she has been asked to put the last shred of family *hygge* on the altar of sacrifice. In *Brand*, as elsewhere,

Figure 2: Agnes giving away the last scrap of children's clothing in *Brand*, Act Four. Production: Nya Teatern (Stockholm), prem. March 24, 1885.

Ibsen used these reversals of Christmas *hygge* as a convenient way of undermining the cultural attachment to home in its most instinctive form.

It remains to evaluate how these viewpoints are positioned within the entire dramatic poem, given that the depiction of Brand's all-or-nothing sacrifice of family love at the altar of his demanding god is presented so equivocally. A well-worn line of Ibsenian criticism has put great weight on the contradicting final voice proclaiming a god of love instead.[73] But even if one accepts the line of criticism that sees the ultimate stance of the poem as a critique of Brand's extremism, it is hard to find a viable notion of home that can be rescued from the dramatic world depicted here. Both of Brand's homes are cold and dark, where signs of potential *hygge* slide quickly into their opposites. For the fickle crowd of townsfolk, who start to follow Brand away from town at the end of the play, but then abandon him when he pushes them beyond their limits, "hearth and home" is moreover the place of retreat and compromise. In the end, the Dean (*Provsten*) welcomes their return to society by saying,

> Oh, my children! Oh, my sheep!
> Now you return to hearth and home [*Hjemmets Arne*]
> let regret clear your eyes
> and you will see how well it goes.[74]

This can hardly be taken as a ringing endorsement of home, no matter how one feels about Brand's extreme, uncompromising demands. The most scathing image, however, comes when Ibsen depicts the human-made god that Brand despises as a kind of wishy-washy god of *hygge*: a deity dressed in slippers, reading glasses, and a skullcap, a kind of Jørgen Tesman of the skies: "Yes, that is exactly how he looks, / our country's and our people's family god [*Familiegud*]."[75] With critiques of domesticity this potent and vivid, little can be salvaged from the home.

In all of these examples, Christmas settings present Ibsen with a concentrated expression of family *hygge* that amplifies the power of his critique. One gets a full sense of Ibsen's strategy when the appealing Christmas tableau of church bells, cottage, and family hearth in "On the Heights" turns suddenly into a scene of flaming destruction, or when the idyllic family scene from *Brand* turns grim from one year to the next. Christmas was not only the season of battle for Ibsen, as he said in his response to the 1881 holiday *skål*, but it was a well-chosen scene even so. If one is looking to pick a fight with *hygge*, there is no better setting than Christmas Eve.

"The master of *uhygge*"

Ibsen's invocation of attractive domestic scenes as starting points in plays and poems prepares the ground for sudden reversals of effect in which *hygge* slides into *uhygge*, while still maintaining the ostensibly realist basis for the play in question. On stage, the effect is generally all the more striking, since a constant physical space gradually reveals a much different atmospheric potential. When one looks at reviews and critical accounts, it is clear that the initial positive reactions to the setting of Ibsen's opening scenes rarely lasted to the end of each performance. Ibsen exploited Freud's insight *avant la lettre*; it is precisely the ambiguous instability of the uncanny as a phenomenon that links *hygge* and *uhygge* in some essential way: "Thus *heimlich* is a word the meaning of which develops in the direction of ambivalence, until it finally coincides with its opposite, *unheimlich*."[76] Or to put it another way: the effect of the *unheimlich* depends on a secure and comfortable starting point, an anchor of domestic comfort. Otherwise, there is nothing to unsettle.

This is perhaps the best argument for thinking of Ibsen as a master of the uncanny, since the trajectory of "unsettling" is central to all of his plays. The intensely negative response to many of Ibsen's plays often came from the same readers and viewers who responded so positively to the initial *hyggelig* atmosphere. The Danish author M. V. Brun, the reviewer cited earlier who reacted initially to *A Doll House* almost as he would to a holiday play, was for that same reason all the more indignant at its conclusion. Toward the end of his review, he concludes:

> All of the pleasure he provides us in the first acts evaporates in the third, and one sits there in the most painful frame of mind [*den pinligste Stemning*], sickened by a catastrophe that departs from universal values in the harshest manner in order to pay homage to that which is untrue, something that in aesthetic, psychological, and dramatic respects is equally outrageous. I ask straight out: Is there one mother among thousands of mothers, one wife among thousands of wives, who would behave as Nora does, who would leave husband, children and home in order to herself first and foremost become "a human being"? And I answer definitively: No, and once again, no![77]

This critical reaction to *A Doll House* is most often cited for its reactionary content, to smugly mark the distance between the conservative social positions of Ibsen's day and later, more progressive opinions about the woman question. More interesting for my purposes, however, is the physical pain that is described as the initial pleasure has given way, leaving the reviewer "sickened" by the catastrophe witnessed on stage. Many such reactions were described in the press, especially in response to *A Doll House, Ghosts*, and *The Wild Duck*, that suite of plays in the early 1880s in which audiences began to assimilate a particular expectation for Ibsen's plays: *hygge* as a prelude to pain.

These reactions are worth special attention here because they have not been emphasized adequately in past studies, a somewhat surprising fact given the intensity of the rhetoric. For example, how can one ignore the fact that a Norwegian reviewer of the Christiania premiere of *A Doll House* in January 1880 claimed the effect of Krogstad's entrance into the idyllic Helmer home to be the same as "to tear into living flesh [*at flænge i levende Kjød*]"?[78] The intensity of the comment points to the corporeal aspect of live theater, underscoring the phenomenological and spatial attachment to *hygge* that could be developed in several ways in the performed versions of the play. This same intensity can be found in another reaction to this performance; it mentions that even when one is familiar with the plot of the play from prior reading, the effect on stage for some viewers resembles "the sight of a vivisection that they find it painful to endure [*Synet af et Slags Vivisektion, som de finder det pinligt at overvære*]."[79] One reviewer of the Copenhagen premiere performance in December 1879 writes of the experience of watching the play as time on the "torture rack [*Pinebænken*],"[80] prompting a counterreaction that admits the intensity of the suffering but chides critics for not seeing the higher purpose of the drama, as Christians did in the age of martyrs.[81] In Denmark, the popular conversation in the vicinity of the Royal Theater after the premiere reportedly included the comment, "I have never before been so tortured [*forpint*] in a theater."[82]

One does not typically think of the original audience for *A Doll House* as writhing in pain – only indignation – so one might be forgiven for simply discounting this rhetoric as excessive. It should not simply be waved off, however; it is a fact of the discourse generated by the play that writers frequently indulged in this kind of description of the audience's suffering. This focus on the pain of the response was present even in less flamboyant accounts of the play:

> And it is such a painful and depressing [*pinligt og nedslaaende*] impression that one cannot shake it off later – it casts its shadow over daily life and gives us the feeling that the stench of lies and deception from *A Doll House* still encircles us. It is naturally different for each individual: but every thinking person would have to feel painfully moved [*pinligt berørt*] at seeing *A Doll House* on stage. And to the extent that one does not attend the theater only in order to suffer and be shaken up [*pines og rystes*], one could expect that a writer of Ibsen's great talent, instead of only assaulting us [*at slaa os*] also gave us something to please our minds.[83]

One catches a glimpse here of a trace of the baseline attitude that Scandinavian theatergoers brought to *A Doll House*: an expectation of pleasure ("something to please our minds"). When that expectation was reinforced by the initial spatial and atmospheric impressions of Ibsen's opening scenes, it only made the eventual assault on the audience more torturous. A final example can sum up this response to *A Doll House*:

> The scenes in the first and second acts in which the sun-filled "doll home's" comfort and happiness are depicted, and in which the songbird romps around with the children, decorates the Christmas tree, and plays hide-and-seek, belong to the most lovely scenes one can imagine depicted on stage. This luster and charm make an even deeper impression in contrast to the darker and darker shadows that eventually spread over the home, until the most unpleasant impression [*det Uhyggeligste*] gains the upper hand to such a degree, that it becomes torturous for the spectators.[84]

Ghosts upped the ante. Actual performance of the play exceeded what any of the national theaters dared, at least in the usual window after its initial publication, so there are no corresponding immediate impressions recorded from the established theater audiences of the sort one can find for *A Doll House*. Even so, the mere act of reading it produced similar hyperboles of pain. One reviewer wrote, "We suffered from its ghastly horror [*grufuldes Uhygge*]" and said that the Christiania Theater was right in rejecting the play for that reason.[85] When the play was eventually staged by the independent touring troupe led by August Lindberg, these effects only escalated. From the same 1883 performance of *Ghosts* in Helsingborg (mentioned earlier) where the audience was presented initially with "a pleasant [*hyggelig*] room with Nordic comfort," we get this view from a different visiting Norwegian reporter: "On the other hand it is certain enough that the enjoyment [of the play] was *extremely taxing and not very pleasant* [*anstrengende og lidet hyggelig*]: many had to wipe cold sweat from their brow, and there will surely only be a few who wish to see *Ghosts* very often" (original emphasis).[86] Figure 3 is a studio photograph of Lindberg himself as Osvald and Hedvig Winterhjelm as Helene Alving recreating the final scene of *Ghosts* for a studio portrait, giving some sense of the pathos and pain elicted by the ending of that play.

The renowned Danish author Herman Bang, who also attended the Lindberg production in Helsingborg (and would later himself play the role of Osvald in that play in 1885), gave this famous account of his feverish response to the play, which he projects onto the surrounding audience as well:

> There is no other way to describe my impression than this: there was not enough air in the large and empty theater. One gasped as if under a weight on the chest. There is one single scene that was performed with all the recklessness that Ibsen has demanded, which allows this anguished terror to climb almost to mortal fear. I doubt that our public could bear this scene. It is when Osvald wants to convince his mother to give him the capsules.[87]

48 Ibsen's uncanny

Figure 3: Studio photograph of August Lindberg as Osvald and Hedvig Winterhjelm as Mrs. Alving in *Ghosts*. Production: August Lindberg Scandinavian touring production, August 1883–May 1884.

An eventual visit by Lindberg's itinerant troupe to Kristianstad, Sweden, reportedly produced similar effects: "The audience sweated and shuddered, and it will certainly not forget *Ghosts* soon."[88]

This composite picture of a sweating, shuddering, gasping, tortured, aghast, and sickened audience is not as important to verify factually as it is to appreciate for its "tellability." That is, it may not be the case that most audience members actually found *Ghosts* physically unbearable, though there is mention of some spectators in Copenhagen having to leave during the final act.[89] More interesting, however, is the fact that this kind of anecdote had legs in the discourse surrounding the play and was worth retelling until it became an inherent part of the story. It seems likely that the vivid description of the audience's pain was a way of making sense of its thwarted expectations, of that initially *hyggelig* home turned desolate. Perhaps every Ibsenian home was experienced as sharing the fate of Dr. Stockmann's in *An Enemy of the People*, in which the opening cheery toddy party turns into an uninhabitable wreck of a home with the wind blowing through the smashed windows by the end of the play. The audience's pain was surely intensified by the loss of the initial, relatively cheery home by means of the typical Ibsenian ambush partway through each play, which apparently "hit home" with tremendous force when Ibsen's plays were first performed.

The tension between *hygge* and *uhygge* came to a head in the reaction to *The Wild Duck*; none of the other plays generated such explicit commentary on the subject, thanks in large part to two productions of the play, one in Bergen and the other in Christiania in January 1885. The opening salvo came in a forceful articulation of the issue by the Norwegian critic, journalist, literary historian, and eventual Ibsen biographer Henrik Jæger. Jæger had been quite negative in his critique of *Ghosts* and had only begun to come around to an appreciation of Ibsen when reviewing *The Wild Duck*.[90]

His assessment repeats some of the rhetoric of pain as cited earlier from the other plays, but it adds a foregrounded sense of the uncanny/unhomely aspects of the play in his review of the Christiania production:

> It has been said about Henrik Ibsen that he is the poet of unease [*Uhygge*], and *The Wild Duck* shows better than any of his other works how true this observation is. It is a piece of great scenic effect, but the effect is from start to finish that of unease [*Uhygge*]. That is the basic mood of the piece, and it is varied with unbelievable virtuosity, with a real demonic mastery, compared to which Paganini's "Witches' Dance" or Böcklin's eeriest [*uhyggeligste*] images from the world of sagas and fairy tales count for nothing. Ibsen is a master of unease [*Uhygge*]. It cuts through the cheery party in the first act

in the form of Old Ekdal's worn-out figure, not like a knife – no, tearing and ripping like a shard of glass through living flesh.⁹¹

Jæger's review ends in much the same vein: "Unease added to unease, from beginning to end; there is a veritable wallowing in unease, in a manner that is both refined and intense [*Uhygge og atter Uhygge fra først til sidst; der fraadses formelig i Uhygge, raffineret og umaadelig*]."⁹²

These are rich passages, with several aspects worthy of closer analysis. My translation of the Norwegian word *Uhygge* as "unease" in the quotation feels contextually correct but connotationally impoverished, since that word in English misses the associate meanings of gloom and visceral unpleasantness contained in the term. Many of Ibsen's reviewers (and not just of *The Wild Duck*) use the term *Uhygge* in that general way to convey the feelings of unrelenting physical oppression that often marked the performance atmosphere of plays like *Ghosts* and *Rosmersholm*; in those cases, one might prefer to translate *Uhygge* in any number of other ways – as "gloom," "oppressiveness," "unpleasantness," or "discomfort."⁹³ This is what seems best for another review of *The Wild Duck* not written by Jæger that called it one of Ibsen's "most unpleasant and dreary [*uhyggeligste og trøsteløse*]" plays.⁹⁴

I would argue in Jæger's case, however, that the term *Uhygge* is used more strategically to convey a specific sense of the uncanny, especially in the widened sense of the "unhomely" that was discussed earlier. I have conveyed that sense here by translating it as "unease" in his review, since the sense of "unhousing" inherent in the experience of the uncanny is clearly what Jæger had in mind by piling up his mentions of the term. In *The Wild Duck*, Jæger sees a home that is not a home, a family façade that hides some very unpleasant truths, and a lack of any redeeming meaning in the suffering on stage. These are all forms of "unsettling" the domestic world and putting the spectator in a position of unease and estrangement.

The physical aspect of *Uhygge* as a special effect of theatrical *performance* is clear when one examines Jæger's published reviews of the *book* version of *The Wild Duck*, which he published in a series of articles in November 1884.⁹⁵ As mentioned earlier, he speed-read the play to be the first to review it as a literary publication, so it may simply be that the uncanny perspectives in the material take some time to recognize. At any rate, in Jæger's role as literary critic in the debate about "journalistic" criticism during the week of November 12, 1884, there was not a hint of the uncanny reading of the play he would give as a *theater* critic two months later when he saw it on stage in Christiania; instead, it is a straightforward reading of the play in the context of Ibsen's earlier thematics. It is tempting to attribute this change more to the physical immediacy of theater than the interpretive space of a more leisurely reading.

It is also interesting that Jæger reveals at the outset of the January article that others before him have regarded Ibsen as a "poet of *Uhygge*"; by making that claim, he is apparently consciously joining an ongoing discussion on the topic in the cultural discourse of the time. When Jæger calls attention to the frequent repetition of the term, however, it seems to add up to more than a public consensus that Ibsen was depressing or pessimistic. The term has a more technical function in Jæger's discussion that, even if less complex than the Freudian model of the uncanny, nevertheless incorporates some of its same aspects of domestic dislocation and vestigial, temporal layering. It is for this reason, for example, that Jæger emphasizes the painful discordance of Old Ekdal's broken-down figure appearing out of place (and in his decrepit state, out of time as well) in a cheerful, contemporary high-society party. Interestingly, Jæger makes use of the same hyperbolic image of ripping flesh to describe the effect of Old Ekdal's uncanny appearance on spectators. Furthermore, if Paganini and Böcklin are the closest neighbors to the kind of *Uhygge* that Jæger is describing, it is clear that this is not simply another claim that Ibsen is gloomy: there is a much stronger presence of eerie haunting in Jæger's use of the term.

If we think of *Uhygge* in its architectural sense of unhomeliness, then Jæger's comments on scenography also become quite interesting. He finds the Ekdal home to be extremely unsettling, provoking in him a surprisingly intense reaction to the physical space that is worth quoting at length. Attributing a kind of agency to the idea of *Uhygge*, Jæger writes:

> It [*Uhygge* itself] arranges the stage in the following acts in the shape of Hjalmar Ekdal's studio, this uncanny [*uhyggelige*] hybrid of a living room, a dining room and a workroom, just as devoid of a living room's cozy hominess as of a dining room's well-being and a workroom's busy activity; this repulsive bastard of a room [*denne Modbydelige Bastard af et Rum*], in which the odor of collodion and other photographic chemicals mixes in with the aroma of food, the smell of beer, and the reek of liquor, in which everyday clothing, photographic equipment, plates, bottles, glasses, and living-room furniture have gathered to meet, and in which the fantastic old loft sends its icy cold in from the one corner, while the great, cold glass studio roof spreads unease [*Uhygge*] from another, sometimes in the form of pale moonlight, which disturbs the harmony of the subdued lamplight, and at other times in the form of a cold-grey daylight and melting slush.[96]

The mixed function of the "bastard room" that the Ekdals call home challenges the received notion of the home as a protected, unified nest, a beacon of light set off against the darkness of the exterior world. Jæger amplifies that effect in his reaction, which in its vehemence provides us in turn with a measure of the expectations of harmony that had been thwarted. Instead of a peaceful domestic haven, one gets a room that is an "uncanny in-between thing" in every way: in function, in lighting, in its furnishing and other trappings.

No photographs of the 1885 production in Christiania survive, but there are some ways to get an idea of the effect of the play on stage. An illustration of the Ekdal interior was published in the Norwegian weekly periodical *Ny Illustreret Tidende* in April of that year (Figure 4). For the most part, this drawing conveys a fairly faithful rendition of Ibsen's stage directions for the play, with some minor adjustments to the described placement of the doors and a bit less clutter than one might expect, given Ibsen's written stage directions. Also, here the sliding doors opening onto the attic in the rear are either wallpapered or painted with flowers and a

Figure 4: Hedvig's body is carried out from the attic in the final scene of *The Wild Duck*. Production: Christiania Theater, prem. January 11, 1885.

Figure 5: Set photograph from a later production of *The Wild Duck*, showing recycled elements from the Christiania Theater set. Production: National Theater (Oslo), prem. March 16, 1904.

balustrade for a mild *trompe l'oeil* effect, a visual flourish not in the original text, which does not describe the attic doors in detail.

It is important not to be too trusting of stage illustrations drawn from memory by correspondents and illustrators, but in this case one can with some confidence confirm a number of the details of this drawing by looking at Anders Wilse's photograph of the National Theater's 1904 production of *The Wild Duck* (Figure 5), which seems to have largely reused the scenography from the earlier production at the Christiania Theater. One can see the repetition of the décor on the walls, the placement of the furniture, the coat rack in the back, the angle of the glass roof, and the same painted scene on the sliding doors in the back, the added detail that seems to link the two set depictions most strongly. From the later photograph, then, one can through a kind of relay confirm with a sharper picture the probable look of the set in 1885.

In looking at this set, it is hard to recreate Jæger's feeling of disgust and revulsion about the mixing of spaces, at least from its architectural qualities alone, and in that sense it is a bit hard to understand his reaction. And when one looks at other reviews of the same production, one finds some disagreement about Jæger's characterization of the space as *uhyggelig*. There could be a class-based dimension to Jæger's reaction, since the working classes at the time almost always lived in "bastard" spaces too small to afford supposedly "proper" divisions of function. Since Jæger came from a lower-middle-class background and never made a very secure living as a writer himself, the constant threat of falling into poverty might partly explain his unusually intense rhetoric in seeing this kind of hybrid living space represented on stage. Showing such a mixed space on stage was also something of a novelty at this point in time, so perhaps a certain upsetting of theatrical habit is at work in his reaction as well.

It was most likely this article by Jæger from January 13, 1885, that prompted the response on the other side of the debate, the review by "H. H." that was introduced earlier ("The opinion of some that finds the Ekdal home to be *uhyggeligt*"). That review's willful reading of Act Two as a positive, cozy family scene stands in contrast to Jæger's claim that the play positively "wallowed" in *uhygge*. After all, the reviews came only a week apart and, most importantly, were written in response to the very same production and stage setting. "H. H." cites the general mood of the audience at the Christiania Theater as evidence, noting the cheerfulness of the audience and its lively response to the comic elements of the play, as well as the "quite homey" set. Since these would seem to be elements of the physical theater experience, and thus not be so open to interpretive disagreement, it is all the more interesting that Jæger's response is so emphatic in its perception of *uhygge*.

The best explanation for such disparities in reaction is that this play, more than any other of Ibsen's dramas, contains strong elements of both. It is common to describe the play as a tragicomedy; a slight shift of emphasis allows us to see in that term the culmination of the dynamic of the uncanny. *The Wild Duck* is a hybrid of *hygge* and *uhygge* as well, an "*uhyggelig* in-between thing" not only in terms of genre but also in terms of architectural setting. Although I certainly find Jæger's assessment to be more persuasive now than the naively happy reading of the play – it is fairer to say that textual evidence of the play tips more strongly toward the "unhomely" reading – the interesting historical point is that Ibsen's contemporaries, armed with the determined expectation of finding a more centered home on stage, actually did find it there. These now-eccentric viewers placed what one today would see as an inappropriate emphasis on the play's more cheerful tendencies and came away with scenes of *hygge* playing in their heads. That they did this in spite of what they must have regarded as that unfortunate bit about Hedvig at the end simply shows the extent and power of the audience's "homey" expectations.

We can see this tension played out in a review of the play at the Royal Theater in Copenhagen, with Betty Hennings in the role of Hedvig.[97] The commentator, Arthur Rothenburg-Mens, clearly understood that to perform the play correctly, one had to give spectators a contrast between *hygge* and *uhygge*. His main criticism of this production was that the play demands a stronger chiaroscuro effect than what was possible on the massive Copenhagen stage:

> Act Two is supposed to present a modest, but pleasantly [*hyggeligt*] arranged and furnished room ... The important atmospheric background that Ibsen has given the attic space lay there unused. It was arranged with an insistent clarity; there was nothing dusky or ghostly about it; ... In this *mise-en-scène* there was no eeriness [*Uhygge*] or horror in the attic space, just as its human counterpart, the idyllic Ekdal family life, was erased.[98]

The objection to the flattening of contrasts shows that some critics understood quite well what the play was about: the kind of "ripping flesh" that accompanies a jarring, precipitous slide from *hygge* into its opposite.

Perhaps the view that opens up for commentators such as Jæger and Rothenberg-Mens, the insight that becomes "tellable" in this particularly painful way, was a shared glimpse with Ibsen into the surprising tenuousness of one's sense of belonging in a home. By subjecting supposedly instinctive forms of family intimacy to sudden reversals and estrangement, he reveals the arbitrary and constructed aspects that might underpin one's sense of belonging, creating a distinct impression of unease. By observing the familiar at a distance, as if through the hunter's framing hands in "On the Heights," Ibsen is able to turn *hygge* from a given cultural norm into a proper subject for his probing form of theater. It is this issue of the theatrical home and its unmasking that will guide my analysis in the next chapter.

CHAPTER 2

Façades unmasked

During the summer of 1864, amidst the flood of impressions from his first summer in Italy, Ibsen wrote a short poem entitled "*Fra Mit Husliv.*"[1] Translated literally, the title would read "From My House-Life," although "From My Domestic Life" would be kinder to the English ear. In four 5-line stanzas, the poem treats two sudden shifts in mood in a domestic scene. It begins with the house interior quiet and the street outside "dead," the living room wrapped in soft shadows. It is a time of contemplation and implied intellectual reflection. Suddenly, the narrator's children come tumbling into the room, freshly scrubbed and lively, and the mood shifts to laughter and tumult. Then, just as suddenly, "just as the game was moving along at its best," the narrator catches a glimpse in a mirror of a "stocky guest" looking back at him with leaden eyes, a closed vest, and slippers. At this moment, a weight falls on both the narrator and the happy children, who suddenly turn shy, clumsy, and subdued "in the proximity of a stranger."

Herleiv Dahl's reading of the poem in his classic 1958 overview study of Ibsen's poetic production concurs with those who interpret the "wild flock" symbolically, with the children standing in for the untameable characters from Ibsen's frustrating work on "Epic Brand" in 1864.[2] In a brief mention of the poem in the Centenary Edition of Ibsen's collected works, Didrik Arup Seip reads it biographically instead, as an example of Ibsenian self-criticism and a hint of his sense of failure on the family front.[3] Seen in that light, the emphasis would land on a poet plagued by self-reflection and melancholy, unable to participate fully in the joys of family life. One might also see continuity in theme from "On the Heights," written five years earlier, in which ties to family had to be sacrificed for the sake of an artistic calling. There, the "higher" perspective involved the ability to view dispassionately through an aesthetic frame the burning of the family home. Here, the family tableau of giggling children fresh from the bath, for all its charm, cannot withstand the power of an artist's sudden introspective glance.

Façades unmasked 57

Ibsen's ongoing attention to the theme of *hygge* and the uncanny, as discussed in the previous chapter, adds an extra layer of meaning to the poem. Key to my reading would be the suddenness of the reversals – the explosion of "madcap [*viltre*]" children into the poet's room of solitary contemplation, followed by the equally abrupt intrusion of a second self, a double in the mirror who can logically be no one other than the narrator himself, yet is identified as a stranger.[4] This unsettling appearance of the strange within the familiar immediately turns the mood literally and figuratively *un*familiar – outside the family – and points to the fundamental instability of the demarcated and protected intimate sphere. In the presence of strangers, the poem states, even the most lively (*de raskeste*) boys become subdued. In this poem, the super-*hyggelig* becomes the super-*uhyggelig*.

The unease of the children in the poem is reminiscent of two scenes from Ibsen's early prose plays, written a decade or more later. The first occurs in *A Doll House*, where Nora is playing a lively game of hide and seek with her children and the game is interrupted by the loan shark Nils Krogstad's first entrance. The mood changes immediately. Nora tells the children, whom she has just described as having cheeks "like apples and roses," that "the strange man won't do mommy any harm."[5] As in the poem's line "just when the game was moving along at its best," in the play the intrusion of a stranger disrupts the happy family game of hide and seek. The second echo of the poem can be found in *The Wild Duck*. There, the intrusive stranger is Gregers, who makes his first entrance into the Ekdal apartment in much the same manner, in the midst of what might be called the "Family Tableau with Beer and Flute." Again, the intrusion happens just as the "game" is going well. Hedvig's line at the beginning of Act Four, when the sum total of the Ekdals' performative family routines has been definitively disrupted by Gregers, echoes the suddenly clumsy children in the poem: "it's turned so strange [*underligt*] here."[6] These examples all depict the potential for sudden alienation, even inside the domestic sphere.

The poem's use of the mirror as a sudden pivot point deserves comment because that objective reflection of the narrator's image introduces self-consciousness into family life for both the narrator and the children. This is contrasted to the immersive experience of being in the middle of the "game." At the moment of greatest absorption, the mirror reminds the narrator of his position in the scene and his performance of a role. Once one sees clearly, the poem seems to suggest, the game cannot proceed unaffected: self-awareness and consciousness rupture the absorption of performance. The parallels to Heinrich von Kleist's essay "On the Marionette Theater" (*Über das Marionettentheater*) from 1810 are suggestive (there the

:dote concerns a young dancer who becomes conscious of himself moving ?fully in a mirror and then cannot intentionally repeat the motion).⁷ In this updated, more thoroughly bourgeois scene, family *hygge* is the illusion that can easily be disrupted – all it takes is a single look back from the mirror.

In the preceding chapter, I showed that Ibsen's interrogation of *hygge* entailed consistent reversals of otherwise reliable signifiers of family happiness and comfort. Here, I explore more fully the consequences of unmasking the home, focusing on the ways in which Ibsen activates the idea of walls and façades in the source domain of his architectural metaphor system. His central questions are these: Can the home absorb the fundamental shift in consciousness that an "unmasking" entails, or is "home" the kind of performance that does not tolerate such interruptions? Further, in most metaphoric systems, façades are assumed to be false or misleading, so what does one find when one removes them? If something of substance is possible behind the domestic façade, how does one then create a building that is consistent inside and out? In what ways might the rhetoric of unmasking be compatible with the idea of reform? Or is the act of exposure too destabilizing and destructive? In this chapter, I concentrate my analysis on the first two plays of Ibsen's prose cycle, *Pillars of Society* and *A Doll House*, together with relevant reception material. These two plays contain some of the most overt use of architectural metaphor in Ibsen's *oeuvre* (only *The Master Builder* rivals them on that account). They also share a strong interest in façades and their unmasking. The dramatic fallout is not identical (Nora's slammed door does make a difference), but both plays differ from those that follow by holding out the (fading) possibility of rebuilding (something) on true foundations.

The unmasking that takes place in Ibsen's plays, the shift of consciousness that changes everything for characters, can be represented by a single word pair: the difference between "home" and "house." In the poem just cited, "home" is most easily associated with the participatory mode of the *hyggelig* scene with the children, games, and smoke-filled room, and "house" with the unmasking glance in the mirror. "Home" implies the smooth and absorbed performance of family roles that is set in motion the moment the children come tumbling in; "house" reflects the more analytical facts of the situation (stripped of emotional content, the room contains only a stocky man in vest and slippers and suddenly awkward children). Or to put it in art historian Michael Fried's terms, "home" is absorption, whereas "house" is theatricality.⁸ This is a complicated claim that will require a detailed argument. The first part of that argument, the focus of the present chapter, concerns the aesthetics of unmasking. The second, which occupies the following chapter, charts the growing denigration of domesticity in Ibsen's plays and the emergence of alternative modes of inhabitation.

First, though, a few commonsense observations about house and home will suggest why these terms lend themselves to this kind of thinking. As in most Germanic languages (English included), common usage in Norwegian would understand "house [*hus*]" as a lesser version of "home [*hjem*]." "House" is often taken to be the more neutral descriptor that denotes the factual, physical domestic structure. Given that word as a semantic anchor, "home" is then free to attract all of the surplus meanings of domesticity, such as connotations of childhood origin, security, protection, familial connection, ethnic roots, cultural tradition, or national identity. In Norwegian as in English, that is, "home" is simply "house" augmented by some positive sense of attachment.

One gets a hint of this potential already in "On the Heights" from 1859. As we have seen, in that early poem the mentor braces the poem's narrator during the personal test of the Christmas conflagration scene by encouraging him to see the loss of his childhood home in more neutral terms: "After all, the old house is merely burning up."[9] At first glance, this seems to tap into the usual distinction between house and home (in the sense that losing an old house would not be as disastrous as losing a home). There is more than that going on here, however, because that phrase – *det brænder jo bare, det gamle hus* – could also be seen as a kind of artist's motto. The ability to call the home a *house* is the precondition for seeing life stripped of its feeling (in the same way that to call a house a *home* is to activate the whole range of ethical and social obligations that aesthetic distance would ignore). If the poem's narrator can watch the scene through the frame of his hand – a picture frame – he can free himself for what he takes to be higher pursuits than family, cozy furs, cats, and Christmas beer. We in turn might say today that by creating a position of observation, Ibsen makes visible the ideological status of the term "home" and thereby deprives it of its automatic function as a consensus social ideal. The unmasking allows readers and viewers to see the less desirable aspects of that ideal and to imagine positions outside the home, such as that of the artist.

The very attempt to describe such a position in language reveals some of the difficulties Ibsen faced, however: to describe it as "homelessness [*hjemløshet*]" casts the issue too clearly as a matter of loss and captures none of the gains Ibsen saw in leaving the home. An invented (and awkward) phrase such as "to become un-homed" is more precise and gets closer to a positive notion of a newly disencumbered individual, but that too depends on readers and viewers agreeing in advance that "home" is damaging or limiting more than it is protective. The fact that there is not a ready term for this process of detachment that explains itself without the help of a gloss simply demonstrates the degree to which Ibsen's project was (and remains) positioned in difficult conceptual (and therefore new semantic) territory. The question goes beyond simple "homelessness," asking instead what exactly one can inhabit outside the home.

In the early prose plays under consideration in this chapter, Ibsen concentrates his attention on a redefinition of home as an alternative, unrealized ideal. In his first attempts at unmasking, that is, Ibsen removes a given home's false façade to invoke a truer home elsewhere, a home based in fantasies of absolute structural integrity. The rhetoric of foundations, pillars, and windows is most relevant to this first stage, since that set of images is so well suited to expressing the disparity between public appearance and private reality.

The model home

Early in the text of *Pillars of Society*, the first play of Ibsen's prose cycle, the schoolmaster Rørlund leads a ladies' group in a discussion of a book entitled *Woman as the Servant of Society*.[10] As this self-appointed "moral pillar" lectures the prim and proper ladies of the "Society for the Morally Corrupt"[11] – none of whom see any irony in the name – he introduces one of the central metaphors of the play: the ideal of the structurally sound social building. Clearly enjoying hearing himself talk, Rørlund expounds on the dangers of the rapidly modernizing society outside their small coastal Norwegian town:

> This gilded, cosmetic exterior [*Denne forgylte og sminkede yderside*] that the great societies present to view, – what does it actually conceal? Hollowness and rottenness, I dare say. No moral foundation under one's feet. In a single word – they are whitewashed sepulchers, these great societies of our day.[12]

Note the intriguing blend of theatrical and architectural imagery here: cosmetics mixed with hollow façades, rotting foundations, and whitewashed sepulchers. As Toril Moi has pointed out, a mix of theatrical and religious metaphor allows us to appraise Rørlund at once as "antitheatrical, idealist, and completely bigoted."[13] I would only add that among Ibsen's fictional characters, Rørlund is one of the strongest proponents of the social building metaphor as well. As he continues in this vein throughout the first act of the play, he describes how family life is "undermined" in modern society and how truths are challenged by "reckless desires to overthrow [*frække omstyrtningslyster*]."[14] He suggests to Martha Bernick that a life full of sacrifice gives "a firmer foundation to stand on" than the "great roiling human society, where so many go to ruin."[15]

Rørlund's growing architectural euphoria throughout this first scene is about to culminate in this way: "And in a house like this, – in a good and pure home, where family life appears in its most beautiful guise, where peace and harmony rule,"[16] at which point comes the first of many Ibsenian deflations in the play, namely an audible commotion from Bernick's study that flatly contradicts what Rørlund has just said. In fact, peace and harmony do not rule in this home's interior, where at that very moment a railroad development scheme is being hashed out by Bernick and his partners.

With this first unmasking, Ibsen sets the tone for a play in which every equation of moral rectitude with architectural stability turns out to have the logic of a false façade. The "pillars of the community" – Bernick and his three partners – are deceptive land speculators. Rørlund's own "foundation" of moral self-sacrifice shows itself to be guided by various forms of self-interest. The Bernick household as a "model [*mønster*] for our fellow citizens" turns out to be based on a crucial lie in the past.[17] The ideal model is constantly unmasked to contain real contradictions instead; the play's recurring and excessive architectural metaphors all concern an apparent solidity that gives way under the pressures of plot. This is the way hypocrisy most commonly gets imagined in architectural terms, either as a disparity between superstructure and foundation or between façade and interior. The first operates on a vertical axis and the second on a horizontal, but both posit a deceptive surface that conceals the moral lack located "beneath" or "behind."

Ibsen's vertical imagination was noticed early on by William Archer, who produced an adapted translation of the play in Britain in 1880. He gave it the title *Quicksands (The Supports of Society)*.[18] Although one might wonder about the adapted title, it does have the virtue of cutting to the quick of the play's metaphoric system by giving away from the start the result of the eventual unmasking. The pillar metaphor depends for its persuasiveness in our daily architectural experience on the expectation of solidity; we expect buildings to stand and floors not to give way. The quicksand metaphor, though cliché, has enduring appeal to the imagination because a special, elemental horror attaches to the idea of an apparently solid ground that conceals an abyss. In many ways, the opening act of *Pillars of Society* fits neatly into fairly traditional notions of quicksand as a moral metaphor (another version of this abyss image will appear in connection with *A Doll House*).

As for the horizontal equivalent – the façade and what it conceals – Asbjørn Aarseth has pointed out that the idea of seeing through façades has been commonly associated with the activity of theatergoing throughout history.[19] Especially in the dramatic tradition that culminated with Ibsen in the late nineteenth century, a play presented spectators with an initial appearance that changed when subjected to the pressures of dramatic elaboration. If the façade were sufficient in itself, there would be no need to explore the building's interior, so to speak, nothing further for the theater to discover through its processes of exposition, conflict, and resolution. Nowhere is this truer than in the form of analytic drama that Ibsen developed and perfected. In his mode of theater, initial appearances are categorically deceptive, and the drama's task is to dismantle the façade to find out what lies behind it, if anything. (This kind of layered drama of surface and depth was abandoned in many [not all] forms of twentieth-century drama, in which more existential approaches offer the stage as all that exists.) The analytic drama thus almost always entails a system of architectural metaphor built around the idea of *apparent* solidity. In this regard, Ibsen's dramas show close kinship to novels of the period that similarly thematize the deceptive aspects of façade architecture, with the Danish writer Herman Bang providing the prime example in his 1887 novel *Stucco*.[20]

The structuring of a play such as *Pillars of Society* around the logic of the façade also gives it a metatheatrical aspect, as can be seen in the play's striking scenography. The main element is the large glass wall upstage that separates the home from the garden where the crowd gathers to celebrate Bernick as a pillar of the community in the last act of the play. The curtains that cover the transparent back wall of windows – mentioned with overt emphasis by the characters at several points in the play – mimic the stage curtain that covers the transparent fourth wall separating audience and stage, in effect creating a stage playing area with audience space on both sides. To put it another way, we are not just dealing with the "invisible fourth wall" separating the realistic stage from the audience, but a fictional "invisible third wall" as well, separating the main characters inside the home from the larger fictional world outside it. Figure 6 shows how that ambitious spatial arrangement – surely the most detailed and layered scenography in all of Ibsen's works judging from the almost novelistic detail of the set decription in the text – was realized in an early Danish production at the Royal Theater. The actual theater audience has an advantage over the depicted audience of the staged crowd, since it has access to all the private dealings of the family and can see both the family and the fictional audience without being seen in return, as is dictated by the

Figure 6: Act Two of *Pillars of Society*, showing the "invisible third wall" in the back of the set. Production: Royal Theater (Copenhagen), prem. November 18, 1877.

conventions of realism. Aarseth finds the physical arrangement of the stage in this play to be such a compelling expression of the fundamental assumptions of Ibsenian theater that he subtitles his excellent study of Ibsen's scenography *En Studie i Glasskapets Dramaturgi*, which would translate literally as "a study in the dramaturgy of the display case."

Aarseth's organizing metaphor is the *glasskab* (I retain the original spelling from Ibsen's text in the following discussion), the piece of furniture common to middle-class homes in which objects of value are put on display for guests ("vitrine" or "glass cabinet" are possible translations). The image comes from the oft-cited exchange between Lona Hessel and Mr. Rummel late in the play, just as the crowd is about to gather under torchlight to celebrate the town's leading citizen and his family. The complications of the dramatic action have by this point in the play thoroughly discredited the initial happy façade of family life presented in Act One; readers and viewers both know by this point that Bernick's family life and reputation have been built on deception and that the home is not the model it is generally taken to be. It is at this juncture that Mr. Rummel, pillar of the community and political *metteur-en-scène*, prepares for the evening's planned program:

RUMMEL: Damn these newfangled contraptions; I can't get the curtains down.
LONA HESSEL: Are they coming down? I thought instead –
RUMMEL: First down, Miss. You do know what is supposed to happen, right?
LONA HESSEL: I see. Let me help (grabs the drawstrings); I'll let the curtains go down for my brother-in-law, – although I'd rather raise them.
RUMMEL: You can do that later as well. When the garden is filled with the teeming crowd, the curtains go up and one looks in on a surprised and happy family; – a citizen's home should be like a display case [*glasskab*].[21]

The metatheatrical aspects of this scene have been thoroughly discussed in several previous studies, where commentary has focused on the obvious parallels between Rummel's public display of the private family and the many family lives put on stage by the nineteenth-century realist theater more generally. Also of interest has been the disparity between the ideal tableau Rummel imagines and the dealings on the fictional "backstage" in *Pillars of Society*. As Aarseth points out, Rummel wants to present an ideal, static tableau, not a full dramatization of family life in all of its complexity and contradictions – that would be closer to what Ibsen *actually* gives the audience sitting in the theater in *Pillars*.[22]

Toril Moi, using Aarseth's analysis as a point of departure, elaborates on the implications of the *glasskab* sequence for models of theatricality. This line of research, originating in Michael Fried's influential discussion of "absorption" and "theatricality," has been productive in Ibsen studies for more than a decade now.[23] The main interest of this research has been to understand Ibsen's peculiar combination of realist aesthetics, which lean toward the absorption side of Fried's schema (in the *Pillars* example, this could be found in the "surprised" element of the family caught unawares), and metatheatrical elements, which demonstrate a more theatrical consciousness (conveyed in the careful posing of the family to create that effect of surprise for the public). In Moi's analysis of this problem in *Pillars of Society*, it is "unlivable ideals" that produce Bernick's theatricality (this is in line with her overall thesis that Ibsen's modernism is best seen as the result of his break with idealist philosophy and aesthetics).[24] It is important to note that the model she invokes is not the more celebratory view of performative role-play common in postmodernism – instead, it is the theatricality of insincerity and false performance, evaluated from an ethical standpoint. To put it another way, it is the kind of theatricality that is generated by the disparity between appearance and reality, which always carries an ethical valence. For Moi, Ibsen's modernism consists in his recognizing and depicting theatricality as a philosophical and moral problem, not in espousing it as a positive aesthetic as one might find with more postmodernist sensibilities.

Sincerity and integrity are not only theatrical issues, however – they have architectural resonance as well. When Bernick performs his public confession, he says that before he is entrusted with leading the community in the future, his fellow citizens must get to know him thoroughly, "to the depths [*tilbunds*]."[25] The promised unmasking of his personality's true foundation shows that the long-standing dream of "being" instead of "seeming" is as easily expressed by metaphors of foundations and buildings (or interiors and façades) as it is by that of souls and masks. The advantage of the architectural register is that it more easily figures integrity as a social issue, since buildings are shared spaces that exceed individual subjectivity. The revelation of a building's foundation thus seems more socially consequential than the unmasking of a single individual's true motives.

For this reason, it is interesting to see the way in which Lona Hessel corrects Bernick's attempt to redefine the metaphor of "pillar of society" as the play closes. Bernick claims to have learned that he and his speculator colleagues are not the true pillars of society, but that women have that potential instead. Lona implies that this is a limited sort of lesson, hinting that Bernick's transformation was not yet complete. This point was clearly understood even in the earliest commentary on *Pillars of Society*, and since that time readers and viewers have often been suspicious of Bernick's final stance. Even early reviews seized on the fact that although he has come clean about the backroom railroad deal and the affair fifteen years earlier, at no point does he admit to the crowd that he knowingly just sent out an unseaworthy ship to its near-certain doom.[26] Perhaps for that reason as well, Lona immediately redirects his pillar metaphor in a more abstract direction, claiming that society's true building cannot be based on individual people at all. Instead, in the famous closing line of the play, Lona claims, "the spirit of truth and of freedom, – *those* are the pillars of society."[27]

Lona Hessel's invocation of freedom and truth as the most dependable pillars of society is an important gesture with several conceptual implications. Most obvious is that she does not reject the metaphor that compares society to a building, as several of Ibsen's later, more radical characters will do – in her view it is just a matter of finding the right building materials. Stepping outside the architectural metaphoric source domain will provide some useful leverage on the idea of "pillars." As mentioned in the Introduction, other possible source domains could be used to increase the legibility of the abstract concept "society," the target domain. Society could be compared to a body, or a machine, or a plant, all of which would entail a different literary figuration were they to be chosen as the play's central metaphor. We might then have Bernick appearing as the lead in *The Legs of Society*. Or perhaps *The Wheels of Society*? Or to reimagine the concluding line, we would get "The sprouts of society are truth and freedom." This substitution exercise is not only facetious, though it is that as well. It helps put some pressure on the rhetorical choice that Ibsen acctually did make and that was accepted so readily in this early prose play: society is a building, and the pillars supporting it, which are originally assumed in a conventional way to be the leading men of the community, turn out to be abstract principles instead.

The consensus around that metaphor is what allowed reviewers to respond positively to the play's essentially "constructive" stance. For example, Carl Thrane's account of the Royal Theater's production of the play in Copenhagen in the fall of 1877 mentions approvingly, "This piece thus does not just tear down, but builds up" and speaks of "truth as the correct foundation for happiness [*Lykkens rette Grundvold*]."[28] This is almost an exact echo of what the Norwegian writer Arne Garborg wrote about the play, as quoted at the outset of this book. Here is the elaboration of Garborg's comments:

> The "upbuilding thought" that Ibsen has achieved is not new; but it is good. It is namely that they who call themselves the *pillars* of society [*Samfundsstyttur*] are merely the *tools* of society [*Samfundsreidskapar*], and that it is "*the spirit of truth and freedom* that are the pillars of society." We need to hear that here, where so many would like to prop up society with *artificial* pillars and frames and scaffolding [*kunstiga Støttur og Stengslur og Stellingar*], and believe that freedom is *dangerous* for society. [orig. emphasis][29]

Garborg imposes a hierarchy of pillars here when he claims that no one person could alone be adequate to support the social building, which must be built on higher principles (more *authentic* pillars) than the personal. In his view, individuals can only be the subordinated *tools* of society, not its pillars. Further, his insistence on natural, true, or otherwise authentic building materials in place of false ones makes a distinction between structurally sound societies that can stand on their own and those that would fall if not propped up artificially. Both of these points are in complete agreement with the stance Lona Hessel takes at the end of the play and demonstrate that in Garborg's view, Ibsen was still working securely within an essentially constructive architectural framework. In Garborg's commentary as well, the relevance of the architectural metaphor is not in question.

It is also clear from that response that the theatrical and architectural metaphors reinforce each other at the end of the play. No more masks! In the future, Bernick seems to indicate, private lives of complete integrity will be open to the public eye. No more façades, either! The new age will usher in a transparent architecture without backroom deals. This will indeed be a glass-walled house, but it will be Lona's unposed version in which the curtains are constantly open, not Rummel's artfully arranged ideal tableau (their awkward agreement about the need to raise the curtains – for entirely different reasons – shows the essential ambiguity of the unmasking gesture). The interior of the home is thus equated with perfectly transparent moral conduct, and a fantasy of complete integrity is imagined for them both.

What is left unresolved in *Pillars of Society* is the relationship of this imagined social building to the forces of modernity. Bernick's and Lona's rhetoric of pillars and foundations makes clear that the play expresses a simple reversal: at the start of the play, the schoolteacher Rørlund identified the new social impulses of the wider modern world as hollow and shaky, as a "white washed sepulcher" in which an attractive façade hides the corruption behind. By the end of the play, the duplicitous social structure of the traditional small town has come to be identified in the same terms, as a former age now put to rest. Bernick even proposes creating a kind of hypocrisy museum that will ensure the death of all forms of public deception and disparity: "The old [age], with its cosmetics, with its hypocrisy and its hollowness, with its deceptive propriety and its miserable deference, shall seem like a museum to us, open for instruction."[30] If the past can be treated as a museum, Bernick implies, one can ensure its death and cooperative burial. An Enlightenment confidence accompanies this image, since it proposes that the entombment of the past will make it available for safe observation and instruction. (As we will see in Chapter 4's discussion of *Ghosts*, the museum-memorial effort develops its own uncanny side effects.)

Interestingly, Bernick's metaphorical museum is given a strongly material turn as Bernick asks his three fellow "pillars of the community" to donate the actual honorary gifts they have received from the townspeople that evening: the tea set, the goblet, the album, and the collection of sermons. These would be fitting starter pieces for the Karsten Bernick Museum of Hypocrisy because they are precisely the sorts of objects that might be found on display in a bourgeois *glasskab*. Bernick begins by suggesting a figurative museum, but the metaphor's material turn brings it closer to architectural-theatrical practice, especially when the stage before the audience's eyes is itself conceived of as one giant display case.

When Bernick suggests the museum, Rummel's notion of an artificially composed tableau of ideal family life is with one stroke equated with a display in the past and put to rest – if one imagines that all those newly self-examining townspeople really would go home and upon reflection come to the same reasonable conclusion. What is left uncertain is this: if the old age seemed authentic but turned out to be false, can the new age that was intitially claimed to be hollow and superficial at the start of the play now take its place unproblematically as a burgeoning age of sincerity and authenticity? Is there really no residue of suspicion about that substitution? Ibsen's ongoing tussle with architectural metaphor in subsequent plays demonstrates the difficulty of defining the new in architectural terms by replacing old structures with new ones. The final consensus position reached at the end of this play about society's true pillars is undercut slyly by an offhand comment from young Olav, the future of the Bernick family, who rejects the idea of being a "pillar of society" when he grows up: "because I think it must be so boring."[31]

In Ibsen's first prose play that really engages with architectural metaphor in a sustained way, then, we see a consensus metaphor of the social building being contested by the fictional characters, but not in any radical sense. When the discussion among the characters centers on what the pillars should signify, and not on whether there should be any pillars at all, the basic architectural thought structure set up at the start of the play remains intact. Similarly, when Ibsen's contemporaries (such as Thrane and Garborg) in response to the play praise Ibsen for his "constructive" impulse in this play, they perceive a structure in which some pillars are solid and some artificial and claim the task of the author to be essentially that of a building inspector pointing out code violations and where the structure could be improved.

Doll housing

A Doll House (1879) continues an overt foregrounding of the architectural, and not just superficially in the title of the play. As in *Pillars of Society*,

Ibsen asks how one best might imagine a true home on a solid foundation. The home of perfect structural integrity, however, is more elusive in *A Doll House* than in the final redemptive (and ultimately misleading) tableau of the previous play. *A Doll House* has no positive architectural finale; in place of a positive redefinition of the key metaphor, as in the previous play, there is here the famous slamming of the door. Even so, the implicit social critique in Ibsen's best-known drama depends on a comparison with a fuller, more authentic form of home.

Nora's final door slam and departure from the home signifies on several levels. On the one hand, it is the logical outcome of a specific configuration of plot and character, which is to say, Nora slams the door on Torvald and leaves home because the fictional trajectory demands that ending. Although some early reviewers outside Norway tried to restrict the ending's sense of universal necessity, claiming that the play's outcome reflected specifically Norwegian cultural conditions,[32] Nora's departure has more often resonated as a late nineteenth-century woman's paradigmatic rejection of a bourgeois, patriarchal form of marriage.[33] The door slam can also be read metatheatrically on the level of architectural metaphor, however, as a powerful challenge to the notion that the human subject – especially but not exclusively the female subject – can ultimately reconcile itself to constraint within architectural structure and what it represents. But what does that freedom look like when it is imagined outside the home? What are the poetics of detachment, and of possible reattachment? *A Doll House* extends Ibsen's thinking on all of these questions.

As was the case with *Pillars of Society*, it is possible to begin the analysis of *A Doll House* with its overtly architectural title. The first thing to emphasize is its fundamental strangeness in Norwegian, for the word *dukkehjem* (literally "doll home") is a neologism. Ibsen reportedly used the term in a personal context in the 1870s as an invented diminutive describing the home of an acquaintance, Laura Kieler, who would later also serve as the model for Nora in the play. The source is a retrospective account that claims, "She was even visited by the famous author in their [the Kielers'] home in Hillerød, which on that occasion he characterized as a doll home [*et dukkehjem*]."[34] Ibsen himself claims the word as his invention in a letter on January 3, 1880, to his Swedish translator, Erik af Edholm: "the situation is exactly as you have surmised, Lord Chamberlain, that the title of my play, 'A Doll Home,' is a new word, which I myself have invented, and I would be pleased if the word were reproduced in Swedish in direct translation."[35]

The word *dukkehjem* is not listed in the current *Bokmålsordbok*, and the older *Riksmålsordbok* lists it only in reference to Ibsen, marking its literary status and defining it thus (translated here from the Norwegian): "an apparently idyllic home where the husband spoils his wife, but doesn't treat her as an independent personality."[36] In other words, the dictionary definition of the word *dukkehjem*, when it is listed at all, has no real referent beyond the context of Ibsen's play, and the word *dukkehjem*, for all its current fame, remains mainly an Ibsenian term.

My interest here is in the first part of the dictionary definition, an "apparently happy home," since that can serve as a concentrated expression of the problem of façades. It is worth asking why Ibsen did not use the common word for a miniature toy house, *dukkestue*, since he does have Nora use that word at a crucial point in the first full draft of the play, when Nora says to Torvald, "Our home has been a dollhouse [*Vort hjem har været en dukkestue*]."[37] In the final published version of the play, the key word in this line gets changed to *legestue* (Rolf Fjelde translates this into English as "playpen," but literally it has the stronger architectural dimension of "playroom").[38] In both the draft and the final version, Nora's speech at this same juncture reinforces the dollhouse metaphor with her realization that as Torvald's wife she has really only been a "doll wife [*dukkehustru*]" and a "doll child [*dukkebarn*]."[39] By the time Ibsen finished his final draft, however, the only remaining invocation of the doll home phrase as an architectural structure was in the title.

Given Ibsen's pointed instructions to the Swedish theater to retain the term in translation, it is interesting that no published English translation that I am aware of renders the title literally as *A Doll Home*.[40] Instead, the attention to the title in English has centered on the question of whether to call the play *A Doll House* or *A Doll's House*.[41] The distinction is primarily one of language conventions in American and British English, respectively, but neither of those translated titles captures Ibsen's slightly jarring original combination of the words *dukke* and *hjem*: the neologism pits the doll's association with an empty mimesis against the presumed authenticity and rooted emotional depth of the home. By using his own term instead of the usual *dukkestue* for his title, then, Ibsen foregrounds a clash of perspectives that challenges widely held assumptions about "home"; readers are left to consider which half of the term – the "doll" or the "home" – overcomes the other rhetorically.

Taking the doll side of the neologism first, several considerations are relevant. As Moi has pointed out, one set of associations with the doll is the philosophical "problem of other minds," namely this: how to be sure in one's interaction with the world that one is dealing with subjectivities as full as one's own.[42] How can one know in a philosophical sense that others

Doll housing

are not merely convincing automata or dolls? Moi brings out the ethical aspect of this question, especially as it pertains to gender relations. Approaching Ibsen's doll imagery from this angle helps foreground traditional gender hierarchies that have assigned doll-like subjectivities to women. It also advances Moi's overriding philosophical considerations about the full recognition of "others" being at the center of Ibsen's concerns.

Moi also gestures in the direction of the uncanny by mentioning the tradition that regards the doll as an object of simultaneous horror and fascination precisely because of the potentially evacuated subjectivity of the human figure (E. T. A. Hoffmann's Olympia figure comes most readily to mind). That said, it seems unproductive to emphasize the *dukke* at the expense of the *hjem* when examining the title. If a strong connection is to be made with the uncanny in *A Doll House*, it is in the realm of the modern unhomely rather than a traditional understanding of the uncanny – the "doll" of the dollhouse does not signify an eerie form of experience, just an evacuated and miniature one. Ibsen's introduction of the doll metaphor goes beyond a reference to Nora's own diminutive existence in the marriage – it extends quite quickly to include the entire familial, social, and architectural system, which is the effect when the *dukke*-compound words (dollhouses, doll wives, doll children, etc.) proliferate in Nora's speech during her confrontation with Torvald. (Frode Helland makes a similar generalizing gesture in his sociopolitical interpretation of another Ibsenian doll motif in *The Master Builder* [the nine dolls Mrs. Solness lost in the catastrophic fire]: the doll not only represents Aline's immaturity and the incapability of a child, but also alienation, or *fremmedhet* more generally.[43])

Nora's (and Torvald's) whole situation is doll-like, if one takes the metaphor to mean inauthentic, façade-like, and performative (when used in the pejorative sense of "empty" and devoid of real feeling). This is what Aarseth takes as the main point of the doll metaphor, which shares with the Alving home in *Ghosts* and the loft apartment in *The Wild Duck* the quality of an "artificially protected sphere."[44] This gives Nora's experience of sudden estrangement the stamp of relative authenticity; the home's façade is the source of that artificial protection, and when that is lifted, it is assumed, one is given access to the real and the natural Nora instead. But the central ambiguity of *A Doll House* remains precisely this problem of what one finds behind the façade. Is it only Torvald Helmer's kind of home that has been exposed as false, or does the critique not stop there? To put it in the terms of the previous play, has one kind of pillar simply been substituted with another? Or does the whole complex of ideological entanglements that create the effect of "home" get taken down with the lifting of the façade? If it all gets pulled into the wake of this specific critique of the Helmer household, then the very idea of home is a casualty of the unmasking. Given the nature of synechdoche, which leaves unstated the extent of the whole for which the part stands in, the represented slice-of-life in Nora and Torvald's marriage could either be limited or vast in its reference, and that is exactly the rhetorical uncertainty that generated so much debate. If there were thousands of households like the Helmers', then the slamming of the door would have much wider "unhomely" and "un*familiar*" consequences, with Nora's specific departure from her family being only the most literal manifestation. Seen in this light, the play and its effects were "unhomely" in a much wider sense.

One can infer some of these possible meanings from the usual, well-worn connotations of doll imagery, but what were the available cultural meanings of the "dollhouse" at the time Ibsen was writing? It was with considerable surprise that I realized recently that in all of the time I had worked with Ibsen's *A Doll House* over the years, I had never once asked myself what the material object referred to with the term actually looked like in Ibsen's day – what was the lived experience of dollhouses among Ibsen's cultural interlocutors? I had always assumed that he and I were working with the same mental image as the source domain for the metaphor, namely the sort of interactive children's toy that might fit on a tabletop or be played with on the floor, in other words a strongly miniaturized model house. However, a *dukkestue* in late nineteenth-century Scandinavia was much more likely to be a substantial piece of furniture than a toy. One example comes from the exhibit of the *Wessels gate 15* building at the Norwegian Folk Museum.[45]

Some quick background on this exhibit will be useful: the building on display at the museum was itself originally located in the Oslo city center but was painstakingly dismantled, moved from its original location a short ways out to the Norwegian Folk Museum on the Bygdøy peninsula, and rebuilt there between 1999 and 2001. The eight interior apartments have been staged to represent daily life in Oslo at different points in time over the last 125 years. This creative approach gives what otherwise might be a static museum object like a building a temporal dynamism more representative of its actual multi-generational life. The most recent time period represented is that of a Pakistani immigrant family from 2002, and the earliest, entitled "Et Dukkehjem – 1879" ("A Doll Home – 1879") models its suite of rooms after Ibsen's stage directions for his most famous play. Since it is an actual apartment, the floor plan goes beyond the one room that would be seen on stage; here, there is also a kitchen, a dining room, a

Actual dollhouse

Figure 7: *Dukkestue* used in the Norwegian Folk Museum's display of "The Doll's House 1879" interior in the *Wessels gate 15* exhibit.

maid's room, and a nursery. The resulting hybrid of museum and theater is perhaps conceptually not so far from the imagined Karsten Bernick Museum of Hypocrisy, in the sense that this exhibit presents the architectural attitudes of past moments in time to make them "open for instruction" (the Folk Museum's curation of the 1879 room, for example, instructs visitors about the disparity between public and private space in the home).

In one corner of the "Helmer" apartment in the *Wessels gate 15* exhibit stands a dollhouse (a *dukkestue*) from the museum's toy collection (Figure 7). It is nearly 4 1/2 feet high and is split into three levels. The first depicts an imagined view from the street, and the upper two the interior rooms of the house. It was originally custom-built by a watchmaker for a Kristiansand family in the 1860s, and the piece came into the museum's possession in 1937.[46] It was moved from the museum's toy collection into the *Wessels gate 15* exhibit when the Doll Home room was prepared. The choice is appropriate, for once one has decided to base the design of the exhibit on descriptions from the play, it seems fitting to have a dollhouse standing in the corner of a re-created Helmer apartment; the toys are mentioned as Christmas presents in the first scene of the play and then thematized metaphorically in the final discussion scene as well. The elements of meta-theater from the original play here translate evocatively into a kind of meta-museum: a dollhouse from the museum's own collection is depicted within the "A Doll Home – 1879" apartment of *Wessels gate 15*, a building that is itself like a gigantic, walk-in dollhouse.

The dollhouse piece at the Norwegian Folk Museum is typical of the period for upper-middle-class families, the only ones who could afford to custom-order such an expensive item in the years before mass production. One gets a better sense of the period dollhouses as a genre by comparing the Norwegian example to a display of Swedish dollhouses at the Nordic Museum in Stockholm.[47] Some of these pieces in that exhibit are quite large, and in particular the one shown in Figure 8 corresponds in age, size, and style to the one in Oslo.[48] This dollhouse belonged to a Swedish middle-class family with parents who married in 1856 and eventually had thirteen children. The dollhouse was on display for the children in their home during the 1860s and 70s.[49]

The word for a dollhouse in Swedish (*dockskåp*, "doll cabinet") underscores the most obvious characteristic of the high-end dollhouses: larger than a child, their scale was imposing. Moreover, information from the Nordic Museum indicates that in some families at least these dollhouses were not intended for hands-on play but rather primarily for display (that was true of the piece shown in Figure 8).[50] This is clear from the see-through glass doors (the doors on the Norwegian piece have been removed, but they too were likely of glass).[51] In other words, these high-end dollhouses are functionally the same and physically similar to the *glasskab*, or vitrine, mentioned in *Pillars of Society*: they are status objects used to display an image of bourgeois material life through a transparent glass wall. In this sense, it does not matter whether the object is called a *dukkestue* or a *dockskåp* or *glasskab* – the important point is that the material characteristics of these objects had a strongly observational and representational function for family life. They encouraged an analogy between careful display and family structure.

If this was the image Ibsen had in mind when he carried the doll-home metaphor over to his play, one can see a strong line of continuity from the architectural imagery of *Pillars of Society*. Aarseth has suggested this connection on a thematic level,[52] but it is interesting to see the shared material basis for both the glasshouse and the dollhouse metaphors as well. Whereas Rummel's *glasskab* in *Pillars of Society* was redirected and rehabilitated by Lona to refer to her newly renovated, imagined transparent house of

Figure 8: Swedish *dockskåp* from the 1860s–70s, from the display of dollhouses at the Nordic Museum.

integrity, the dollhouse metaphor in the following play has little such positive potential; in that sense, the choice of the metaphor matters. In *A Doll House*, the idea of a transparent home competes with the added diminutive qualities of the metaphor's referent. It is simply too hard to reconceive of a "doll life" as a life of authenticity and substance. That is why it proves such an effective weapon for Nora at the end of the play: when she tells Torvald that she has "merely" been a doll wife and doll child, he has no obvious way to argue against or redirect her metaphor (it is not possible to conceive of a "truer" doll existence in the same way that one can imagine "truer" pillars, or the way Lona Hessel flipped the image of the theatrical glass cabinet to create a positive sense of transparency and integrity). Here, Torvald can only object with bluster and reject the term.

One would think that the second half of Ibsen's neologism – home, or *hjem* – would be equally potent in its associations, if not more so. After all, as we have seen from the reception material in the previous chapter, Ibsen was very successful at presenting a seductive, if temporary, image of the ideal home to the readers and viewers of *A Doll House* who invested the home depicted in the first two acts with their own associations of *hygge* and beauty. What then is the process in the play that empties the term "home" of its positive content? A closer look at the use of the term *hjem* reveals a degree of willful assertion in Nora right from the start, showing the happy home to be only an "apparently happy home," to use the phrase that was repeated in many reviews of the time, and eventually in the very dictionary definition of Ibsen's neologistic title. At the beginning of the play, Nora piles up reassuring adjectives around the word "home," almost as if to protect the term from scrutiny by calling up its habitual connotations. She confides to Fru Linde in Act One that Torvald must not find out her secret, for "It would completely shake up the relationship between us; our beautiful, happy home [*vort skønne lykkelige hjem*] would no longer be what it is now."[53] Later, when trying to win Krogstad's job back for him, she adds no fewer than five positive qualifiers to the idea when she begs Torvald, "We could have it so nice now, so calm and happy here in our peaceful and carefree home [*så godt, så roligt og lykkeligt her i vort fredelige og sorgløse hjem*]."[54]

Since this happy notion of home is already under some pressure when it makes its debut in the play (from the start, the "snake" is in the garden of paradise, as M. V. Brun put it),[55] it is interesting that readers and especially spectators nevertheless accepted so uncritically the happy home and fought off any inklings of the on-marching catastrophe. When one further considers that despite the immediate notoriety of the published version of play, whose outcome was already well known by the time of its performance weeks later, audience members in the theater nevertheless held on tightly to the initial impressions of family cheer, though they must have known it to be doomed in advance. In spite of that foreknowledge, the idea of home had an almost irresistible and instinctive appeal, hard to counteract with rational distance. When the play's catastrophe hits, one of the immediate collateral effects – in addition to Nora's disillusionment about "the wonderful thing [*det vidunderlige*]" and Torvald's expected heroism[56] – is the sudden tilt in emphasis in the hybrid title of the play from "home" to "doll." Readers and viewers who had latched on to the positive potential of "home" were unnerved to find it increasingly contaminated by the empty associations of the doll. In Ibsen's play, "doll" trumps "home."

As the play progresses to the immediate aftermath of Krogstad's first letter, the word "house [*hus*]" begins to make headway in the text as an alternative. It appears, for example, in Torvald's feverish attempt to talk his way through the potential blackmail: "And concerning you and me, everything has to look as if everything between us were exactly as before. But of course only in the eyes of the world. You will stay here in the house; that much is clear."[57] What remains for the Helmers in the future is the reality of going on living in a house that for Torvald can only be seen as a much reduced form of existence. "Going on living in a house" with Nora is an extremely painful prospect for him, the equivalent of "saving the remnants, the fragments, the appearance [*at redde resterne, stumperne, skinnet*]," as he says immediately afterward. From Torvald's perspective, the house can only be conceived of as a ruined *home*, a home evacuated of all its *hygge* and other pleasures. It is indeed a home *manqué*.

All the more surprising, then, is the way Torvald positively rushes back into the embrace of the term "home" after Krogstad's second letter famously saves first only *him*, and then both of them, which Ibsen ingeniously depicts as an afterthought for Torvald. He says, as if nothing has happened, "Oh, how our home is cozy and beautiful [*hvor vort hjem er lunt og smukt*], Nora. Here is shelter for you; I will protect you like a hunted dove that I have saved from the hawk's claws."[58] For both readers and audience members, the rhetorical reappearance of the snug and cozy home comes as a shock at this point, given what has just transpired; today, one might even see in Torvald's quick return to the rhetoric of "home" the unnerving language of an abuser. How can the original idea of home really emerge from such a terrible onslaught unscathed? After such a sudden unmasking of the violence behind the façade in the home, after such a sudden detachment from the domestic ideal, is it really possible to reattach to it so effortlessly, as Torvald asks us to do? Nora's near-silent, open-mouth bewilderment at the return of the cozy rhetoric is really the only understandable response to this abrupt reversal. Even if Torvald's words convince him that all is as it was before, it is hard to see them convincing readers or audiences, who most likely share Nora's amazement. If one analyzes that reaction carefully, it becomes clear that both readers and viewers have been carefully led by Ibsen into a double reversal of meaning to estrange them from a widespread, accepted rhetoric of the home and make it highly difficult to reinhabit unproblematically that once-natural discourse. By having Torvald reintroduce the earlier rhetoric as if nothing has happened, Ibsen is able to return familiar phrases to the reader and viewer in uncanny form (emptied of life, repetitive, out of proper time and place) at the end of the play. For those of Ibsen's contemporaries who were especially invested in the rhetoric of domestic comfort, that must have been an intensely *un*comfortable experience. Entrapment by metaphor – the way Ibsen maneuvers his audience into non-intuitive associations with the home – goes far in explaining the intensely negative physical reactions to the play presented in my previous chapter.

What is at stake here is a poetics of detachment, or to put it differently, a poetics of unmasking: what is the effect of "exposure" on ideals? Logically, it either entails a rejection of all ideals as deceptive or the substitution of better, stronger ones in their place, as was the case at the end of *Pillars of Society*, but there is little sense in Ibsen's worldview that ideals can survive the light of day, a notion that grew stronger in the transition to *A Doll House*. Ibsen's contemporaries sensed that something new was afoot in this play as well. A more pessimistic view of reform can be seen in a prominent review of *A Doll House* written by Edvard Brandes in 1879, soon after the publication of the play. Offering his own version of the quicksand rhetoric, Brandes describes the effects of unmasking in Ibsen's new play in this way:

> Sometimes events occur in our public life that demonstrate in the most unpleasant way how different what one says and does can be and how brutal the passions are that can be hidden beneath the greatest refinement. When something of that sort suddenly becomes apparent one gets the impression that our entire society is built on a sinkhole [*Hængedynd*]. One becomes suspicious beyond one's years, not the least towards those who boldly promote themselves as the official representatives of morality.[59]

When public hypocrisy is "revealed suddenly," Brandes says, this experience is like stepping on a *Hængedynd* (a thin cover of vegetation over a mire or bog that gives a deceptively reassuring, weight-bearing appearance), the effect of which is to make one question all apparently solid surfaces. Whether the idea of unreliability manifests itself as a sinkhole, as quicksand, as a false façade, or a mask, the poetics of detachment depicts such sudden revelations as irreversibly disillusioning. Edvard Brandes and other Modern Breakthrough writers of the late nineteenth century were especially inclined toward this progressive, Enlightenment bias about the simple and irreversible effects of "seeing."

This was Ibsen's mind set, posits Brandes, when he wrote *A Doll House*: he was filled with "a feeling of bitter mistrust [*Mistillid*]." He chose to depict "a bourgeois home that appears to be a dwelling devoted to peace and comfort [*et indviet Bo for Fred og Hygge*]," whose qualities of culture, wealth, beauty, love, and happiness – all Brandes's words – would "blind" the world like a "shining surface [*glimrende Overflade*]."[60] Mixing metaphors, Brandes then writes that although a golden-ripe fruit of happiness hangs above the house, it is fruit with an unnoticed bruise, a mark of the decay that "spreads, eats its way in, undermines and destroys the radiant happiness."[61] Brandes clearly spares no metaphor in describing the full force of a façade aesthetic in which unmasking trumps all. One does not recover from this kind of insight, Brandes suggests – it puts one in a position of permanent skepticism, of "bitter mistrust."

Still, it remains to explain what happened to the position arrived at in Ibsen's previous play, a position in which the stripping away of the home's façade seemed more akin to opening a window for fresh air than it did to the sudden collapse of a sinkhole. If the reassertion of a positive architectural metaphor at the end of *Pillars of Society* seems glib to modern ears, perhaps it is because it provides no dilation of the moment when the initial architectural structure has been taken away, no gazing into the void before quickly rebuilding the structure with the new pillars of "truth" and "freedom." If, as mentioned in the Introduction, the effect of Ibsen's plays was increasingly "to pull back the covering of habit and everyday language from the abyss that they hide,"[62] the stance in *Pillars* provides nothing more than a quick peek (if even that) before looking away. *A Doll House*, by contrast, spends its entire relentless last act in that territory. As Torvald himself puts it, "There has in fact opened an abyss between us. O, but Nora, couldn't it possibly be filled in?"[63]

At the time of the play's initial publication and performances, the intense cultural energy devoted to imagining Nora's future – in the many parodies, sequels, newspaper articles, letters to the editor that appeared in response to the play – demonstrates the sort of reflexive rebuilding instinct that for many came in response to that glimpse into the void. The cultural response resembles Torvald's when confronted with the abyss of unhomeliness: "couldn't it be filled in?" To be sure, the fact that "the public on its own initiative continues the storyline in the newspapers [*digter videre i Aviserne*]" might be due to the new sense of overlap with real life that was encouraged by the aesthetic of the new realistic theater, as one Norwegian reviewer suggested.⁶⁴ It also speaks to the need for closure where none was provided. But "closure," it is worth reminding, is also a metaphor with architectural overtones, and that insight is helpful when thinking about the ending of *A Doll House*. That is, it was not just the uncertainty surrounding Nora's future that incited heated debate; it was also Ibsen's act of stranding a woman outside the architectural structure of the home, which given the bodily basis for metaphor easily created more subliminal reactions as well. Many of the responses seem in some way guided by the almost involuntary need to get Nora back *inside* – somewhere, anywhere.

Thus, scenes in this elaborative discourse – the public discussion that "keeps on composing" – depict an "Act Four" at Mrs. Linde's, or show Nora returning home to Torvald. One such attempt, "The Happiness that Surpasses Understanding – A Sequel," which was serialized in a regional Norwegian west-coast newspaper (*Aalesunds Blad*) in the spring of 1880 and then published in book form as well, does both.⁶⁵ One first finds Mrs. Linde in her room admonishing Nora "to go home to the place where you belong [*hvor Du er sat*]; you cannot stay here with me"⁶⁶ and urging her not to "become a stranger in your own house [*Fremmed i dit eget Hus*]."⁶⁷ The imagined melodramatic coda in this piece ends with Nora being visited by an apparition of her own missing mother who convinces her not to abandon her own children, at which point Nora returns home to Torvald and is forgiven. "The wonderful thing has arrived! [*Det vidunderlige er kommen!*]," she exclaims at the end of this extra act, while Dr. Rank has reappeared to wonder if maybe he should conduct another medical test on himself just to double-check.⁶⁸

There is also Ibsen's own infamous rewriting of the final scene for the German stage, in which Torvald convinces Nora to stay by melodramatically showing her the children one last time. Biographer Michael Meyer reports that the alternative ending came into being when the actress playing Nora at the Thalia Theater in Hamburg, Hedwig Niemann-Raabe, refused to play the scene as written, and that upon receiving the theater's request for permission to revise, Ibsen wrote the alternative ending to maintain a degree of control over any changes.⁶⁹ In an article published in a German literary journal twenty years later, the story appears with a different slant, with the actress claiming retrospectively that she never would have dared to demand that of so famous an author. She says instead that the request to revise came at the instigation of the Thalia Theater's director Chéri Maurice, who had quite independently developed misgivings about the tolerance of his German audience for the ending as written. Her famous statement that she herself "would never leave her children" was not the cause for the revision, according to her later interview, but simply clinched the decision for Maurice. This retrospective account of the incident has to be read through Ibsen's subsequent ascendance into the canon of untouchable authors by the year 1900, so Niemann-Raabe's memory might have altered the story to her advantage in the intervening years, but it is interesting for the purposes of the present argument to see the infamous decision to revise Nora's departure as an issue of audience expectation. As Niemann-Raabe explains in the interview, "a departure like the one Ibsen's Nora had originally would leave the spectators dissatisfied."[70] I would add that this anticipated audience dissatisfaction had its roots in unquestioned, culturally dominant architectural metaphors.

Many of these attempts to rehouse Nora seized on the imagery of the "wonderful thing [*det vidunderlige*]" that Nora guards so cryptically throughout the play as an idiosyncratic private metaphor. In doing so, Nora's critics joined Torvald in his desperate attempt to muster some hope after Nora leaves – "The most wonderful thing [*Det vidunderligste*]?!"[71] – but without including the answering sound of the door slam that is so inextricably tied to that question in the play. The substitution of an ideal marriage and home for the one that has been unmasked is in other words something that the audience continued to do in spite of the open ending that separates *A Doll House* from the resolution in *Pillars of Society*. It is as if readers and viewers, joining in Torvald's desperate hope, attempted to force the idea of "truer pillars" from the previous play onto a notion of a "truer marriage" in this one. A commentator in *Bergens Aftenblad* even carries the earlier metaphor into his reading of the later play, a reflex perhaps more typical of the literary readings than the theatrical viewings:

> The author has unrolled for us a gripping picture of an unhappy marriage, a marriage that even with all its smiling surface is at its base unhappy, unhappy because it was built on fragile pillars [*skjøre Piller*] and lacked the firm foundation [*faste Grundvolde*] of true love, a reciprocal, complete respect, and unqualified trust.[72]

The commentator seems still to be thinking of *Pillars of Society* here, with his façade rhetoric and the suggestion that a marriage building constructed on true principles would provide a firm foundation to replace the defective one that is depicted in the text. He goes on to write that since Nora's decision seemed rash, it is even possible to imagine her returning:

> It might be tempting to believe this and imagine the reconciliation that comes into view at the end as the author's actual solution; the ideal that is contrasted with all of this bungling, all of the confused steps taken during

the conflict, is a marriage where true love forms the foundation for a true life together between people with real ethical worth.[73]

The reviewer is sensitive enough to the facts of the text that he notes his imagined scenario as something one can *almost* believe about the play; he ends by claiming that Ibsen has actually left us "stranded in uncertainty [*staaende i uvissheten*]" and that "nowhere in the play do we find a hint that any higher principle stands behind the confusion of human life."[74] But the strong presence of a residual idealism on the reviewer's reading of the play is actually quite helpful in marking both the difference between *Pillars of Society* and *A Doll House* and the carry-over of reader expectations when encountering the latter play. This observation is entirely in keeping with Moi's main argument about Ibsen's break with philosophical idealism; what the present analysis adds is the observation that the public's continuing attachment to idealistic world views expressed itself so often in architectural terms.

In contrast to the extratextual elaborations of Ibsen's "fellow writers," there is the position that Nora carves out for herself in the text. If leaving home in the middle of the night without a cent does seem conceptually viable, even "inhabitable" as a position in life, it is only as a sort of emergency shelter. In the play itself, once she has seen the house behind the façade of the home, she hangs on to that clarity of vision and embraces it for its sober reality. She refuses to stay at home, both literally and philosophically, a stance that marks a profound difference between Nora and Torvald. Indeed, it almost prevents them from understanding each other in the final scene in a very literal sense. One of the many failures of conversation occurs when Nora mentions offhandedly in her famous dollhouse speech: "Then I came into your house [*Så kom jeg i huset til dig*]," and Torvald interrupts by calling attention to the term itself: "What kind of expression is *that* to use about our marriage? [*Hvad er det for udtryk du bruger om vort ægteskab?*]"[75] Torvald's reaction foregrounds her use of a word – "house" – as a deliberate marker of difference and distance from his world view. The word "home," that is, no longer has any rhetorical power over her, even when Torvald tries to call up its former magic – its unseen ideological power of social assent. He cries out in the final conversation, "Don't you even have a grasp of your position in your own home?"[76]

Nora fends that off not only by pointedly translating Torvald's term "home" into "playroom," as mentioned earlier, but by becoming very cautious about her own use of the word in its former context. When she tells Torvald she is leaving, she catches herself in the old habit and quickly corrects herself: "Tomorrow I am traveling home [*hjem*], – I mean, to where I grew up [*mit gamle hjemsted*]."⁷⁷ In Norwegian, Nora's substitution of *hjemsted* for *hjem* – "home-place" for "home" – is quite brilliant in the way it dilutes with a slight revision any positive emotional affect the latter term might have. As a parting shot, when Torvald asks if she will think of him after she leaves, she responds in terms that seem carefully chosen for their neutrality: "I will certainly think often about you and the children and the house here."⁷⁸ After so suddenly losing her illusions about one home, Nora is clearly not about to call up those of another. Homes are for idealists; Nora has become a distinctly "unhomely" heroine, which is to say, clear-eyed and realistic.

One remarkable aspect of *A Doll House* is that by using reality criteria as the measure of value, Ibsen has inverted the house-and-home dichotomy so that now "house" emerges as the more authentic of the two terms. The authenticity criteria have shifted in Ibsen's hands and have become a question of accurately assessing one's situation, not of the set of prescribed models and feelings that form the consensus conception of a "true home." "Home" has been exposed as the theatrical effect; "house" is the reality left behind when the illusion of home is dispelled under pressure. Many years later, we can now see that we find ourselves on the other side of a conceptual divide, in a position where "home" may have as many negative associations as positive. Errol Durbach has made this point in his book-length study, *A Doll's House*, where he writes:

> If we pride ourselves that we no longer live in dolls' houses, it is because plays like Ibsen's have undermined so thoroughly the Victorian foundations of "home" and "family," exposing them as empty and oppressive shams in a world where such ideals are maintained only at the expense of self-negation and deceit.⁷⁹

It is not overstating the case to say that Ibsen helped introduce this suspicion of the home into Western thought. Judging from the responses to Ibsen's first two prose plays, however, the ideals of home seem to have mostly survived the unmasking; for many, that is, especially those who imagined the happier endings, the force of the critique stopped at the level of the façade. As one tracks the further development of house and home in the remaining dramas, it becomes more difficult for readers and viewers to maintain that position. Increasingly, Ibsen came to expose the contingency of home and *hygge* in ever-more powerful and far-reaching critiques. As we shall see, it was still possible to disagree with the domestic architectural model implied by Ibsen's houses, but as his dramatic housing experiments became more generally familiar across Western culture, it became increasingly difficult for Ibsen's readers to accept the assumption that "home" was a natural and given entity. As will now be shown, in his later plays Ibsen introduced an idea of elective and strategic relationships to built structures that point to a more modern repertoire of housing choices.

CHAPTER 3

Home and house

The title of this chapter is not intended to roll off the tongue. The idiom in English should read "house and home," so phrasing it differently here goes against the grain of verbal habit. The point in reversing the terms is to reflect the process at work in Ibsen's later plays: the dislodging of home from its privileged association with domestic ideals and the testing of "house" as a modern alternative, a more temporary and contingent form of inhabitation. As his dramatic characters and their commentators bandy these two terms about, "home" in Ibsen's plays slides in connotation from the ideal to the trivial. His strategic contamination of the term "home" would strip away its redemptive associations with hearth, origin, and authenticity, gradually elaborating it as the idea of a copy without vitality or substance, the process that Nora began with the insight about her "doll home." This kind of rhetorical reversal creates the possibility that the home might be confining, squelching, or in other ways detrimental to individual freedom.

Many of Ibsen's dramatic characters seem unusually interested in the linguistic distinction between house and home; they both discuss it openly and convey their interest indirectly in their use of domestic metaphor. One might not think that debating the semantics of domesticity would make for compelling dramatic material, but Ibsen's characters do just that. The talk of house and home clearly struck a chord with many of Ibsen's commentators as well, because they continued to dig into the linguistic resonance of "home" in their reviews and discussions of his plays. Along the way, their accounts reveal much about the attitudes and assumptions that propped up those terms. In one sense, the dogged support of the old domestic ideals by some commentators provides a useful corrective to those who would overestimate the efficacy of Ibsen's domestic deconstruction. After all, the entire complex of emotional attachments to home (and the ideological use thereof) in Western culture was not likely to be undone by a single late nineteenth-century Norwegian playwright, no matter how forceful his articulation of the issues. "Home" is a powerful source domain for metaphor. The "evacuation" of home took place primarily within the Ibsenian world of characters, stage sets, and plots; in the real world, people went on living in homes, attempting to make them cozy, and perpetuating domestic ideals. And yet, Ibsen introduced a powerful intellectual legitimacy to the alternative position, a suspicion of the domestic that introduced hesitation and contingency into previously unassailable values. Ibsen's treatment of home and house was an extended experiment that deconstructed the most "natural" domestic ideologies of the late nineteenth century and tested the viability of his opponents' positions. That in itself is no small accomplishment; if the concept of a "dollhouse existence" has become established as a ready-at-hand cultural metaphor for the limitations of prescribed gender roles, to choose just one example, then Ibsen succeeded in establishing an alternative position from which to view that formerly mainstream ideology. Perhaps that is the most that can be required of a writer, after all.

The composite phrase *hus og hjem* is as idiomatic in Norwegian as is "house and home" in English: when the words appear together in that order, they serve to capture the totality of one's domestic situation, including everything from its factual basis to its attendant emotions. This usage is a way of intensifying the idea of the domestic, and Ibsen's characters frequently use the joint idiom in that casual way. Karsten Bernick in *Pillars of Society* links the phrase tightly with "family happiness" and "my whole upstanding reputation [*min hele borgerlige stilling*]."[1] Both Nora's and Mrs. Alving's threatened departures are described as running from house and home, just as Dr. Stockman's increasing involvement in politics in *An Enemy of the People* is said to take him away from the same.[2] In these cases, the phrase usually means something like "all of one's domestic responsibilities" or "house, home, and family." Thus, in *The Wild Duck*, Gina Ekdal can tell Hjalmar, "you became such a good husband as soon as you had gotten house and home."[3]

Given this often mainstream usage of the phrase "house and home" in the plays, it is striking that Ibsen goes to work so doggedly on both terms, moving their semantic boundaries and prying them loose from each other, in some cases staging semantic battles quite directly. Although in common usage, *hjem* was (and still is) assumed to be a positive augmentation of the concept of house, Ibsen attempted to make that association less automatic. Increasingly in Ibsen's later plays, domesticity moves from its association with the intimate warmth of the hearth to its figuration as a sphere of diminished vitality, boredom, suffocation, and even imprisonment. Paired with this rejection of "home" and its usual resonances is an ascendant notion of "house" that is something different and more interesting than a deficient or empty version of "home." Several of Ibsen's characters see a distinct advantage in the neutral ground provided by the term "house," a way of defending oneself from the negative encumbrances of "home."

Ibsen's plays form an unusually coherent set of intertexts, so it should come as no surprise that even after Nora's slammed door, the interest in house and home continues unabated. Nora's dramatic rejection of home settles nothing. Ibsen's ongoing engagement with the issues raised by his doll home/house found much to uncover and replay in dramatic form; the hold of "home" on his imagination was extremely persistent for both him and his cultural interlocutors. While there is not a simple trajectory leading through Ibsen's ten prose plays after *A Doll House*, we might identify three major tendencies that define Ibsen's continuing unease with the concept of "home." The first concerns his depiction of the gradual decline in persuasive authority of the idea of a "true home"; the second involves his increasing denigration of home as the realm of the trivial; and the third concerns the inversion of value between the concepts of "home" and "house." The following section deals with specific scenes in four plays (*Ghosts*, *An Enemy of the People*, *The Wild Duck*, and *The Master Builder*) that put pressure on the ideal of the "true" home and contributed to its demotion from a position of automatic cultural assent.

True homes

The discussion in the previous chapter suggested that reviewers' notions of the ideal home often rushed back in to fill the void left by unmasking a façade. It was also suggested by Edvard Brandes that there were potential difficulties for some in reattaching to that ideal after having become more generally suspicious of domestic façades and sinkholes. In the plays following *A Doll House*, Ibsen explored this aesthetic of wariness, subjecting the concept of a "true home" to the closest scrutiny. Increasingly, Ibsen suggests in his plays that the notion of a true or "proper" home was a borrowed concept, an image, an idea, or an assumption about ideal families that did not proceed from real experience. His idea is that talk of a true home correlates directly with *not* feeling at home; in other words, whatever a true home is, it is not *this* – true homes are always elsewhere. It is quite literally that sense of falling short that motivates the effort to imagine the perfect alternative. In fact, the more "unhomely" the situation becomes, the more frantic the invocation of the home ideal, as is clear in Torvald Helmer's willful reset to the ideal at the end of *A Doll House*. As Ibsen develops the issue, one sees quite clearly a process of evacuation underway, until the concept of a true home is shown to be nothing but a copy and a shell.

The play *Ghosts* contributes in two ways to this complex notion. The first comes in the extended exchange between Pastor Manders and Osvald about the alternative, more Bohemian homelife Osvald witnessed in Paris. Manders provokes the discussion by introducing a normative notion of home, saying that because Osvald was sent away from the Alvings so early on, he "has never had the opportunity to become really acquainted with a proper home [*et ordentligt hjem*]."[4] Osvald objects immediately to this claim, and the ensuing conversation becomes a tussle over competing definitions of "home":

MANDERS: So? I thought you associated almost exclusively with artist circles.
OSVALD: I did.
MANDERS: And mostly with younger artists.
OSVALD: Oh, to be sure.
MANDERS: But I thought that most of those people couldn't afford to start a family and establish a home.
OSVALD: There are many of them who can't afford to marry, Pastor Manders.
MANDERS: But that is precisely what I am saying.
OSVALD: But they can still have a home, even so. And here and there they *do*: and a very tidy [*ordentligt*] and very cozy [*hyggeligt*] home at that. *Mrs. Alving follows along excitedly, nods but says nothing.*
MANDERS: But I'm not talking about a bachelor home. By "home" I mean a family home, where a husband lives with his wife and his children.
OSVALD: Yes, or with his children and his children's mother.
MANDERS: (taken aback; clasps his hands) Merciful heavens![5]

This is an important turning point in the thinking about home in Ibsen's writing, because two competing definitions square off to form a continuing thought dialectic for the remainder of Ibsen's career: Osvald's more expansive definition of home as an elective affiliation, and Manders's restrictive notion of a home as a defense against social change. Note the search for a more precise vocabulary as Manders splits the term *hjem* into two hierarchical variants, "family home [*familjehjem*]" and "bachelor home [*ungkarlshjem*]," to shore up and protect the "proper" definition. The important point is that under the pressure of their discussion, the unmarked term *hjem* can no longer stand on its own as obvious in its own right. Osvald is strategically effective when arguing his view with the terms "tidy" (*ordentligt*) and "cozy" (*hyggeligt*), because they are the usual currency of the traditional discourse of home, as we have seen. Tidy, cozy homes but with unmarried parents – for

Manders and others like him, this disgusting, unheard-of combination was scandalous in its own right, an effect that is harder for us to recover than those generated by discussions of sexually transmitted diseases and euthanasia simply because those social tensions have not melted away in quite the same way over the years. It is impossible now to share Manders's shock at Osvald's idyllic description of the artists' homes; the juxtposition is just not jarring anymore, even for those who might reject that lifestyle. The dissonance for Ibsen's contemporaries, however, was reflexive and immediate, contributing greatly to the almost instinctive reactions against this play.

More devastating still is the relentless undermining of the notion of home throughout the play as the readers and viewers come to understand the accumulating references to "Captain Alving's Home." Readers are first introduced to what we might neutrally call Captain Alving's *house*, which would refer to the play's given setting and the actual Rosenvold estate where the Alvings lived their married life and Osvald his first seven years. The truth of life in that house is this: that Alving Sr. seduced his maid and frequented prostitutes, leading to the syphilis that claimed his life; that Osvald was sent away before he could see his father for what he was, but not before becoming invisibly infected with syphilis himself; that Mrs. Alving has secretly run the household and all of Captain Alving's business dealings for years while hiding her husband's debauchery from the public; and that she is building the orphanage not to revere his name, but to rid herself of the captain's influence once and for all and to keep the secret of his promiscuity hidden from sight.

On the surface, the term "home" used in the new orphanage's name seems entirely appropriate for an institution intended to provide orphaned children with shelter. As the reader quickly discovers, however, picturing the image of Captain Alving standing at the threshold to welcome the orphans "home" is more than a bit incongruous. As it turns out, however, Mrs. Alving's project has not been undertaken to honor the captain, but to build something as powerfully distracting as possible to hide the true legacy of her dead husband behind a respectable façade. To do so, she uses up the money paid for her dowry, which she now regards as the price of her unholy purchase. Her original plan is thus a building built with dirty money and a clean face. If that building had not burned to the ground, it would have become the ultimate in façade architecture, actually a perfect mirror of the captain's public reputation. Such is the value of "home" in the play.

Captain Alving's Home is actually a complicated imagined structure, built up offstage through multiple oblique references strewn throughout the text. Moreover, it is a dynamic structure, since the names for the building dedicated to his memory undergo a steady transformation throughout the play. The first mention by Pastor Manders is the legal name of the orphanage from the official papers mentioned in Act One, "The Captain Alving Memorial [*Kaptejn Alvings minde*]."[6] In subsequent conversations, however, the orphanage is most commonly referred to as an *asyl*, cognate with the English "asylum." (In Ibsen's day, that word's connotation of protection would have been stronger than that of confinement, so it would have been a perfectly normal synonym for "orphanage."[7]) After the catastrophic fire burns down the orphanage, however, we find that the money for the orphanage will be redirected to a different project: the sailor's home being developed by Jakob Engstrand, the scheming worker and Regine's foster father who himself is the picture of hypocrisy in his fawning interaction with Manders. This sailor's home is quite clearly a euphemistic description of a brothel, where one assumes that the real Captain Alving would feel more at home than in an orphanage. Even the name for Engstrand's building project, running parallel to that of Mrs. Alving, shifts from an initial mention of "a kind of sailor's home [*et slags sjømandshjem*]" to Pastor Manders's hybrid term in Act Three, "sailor's asylum [*sømands-asyl*]."[8] Engstrand revises Manders's "asylum" to the loftier status of "Chamberlain Alving's Home [*Kammerherre Alvings Hjem*]," in effect merging the name of the orphanage and the brothel.[9] And by the time we hear of the new project at Regine's last exit, the name has finally morphed into *Kammerherre Alvings Asyl*, which Eva Le Gallienne translates literally as "Captain Alving's Hostel."[10] Intending to build one kind of asylum, a tribute to the public Captain Alving, Helene has instead unintentionally built another kind with the same money, this one a tribute to the captain's private reality.

The effect on the idea of home of Ibsen's intentional terminological slipping and sliding is ruinous. Note that both of the structures called "Captain Alving's Home" are marked by façade disparities: the orphanage by irony, and the brothel by euphemism. But the unveiling of the structures does not leave much possibility for salvaging ideals in its wake. By the end of the play, "home" has become the sort of word that Engstrand can use with a salacious wink and a nod – it has almost become a kind of dirty word. The connotation of "home" has become rhetorically arbitrary by the end of the play, when the term "Captain Alving's Home" can resonate in all directions at once, as it does. The crowning irony is reserved for the end of the play, as the bright rays of the sunrise fill Mrs. Alving's living room, and she tells Osvald, "Now you can truly see your home [*Nu kan du rigtig få se hjemmet*]."[11] He can do no such thing, since one of the symptoms of tertiary syphilis is blindness. The moment of greatest clarity, when the home should finally have become a transparent *glasskab* in Lona Hessel's positive sense, is its moment of greatest opacity instead – that is, "home" at the height of its ideological and rhetorical entanglement. Following Ibsen's lead going forward in his authorship, one might need to reserve the clarity model for "houses," not "homes," if one accepts that term as the more factual of the two. After all of *Ghosts*' interrogations and redefinitions of terminology, a more self-reflexive, ironic glimpse is possible in Mrs. Alving's line: "now you can truly see 'home'" – that is, from a distance, and as a contaminated term.

It is interesting in this regard to see how the sinkhole metaphor becomes more consequential in response to *Ghosts* than in reaction to the preceding plays. In Henrik Jæger's discussion of the publication of the play in his 1888 biography of Ibsen, there is no longer the slightest hint of a foothold once the abyss opens up. He writes:

> [Ibsen] knew on what shaky ground all of society rests. Society's morals were like a great sinkhole [*hængemyr*]; only the lightest beings could walk over it without noticing that there was no solid ground under the feet, and the one who fell through first had the experience that the deeper he sank in, the more unstable the soil. Panic gripped him, he fought to find a foothold; but he found none, there was nothing to find. It was worse than a sinkhole; it was as if the firm, secure ground [*den faste, trygge jord*] had been yanked out from under his feet and he at the same time had been thrown out into the open sea. Such was the impression that *Ghosts* made at its appearance.¹²

The *hængedynd* from Edvard Brandes's earlier review (here called a *hængemyr*) has at this point become an established trope in the Ibsen commentary, with the difference that even that image seems insufficient to Jæger to express the experience of losing one's foundations; one can see that he is searching for something even more debilitating in the image of being left adrift in the open sea. Interesting also is the idea that the "lightest beings" – presumably those unburdened by artistic consciousness – can pass over the thin surface covering without falling in. For travelers like the stocky, endlessly questioning Ibsen, there is not a chance that they could make it across without seeing the abyss opening at their feet.

An Enemy of the People's erosion of *hygge* was discussed in Chapter 1; there is more to say about its conclusion, when the inordinately *hyggelig* toddy party of the first scene seems a distant memory. Stockmann's home has by that point instead become a bunker under siege, with broken window panes and stones piled on the table as evidence of the townspeople's intolerance and willful ignorance. The pile of rocks, says Stockmann, will be the inheritance he leaves to his sons. There will be no traditional family home

Figure 9: Set design from the final act of *An Enemy of the People*, showing the ruined home. Production: National Theater (Oslo), prem. September 2, 1899.

to pass on through generations, only the relics of its destruction; the protected private sphere of the home has clearly been violated by the end of this play.

Figure 9 shows a set photograph from the 1899 production of the play at Norway's National Theater and gives some indication of how one Norwegian production handled the final scene in visual terms with overturned furniture, torn curtains, and the like (although without any clear sign of broken glass, at least in this photograph). Even if this particular version portrays more of a disheveled than a traumatized home, the important point would be to imagine the visual contrast between this and the opening toddy party, something that Henrik Jæger mentioned as the uncanny visual potential of the final scene when he first read the written version of the play: "over the entire act unease [*Uhygge*] spreads from the broken windows and crushed stones, an unease [*Uhygge*] that will certainly be very effective as a contrast to the energy and warmth with which the hero faces all opposition."[13]

Most of the familiar architectural tropes from the other plays surface again here when Stockmann attempts the same kind of unveiling of façades. Here, it is the town's spa project that is polluted, and Stockmann's revelation of that fact is motivated by yet another dream of architectural integrity – namely, to have a resort that is exactly as healthy as it appears to be. This is the familiar refrain that emerges when he compares the baths to a "whitewashed poisonous sepulcher [*en kalket forgiftig grav*]."[14] The sinkhole metaphor makes another appearance here as well: in the raucous town hall meeting, Stockmann links it to the imagery of cleaning the social house:

> But luckily it is only an old hand-me-down folk fable, the idea that culture corrupts. No, it is stupefaction, poverty, ugliness of living conditions that carry out that devil's errand! In a house that isn't aired out and swept every day –; my wife Katrine claims that the floor should be mopped too; but that is open to debate; – anyway – there, in such a house, I dare say that people lose their ability to think and behave morally within two to three years. The lack of oxygen stunts the conscience. And there must be a tremendous oxygen deficit in many, many houses here in town, or so it would seem, since the entire compact majority can be so unscrupulous as to want to build the town's future on a sinkhole of lies and deception [*et hængedynd af løgn og bedrag*].[15]

This is a rich passage, one that is rarely mentioned in discussions of that play's famous town meeting, in which Dr. Stockmann's proto-Nietzschean contempt of majority opinions usually commands most of the critical attention. When one is looking for the development of Ibsen's "truth-in-housing" idea, however, this passage takes on more interest. Stockmann's demand for perfect architectural integrity in the social building now sounds familiar, as does the talk of sinkholes and hypocrisy, which clearly continue Ibsen's earlier dramatic arguments against deceptive façades.

This passage adds something more to the mix, however – an ironic undercutting of what might be called the Lona Hessel position, namely the demand for fresh air and architectural transparency. Here, just as Stockmann's metaphor of a clean social house starts to soar in his rambling speech, Ibsen deflates it with the comically literal aside about Katrine Stockmann's debatable opinions on mopping. When Stockmann tries to pick up the thread of the more idealist metaphoric imagery again ("anyway, –"), the talk of clean houses cannot quite get the same lift. Ibsen estranges readers from a widely accepted imagery (cleaning house being the epitome of a consensus metaphor) by foregrounding its rhetorical status and the disparity between its literal and symbolic registers. The new difference added in this scenario is that the deflation comes at the expense of the zealous reformer, not the conservative defender of façades. To be sure, Ibsen's disdain for the latter is still firmly in place: after all, the most cowardly rearguard characters in the play are members of the "compact majority" defending their respective property values through membership in – what else? – the Homeowners' Association [*huseierforeningen*].¹⁶ Even so, it is as if Ibsen has reserved some of the ridicule he had directed toward Rørlund in the earlier play and pointed it toward Stockmann instead; as a consequence, he adds some conceptual distance to the evaluation of ideal architectural transparency.

This newly undermined ideal creates a restless last act in terms of housing alternatives. The action takes place in a home that has lost its protective shell – windows smashed in by the crowd the night before. Stockmann makes a biting joke about the "drafty [*luftig*]" room himself, and Morten Kiil comments sardonically that Stockmann's home is now certainly not lacking in the oxygen he had mentioned in his speech at the town meeting the night before.¹⁷ But since this is a rental home, not a family possession in the same way as Rosenvold in *Ghosts* or the family estate in *Rosmersholm*, the landlord no longer dares to have them as tenants. The fifth act begins with the Stockmann family being served an eviction notice, the first in what actually becomes a rather hyperbolically comic series of rejections and firings for all of the remaining family members. This is the poetics of detachment played for derisive amusement; everyone associated with the Stockmanns gets cut loose from their former ties to home, school, and work by the end of the act.

The action of the last act thus takes place in a home to which the Stockmanns no longer belong, not even as renters. No matter, because Dr. Stockmann has grand travel plans: to emigrate to the new world, or to some "primitive forest" or "little South-Sea island," if he can find a good deal on one.¹⁸ The conversations with the subsequent series of visitors change those plans, prompting him to reverse course abruptly and play out his role as "enemy of the people" on a local level instead. The only door still open to the Stockmanns in town, however, is that of Captain Horster's home, where the town meeting was held, which Horster has offered to the family as a temporary place to stay. The play thus ends asking us to imagine the evicted family in the borrowed house of an inveterate traveler – quite some conceptual distance from the opening scene's *hyggelig* toddy party and enthusiastic promotion of the hospitable home. After all this casting about for housing alternatives, one senses the sobering aftermath of having lost both the unmasked façade of a house and any ideal, reformed alternative; what fictional space is there left for them to inhabit?

When one turns to the play's contemporary reception material for both its debut publication and premiere performance in Christiania, it is clear that the interpretive discussion of Ibsen's central metaphors continued to occupy his cultural interlocutors. Although Doctor Stockmann's discussion of the exceptional individual as a member of society's "advance troops [*forpostfægtere*]" in the new play prompted several lengthy journalistic explorations of the parameters of that new military metaphor,[19] the play's frontal attack on (or should one say "undermining" of) society and all of its political parties continued the appeal of socio-architectural discourse that had begun with *Pillars of Society* and *A Doll House*. Johan Irgens Hansen, for instance, described Ibsen's links to the thought of John Stuart Mill on the issue of the sovereign individual, concluding that "only through its [the individual's] emphasis can the pillars of society be preserved, and these are the spirit of truth and freedom."[20]

Irgens Hansen continues the more apologetic reading of Ibsen's architectural project in the same series of articles for *Dagbladet* when he writes of *An Enemy of the People*, "In the fourth act he knows what needs to be torn down and wrestles with society, [and] in the fifth act he knows what he wants to build back up; in that sense, the usual (unjustly leveled) complaint about Ibsen, that he does not provide solutions, is inapplicable here."[21] Irgens Hansen somewhat willfully wants to continue to see Ibsen as the architectural reformer he saw in the earlier play, claiming that the playwright gives mankind an assignment that is "within the range of human abilities, realizable within society itself, with the overt goal of infusing the same with a new spirit through a renewal of the individual."[22] Perhaps not surprisingly, a review of the published play in a Lutheran periodical of the time also read the play somewhat against the grain of Ibsen's intent and claimed, "Even if he himself remains stuck in pure negation – because pure individualism is not a social principle; on the contrary, it is a denial of all society – he nevertheless in one sense clears the ground for a truer, more organic social principle."[23]

The reviewer in this case was Johan Michael Færden, the Norwegian priest and editor of *Luthersk Ugeblad* who engaged often in the public theological debates of the day. His deft switch from an architectural to an organic metaphoric register (Ibsen tears down the social building; in its place, something grows) seems to acknowledge the difficulties in imagining a new, substitute building when he abandons one metaphor for another. More complicated still is his remarkable extension of that argument in a more architectural vein:

> But even if Ibsen does not have any stone to carry over into the true society of the future because he is one of those builders [*de Bygningsfolk*] who have rejected the Stone that was intended for and has become the "main Cornerstone," and if the heavy stone of social problems [*Samfundsproblemets Sten*] that he relentlessly rolls up the hill will never come to rest, but only rolls

back down again, he nevertheless is able with great power and remarkable skill to throw the stone down into the lies and misery of our age."[24]

Drawing on two discourses at once in this striking passage, Færden refers both to the Biblical image of Christ as the proper cornerstone for the church and the Greek myth of Sisyphus, implying that without the true foundations of religion, all building work with the "stone of social problems" is condemned to ultimate frustration. The fact that Færden could nevertheless write approvingly of Ibsen's strategic stone throwing is one further example of how both conservative and liberal forces found things to like and hate in *An Enemy of the People*. It further demonstrates the central role that architectural thought structures play in a variety of discourses, including the religious.

To judge from some of these responses to Dr. Stockmann, there were clearly readers and viewers who persisted in reading Ibsen's architectural skepticism in more positive, oblique ways in 1882, but it seems fair to say that *The Wild Duck* completes the demolition of the reformer's version of the social "vitrine." It is common to note that *The Wild Duck* is a turning point in Ibsen's depiction of idealism, and this includes the ideals of home. Here the "housing activist," if one can put it in those terms, is Gregers Werle. He opens the architectural motif with a familiar charge when he says to his father of Hjalmar Ekdal in Act One: "That which he calls a home is built on a lie!"[25] Like Stockmann, Gregers is a devotee of ventilation as well: in the comically inclusive "family lunch" in Act Three, Gregers is asked, "Now how do you like this for a change, sitting here at a well-set table in a happy family circle?"[26] The implication is that Gregers, as an unattached wanderer-activist, is better known for running from door to door with his "claim of the ideal" than he is for any opportunities to enjoy family comfort and cheer. Surely, this situation must be a rare pleasure for him, the other characters assume. Instead, Gregers responds with an abrupt, "I, for my part, don't thrive in swamp air."[27] In Gregers-speak, this is an elaboration of the metaphor he has imposed on the entire Ekdal home: that it is a swamp of deception full of wounded wild ducks. His impulse is to force the home's inhabitants to return to life, as a clever dog might do in fetching a wounded duck from the bottom of the sea. In this sense, his motivation is the same as all of Ibsen's previous unmaskers; like Lona Hessel and Dr. Stockmann, he is working with a model of air-and-light housing hygiene.

Once the life-lies of the Ekdal Family Theater have been exposed, Gregers waits for a tableau of reconciliation between Hjalmar and Gina:

"I had expected so surely that when I came through the door, waiting for me there would be a light of transfiguration [*et forklarelsens lys*] shining from both man and wife."[28] Instead of finding an ideal behind the curtain he has pulled back, he says that he finds only the "dull, heavy, gloomy – [*dumpe, tunge, triste* –]." He has not even finished the sentence when Gina removes the lampshade on a lamp in the room. This masterful rhetorical deflation reduces Gregers's abstract rhetoric of light and dark in the home to a practical question of lighting devices, dramatizing the metaphorical gap between target and source domain experiences.

Joan Templeton elaborates these examples of Gina's corrective "sense" against the male characters' rhetorical "sensibility" in her book *Ibsen's Women*,[29] and her treatment of *The Wild Duck* remains the most thorough and convincing account of the gender dynamics of the play. One of the lasting contributions of her reading is the view that the Ibsen criticism's fixation on the contest between Relling and Gregers to control Hjalmar has obscured what all of the male characters have in common: a fatal weakness for "theorizing and sentimentality."[30] I would only add to this analysis that much of Relling's and Gregers's sentimental rhetorical activity is theorizing about the "home": about what makes it true (Gregers), what makes it comfortable (Hjalmar), or what makes it liveable (Relling). In this view, Gregers's demands for structural integrity and transparency are not so different from Hjalmar's sentimentalizing; both depend on borrowed images rather than the insights taken from the practicalities of living.

Hjalmar, for example, expostulates after the scene we might call "Family Tableau with Flute and Beer" in Act Two: "So what if it is cramped and humble under our roof, Gina. It is home all the same. And *this much* I will say: it is good to be here."[31] On the one hand, the expectations for home seem lowered to a common sentimental threshold: one can hear the echoes of many nineteenth-century humble hearths and homes in Hjalmar's lines. At the same time, Hjalmar's notion of his modest but happy home is as suspect as Gregers's imagined home filled with the light of transfiguring reform; it is a mental image fetched from somewhere outside the place where they actually live. Thus, when Hjalmar responds to Gregers's first mention of swamp air in Act Three, it is actually a response *in kind*, despite their apparent disagreement:

> And there isn't any swamp air here, as you put it. In the poor photographer's home the ceiling is low, I know, – and my means are poor. But I am an inventor, Gregers, and a family provider as well. *That* is what sustains me in spite of my meager conditions.[32]

Who is this "poor photographer" that Hjalmar speaks of in the third person? Both himself and someone else at the same time, perhaps someone from a home he has seen depicted elsewhere. Likewise, the home he describes is both his own and one that he mimics.

This is what makes his notion of home so vulnerable when he finds out the facts of his domestic situation. In no time at all, it seems, he is already exclaiming pathetically, "My home lies in rubble around me [*Hjemmet er styrtet i grus omkring mig*]."[33] The rubble image is also a cliché, and the home's "ruin" might easily be contradicted by the continued devotion of both Gina and Hedvig, but the ready-made image of the ruined home is perfect for Hjalmar precisely because it is so well worn and sentimental. Yet even more rhetorically deflationary is Hjalmar's line in Act Four, after Gregers reveals to Hjalmar the devastating facts of his situation. Hjalmar repeats almost word for word the negative inversion of his earlier line from Act Two about it being "good to be here" in the home: "I thought too, that home was a good place to be. That was a delusion."[34] Figure 10 depicts this moment of reversal and disillusionment from the production at the Royal Theater in Copenhagen in 1885, which was apparently performed by the actor with all of Hjalmar's theatrical gestures intact. The consistency of Hjalmar's maudlin posing throughout the play (at the apparently happy beginning, after his eyes have been opened, and even after his daughter is dead – it makes no difference) is an indication of Ibsen's growing suspicion of "home" in all of its guises.

Relling, too, has his own theory of home, namely that to be liveable, home life must necessarily be founded on lies. His "model" home thus takes the protective aspects of shelter to extremes, arguing that the truths of life are too harsh for these wounded creatures. Like the rabbits and ducks sheltered in the theme space of the studio's attic, the Ekdals find protection in the form of life-lies and illusions. In this sense, "home" saves them from "life." The occupants of this house may have been viable once in the full light of truth, but now they have been thoroughly domesticated; these are not "people turned toward the sun," as mentioned in Chapter 1. To call Doctor Relling's position a theory of the home is simply to recognize that when he dispenses life-lies to everyone in the house (one prescription fits all), he does so out of a belief that homelife for the weak needs to be arranged with tailor-made life-lies as the remedies. His housing theory assumes the necessity of domestication.

At some point, the proliferation of domestic theories in *The Wild Duck* suggests that the question ought to be shifted away from which domestic

Scene af »Vildanden«. 4de Akt. Tegnet af Tom Petersen.

Hjalmar: Ogsaa jeg syntes, at Hjemmet var godt at være i. Det var en Vildfarelse. Hvor henter jeg nu den fornødne Spændstighed fra til at føre Opfindelsen over i Virkelighedens Verden? Kanske dør den med mig, og da er det din Forgangenhed, Gina, som har dræbt den.

Figure 10: From Act Four of *The Wild Duck*, with caption beginning: "Even I thought that home was a good place to be." Production: Royal Theater (Copenhagen), prem. February 22, 1885.

model is best to whether one should be speaking of models at all. Templeton's suggestion that the play's two "housekeepers" (a deliberately contrastive, more neutral term), Gina and Mrs. Sørby, deserve more attention as representatives of a truly alternative position is a fruitful way to think about how Ibsen sets up a positive potential of "house" as a defense against the seductive ideologies of "home."[35] Following Templeton's argument, "housekeeping" is the conceptual position that develops out of the particular experience in a specific house and remains steadfastly focused on present realities. Gina thus suggests one possible stance in response to all of the home building going on around her by men who consistently see the real house only through the filter of some borrowed ideal.

I turn now to a late moment for the rhetoric of "true homes" in Ibsen's career: what we might term "life in the rubble." The play is *The Master Builder* (1892), and the aspect relevant for the immediate discussion is the debilitating effect that the idea of a true home has on both Aline and Halvard Solness, although in different ways. Here too one of Ibsen's poems, written unusually late in his career, is relevant as a preview of the themes in the play. Entitled "They Sat There, Those Two – [*De sad der, de to –*]," it is short enough to cite in its entirety (again in my overly literal translation):

> They sat there, those two, in so cozy a house
> in the fall and the days of winter.
> Then the house burned. Everything lies in rubble.
> Those two can only rake in the ashes.
>
> Because down there a jewel lies hidden, –
> a jewel that can never burn.
> And if they search diligently, it might simply happen
> that it will be found by him or by her.
>
> But even if they, those fire-damaged two,
> find the precious, fire-proof jewel –
> *she* will never find her seared faith,
> *he* never his seared happiness.[36]

Like the house burning from "On the Heights," discussed in Chapter 1, the conflagration here comes on abruptly, and the first three lines create as schematic a reduction of Ibsen's housing scenarios as can be imagined: cozy home → fire → rubble. What, if anything, comes next?

Ibsen is a poet of the aftermath (which is just another way of saying, of the analytic drama), and many of his dramatic characters find themselves in the equivalent of this situation, poking through the ashes and rubble of an ideal that has been destroyed by a fire of one kind or another. Even in plays that are not so overtly architectural as *The Master Builder*, lost ideals often find expression in the idea of a lost home. The reaction of "those two," the couple in this poem, is to search repeatedly and obsessively for what was lost, a jewel "that can never burn." The association of the jewel with some ideal of home life suggests itself, but the interesting dynamic of the poem is that Ibsen indicates that the object of their search misleads them; even if they were to find the lost jewel buried in the ashes, it is not what they need, since the actual underlying losses of faith and happiness cannot be reconstituted no matter how endless their search. *The Master Builder* occupies an end point in Ibsen's thinking about true homes because even if there were an indestructible ideal of the home that could survive all fires, the experience of displacement and estrangement is such that one never gets past the effects. The loss of the original attachment changes the value of the jewel, even when it is technically left unscathed.

In *The Master Builder*, Halvard Solness's current building project in the play is a home intended to replace his wife's family home, which is reported to have been lost in a fire that not only burned everything to the ground, but reportedly also contributed indirectly to the death of the couple's infant twin sons. That home, Solness informs Hilde, was "a great, ugly dark wooden box when seen from the outside. But rather cozy and comfortable inside even so [*en stor, styg, mørk trækasse at sé til udvendig. Men nokså lunt og hyggeligt inde alligevel*]."[37] The house, like the equivocal inheritance that it represents, is at once both oppressive and cozy, *unheimlich* on the outside and *heimlich* on the inside, and its destruction correspondingly brings both relief and regret to Solness. *His* home-building activity – the "homes for people [*hjem for mennesker*]" that he touts as his life's main accomplishment[38] – could not begin until the lot had been cleared of its traditional clutter; however, in eliminating the eyesore home that monopolized the space, the fire also placed the experience of a true, original home out of reach. Once one accepts the idea that only the *original* home can be true, one gets locked into the logic of authenticity that makes loss impossible to replace. By definition, every subsequent home will be a pale copy.

Aline Solness remains frozen in this position: "You can build just as much as you want, Halvard – but for *me* you'll never manage to build up a true home [*noget rigtigt hjem*] again."[39] Frode Helland has effectively discussed Aline's stalemate as another instance of the play's structuring aesthetic of melancholy. He writes:

> For Aline the very thought of a "true home" [*riktigt hjem*] has become an impossibility. For her there can only be talk of a new place to stay [*et nytt tilholdssted*], and not only because of her miserable life together with Halvard. She *has had* a home that now is destroyed, and "the new one" can never make good the loss of the old one, it can't be "rebuilt."[40]

Ibsen uses the term "place to stay [*tilholdssted*]" in the play's text as well; it is introduced by Halvard Solness at the very start of the play to describe the kind of compromises young people have to make to "move into their own place."[41] The term is used quite clearly in that passage to mean a lesser form of home, a simple place to stay that has to serve temporarily until one can obtain something true and proper. Helland's point in introducing that term here is that Aline has come to regard her situation as a fire survivor as deficient in a similar way, except that in her case she sees the change as a painful demotion or regression with no prospect of improvement in the future. Of all of Ibsen's characters, she presents the most extreme case of "the home's impossibility."[42] The impossibility of her reattachment to a home is a leading symptom of the melancholy Helland describes – in the Freudian/Benjaminian sense of the endless repetition of trauma and the loss that can never be made good.

Halvard Solness has also accepted the impossibility of home – for himself, that is. The life-lie that allows him to continue building at all, however, is that he excels at building homes for others. For Solness, this is not simply a matter of building houses in the material sense, but precisely the kind of true home that he has relinquished for himself: "Comfortable, cozy, light-filled homes, where father and mother and the whole flock of children could live with the secure and happy feeling that it is an extremely happy thing to *exist* in the world [*Hyggelige, lune, lyse hjem, hvor far og mor og hele barneflokken kunde leve i tryg og glad fornemmelse af, at det er en svært lykkelig ting, det, at være* til *i verden*]."[43] This belief is counter-indicated on several fronts, however. Helland points to the inflated rhetoric of the passage and encourages the reader's skepticism toward the wishful thinking of a contractor who imagines himself to have any significant influence over the intimate life of the homes' inhabitants.[44] Jørgen Dines Johansen points to even more damning evidence: the stage directions at the beginning of Act Three that describe "low, dilapidated houses [*lave, forfaldne småhus*]," located in the exact spot of the happy villa homes Solness has described for Hilde in the earlier scene.[45] Helland comments further that this dilapidation is rather extreme for a mere ten years of wear and tear, so the houses could not have been so ambitious to start with.[46] Aline's own description of the subdivided lot also seems more in keeping with these other deflationary hints. When she discusses those "homes for people" with Hilde, she pointedly shifts away from Halvard's "homes for people" and speaks of the project as that phrase's alienated mirror image: she says that "they," not her husband, have "built houses for strangers [*bygget huse for fremmede mennesker*]" on the lot that used to be her intimate family space.[47] The disparity between the ideal as Solness describes it and the real evidence on stage and in the text is perhaps the best indication that this play should be regarded as the graveyard of true homes.

Mere homes

In Ibsen's later prose plays, the declining possibility of the true home of warmth, security, and *hygge* is matched by an increasing figuration of home as synonymous with stagnation and vacuity. "Home" becomes domestication in the most pejorative sense, connoting a loss of vitality, wildness, and freedom. As denigrating domestic imagery accumulates in these later plays, it becomes possible for the first time to regard a living situation as *merely* a home, a formulation that would not have made sense in the earlier plays (or in the public discourse at large) where reformers could still think of homes in terms of "true" and "false."

The obvious place to start this discussion is *The Wild Duck*, since its attic loft full of formerly wild inhabitants clearly depicts domestication as a form of wounding. The extended account of the wild duck's provenance comes in the second act, in response to Gregers's question to Old Ekdal: "How is it that a man like you, – such an outdoorsman [*en friluftsmand*], – can live in the middle of a stuffy city, in here between four walls?"[48] The more Gregers presses that point, the more Ekdal urges the others to open the attic and show the creatures living inside: chickens, pigeons, rabbits, and a wild duck. The duck is clearly the most valued, having been retrieved from a pond where it would have drowned after being shot in a hunt that left it maimed and unable to fly. Now that it has become accustomed to its situation in the loft, it actually seems to be thriving and growing fat.

The word used about the duck at several points (*trives*) is cognate with "thrive." It normally carries a positive semantic load: to thrive is to be protected from danger, to get all that one needs (and more), to be able to grow and develop. It is the sign of plenty and abundance. But here, the duck's thriving is instead clearly seen as a kind of plump contentedness, a consolation prize for its lost life in the wild:

GREGERS: And in there in the attic it is thriving really well.
HJALMAR: Yes, incredibly well. It has gotten fat. Of course, it has been in there so long now that it has forgotten the true life in the wild [*det rigtige vilde liv*]; and *that* is what it really depends on.
GREGERS: You are right about that, Hjalmar. Just don't let it ever see sky and ocean again.[49]

The phrase "the true life in the wild" is striking in this passage, because in other contexts in the earlier plays, *det rigtige* (the true, the genuine, the proper) is often associated with ideals of home: a "genuine home [*et rigtigt hjem*]" is what provides leverage for the critique of homes that do not measure up. Here, however, the concept of the genuine has been relocated away from the home out in the wild; "home" is filled instead with connotations of wounding, simulation, forgetting. It is the existence of fat contentment.

Ibsen manages this reversal with a little help from Darwin, according to Aarseth, because that way of thinking created the possibility of regarding domestication as a weakening of the species. Aarseth writes of Ibsen:

> He has made room for an implicit moral-philosophical evaluation of the transition from a wild to a tame state, from natural to artificial existence, from freedom to prison. In that context the wild, natural, and free is experienced as authentic life, while the tame and confined is branded as second-rate.[50]

In other words, Gregers is able to argue that "life between four walls" must be a reduced form of existence because of the Darwinian turn that privileges a free and strong evolution in the wild. The domestic sphere shelters its inhabitants artificially, and by protecting them also weakens them. They grow fat and vulnerable on their *hygge*.

One should not underestimate the contradictions of Gregers's position, however. The standards of truth and freedom that he imposes on the Ekdals are in a sense a fatal collision of the old notion of a true home and the ascendant notion of a strong, viable individual in the wild. He demands that the Ekdal marriage be built on the same ideal pillars of truth, freedom, and transparency that Lona Hessel promoted, but at the same time his model of truth requires that they expose themselves to the full force of a wild existence that they are actually no longer fit enough to survive. The problem is that the remnants of the home ideal are no match for the forces of domestic denigration in the play: even if one takes Relling's side about the utter necessity of a "home-lie," if we can shift his favorite term slightly, it is clear that the previous domestic ideals have been severely eroded by that cynicism. Home has become "second-rate," a compensatory existence for those unable to face facts.

The spatialization of a delegitimized domesticity is the main contribution of *The Lady from the Sea* to my argument. The setting for this 1888 play is liminal in the full sense of the word: all of the action takes place in border zones, with the home's innermost interior and the wild ocean occupying the conceptual extremes of the play. In between, one finds either mentioned or depicted in the play an extraordinarily nuanced gradation of space. Moving from most enclosed to the most open, this sliding scale would move from the undepicted interior of the Wangel home to the garden room, the veranda, the garden, the arbor, the shaded corner of the garden with the carp pond, the viewpoint clearing on the hill, the boat landing, the inner fjord, the outer fjord, the coastal mountain peaks, Ellida's childhood home at the lighthouse on the coast, and finally to the open sea. One might call this a continuum of freedom, or moving in the opposite direction and adopting the play's own eventual terminology, a continuum of responsibility; although until the very ending of the play, the notion of freedom prevails as the play's central concept. This spatial continuum is nowhere visible in the play; one constructs it in one's mind the same way one reorders the details of an Ibsen plot – analytically and retrospectively. The pieces accumulate and fall into place from visible parts of the set (if viewing the play in the theater), from the adjectives in set descriptions (if reading the play), and from dialogue along the way. Thus, Act One takes place in the open garden spaces, Act Two on the hilltop clearing, Acts Three and Five by the carp pond, and Act Four in the garden room.

As one of the few Ibsen prose plays with an exterior setting, *The Lady from the Sea* would seem to be one of the least relevant for an analysis of architectural metaphor. As Aarseth has suggested, however, the play retains many of the characteristics and issues developed in Ibsen's preceding examples of *glasskab* dramaturgy, most particularly the contrast between enclosure and openness.[51] These are architectural concepts, and it makes as much sense to call the many progressive border zones of *The Lady from the Sea* quasi-architectural as it does to call them quasi-natural. With its glass doors and potted plants, the garden room of Act Four is the most architectural of the depicted spaces, but the covered veranda is also enclosed enough that Ellida finds the air there to be oppressively stagnant.[52] The arbor that her husband Wangel built for her farther out in the garden is called a *løvhytte* in the Norwegian stage directions, literally a "leaf-hut," which itself indicates its hybrid combination of the architectural and the natural. (Ellida calls it a *lysthus*, or garden pavilion, but the effect is the same.[53]) The carp pond is also enclosed and stagnant, but even the Act Two setting at the hilltop, with its "large rocks, suitable as seating places," has an architectural aspect.[54] This is the one dramaturgical setting in *Lady from the Sea* that Aarseth excludes from his overall claim,[55] but there is enough of a living-room logic in this natural clearing that it could strengthen his point even further.

As an aside, the same could be said of the outdoor setting in *Little Eyolf* (1894), where the outdoor setting similarly preserves an architectural structure, shown in Figure 11. Dramas such as *Lady from the Sea* and *Little Eyolf* that depict exterior spaces while continuing to emphasize long conversations and psychological dialogue require as a practical matter some sort of seating,

Fra „Lille Eyolf" paa Kristiania teater.
(Aabningsscenen i 2den akt).

Allmers — hr. Halvorsen.   *Asta* — fru Dybwad.

Figure 11: From Act Two of *Little Eyolf*, a trace of the architectural in an outdoor scene. Production: Christiania Theater, prem. January 15, 1895.

so in some sense the preservation of the interior logic in outside settings is forced by the continued reliance on the conversational model. Even so, it can also be seen as a continued engagement with vestigial architectural principles, even as the plays' settings move outside in Ibsen's late dramas (the bench in the snow from *John Gabriel Borkman* would be another example).

In *Lady from the* Sea, the one extreme of this continuum that seems without any architectural definition, the open sea, is referred to many times in the course of the play (the lighthouse at land's end would be the last bit of architecture before reaching the formless waves, in that sense). As the stated object of Ellida's attraction and homesickness,[56] the ocean symbolizes a radically open, free space. It is identified as the realm of the Stranger and Ellida's mystical marriage pact and is the setting for the reported sailor stories.[57] With all of the attention clustering around the imagined outer limit of freedom, though, it is remarkable how little we know of Wangel's family home at the other extreme of the continuum. The qualities of the farthest interior space are cloaked in complete silence in the text – the silence of the grave, one might say, since it still seems to be completely given over to the dead wife (the daughters decorate the house and raise its flag every year on her birthday, despite Wangel's discomfort with the practice). The home seems literally to have been evacuated, with only the structuring absence of the dead wife remaining. The daughters seem instead assigned to defend it from their position on the veranda, to judge from the unusually schematic spatial description of Wangel shuttling back and forth between them there and Ellida sitting in the arbor. The guests in turn come and go in the liminal space of the garden.

Ellida's alienation from the home was noted in one contemporary review by Bredo Morgenstierne, who described Ellida in this way: "She is completely rootless in her husband's home; is pushed outside and lives outside, notices little of what is happening around her, and is no support in that space where as a wife it is her duty to be a support."[58] This conservative comment misses the dramaturgical shift represented by Ellida's relationship to space, however. It is an odd effect of Ibsen's construction of this fictional world that readers and viewers are led to imagine that Ellida never goes into the house, simply because for the duration of the play she is always depicted outside it, even though in realistic terms this would be absurd – she is after all married to Wangel, and despite the figurative talk about her being a mermaid living in the fjord, she must logically be assumed to be living in the house with Wangel. The fact that the play works more symbolically and allegorically with space points ahead to a more modernistic dramaturgy, something more like the "impossible" spatial arrangement in the play *John Gabriel Borkman*, written eight years later. When it is claimed that the title figure in that play *never* leaves his inhabited space, it is in some ways simply the conceptual match with Ellida, who seemingly never *enters* the space she purportedly inhabits.

In more realistic terms, a complete avoidance of the innermost part of the home is only plausible in a Norwegian play set in late summer, the only time of year when the outdoors would offer such a nuanced range of inhabitable positions. But there is something else that is significant about Ibsen's silence about the home interior per se. In one sense, that silence marks the space where the ideal of home used to be located. Ellida's true home is by contrast located far away from the actual house: Wangel suggests that they move "out to a spot by the open sea, – a spot where you can find a true home [*et rigtigt hjem*] of your own liking."[59] There is no more talk of *hjemlig hygge* here. In its place are gradations of outdoor domesticity in which the closer one gets to the interior, the more stagnating the effect – at least when seen from Ellida's perspective. Aarseth notes the connection between stifling air and brackish water, not only in this play but in others,[60] and that is clearly marked as an effect of domestication: the carp in the ponds are called "those poor, tame, domesticated fish [*de stakkars tamme husfiskene*]," in contrast to the "great wild schools of fish [*store vilde fiskestimene*]" out in the ocean.[61] The invented combination in the word *husfisk* (literally, "house-fish") points clearly toward connotations of the domestic sphere as a degraded existence.[62]

The link between the carp pond and the social life of the inner fjord is made quite clear, so it comes as something of a surprise that Ellida is able to re-embrace the domesticated existence with Wangel at the end of the play. Her choice seems to be a counterintuitive turn of events, given the consistently negative associations of domesticity with stagnation throughout. One commentator, Alfred Sinding-Larsen, attempts to redeem this degraded domesticity by linking it to the doll-home imagery earlier in Ibsen's writing, imagery that still relied on the implicit availability of more authentic ideals (this passage also has a reference to Selma from *The League of Youth*, a character who like Nora sees marriage as a doll home): "With Ellida it is the same as with Selma and Nora: her husband has let her lead a doll-home existence [*en Dukkehjemstilværelse*] that could never lead to any intellectual communion between them, could not allow her to be his wife in the true sense of the word."[63] The "true sense" was left unrealized in those earlier two plays, Sinding-Larsen continues, but here in this play he sees its ideal fulfillment:

> But Ellida stays. – She experiences "the wonderful thing" [*det Vidunderlige*], namely, that for her sake and out of love for her, because he truly is her spouse, the husband forsakes himself, gives up his own wishes, is willing to renounce everything, including her, for the sake of her happiness. Wangel is the first husband in Ibsen's plays who is not selfish. For that reason the author has here been able to place a period where one has become accustomed to finding a question mark.

To more modern sensibilities, this recourse to Ibsen's earlier ideals of domesticity might seem unsatisfying, since Sinding-Larsen seems to imply that all of the intervening interrogations of the home (the series of "question marks") of the past ten years do not matter, since in *The Lady from the Sea* Ibsen has returned to the idea of true marriages and true homes built on secure foundations and has settled those issues with a period, the sign of final closure. Sinding-Larsen's positive interpretation of the play is not really satisfying as a reading, however; it is not a simple thing to imagine a happy future for Ellida by the carp pond, no matter how well she and Wangel manage the balance between freedom and responsibility. The negative connotative aspects of the stagnation imagery do not really go away, but linger in the interpretive activity even after the curtain falls.

Toril Moi makes *The Lady from the Sea* the climax of a different argument, one that sees in the disciplined reconciliation scene an ethical negotiation of otherness that is lacking in the other plays. In Moi's treatment, the "healing power of ordinary human conversation" makes possible Ellida's transformation and reconciliation to a domestic sphere that is not denigrated, but "ordinary" and "everyday" in quite positive senses of those terms (whose recuperation in current critical discourse creates another important shift in possibilities for interpreting Ibsen).[64] The plays after *The Lady from the Sea* thus constitute the Epilogue section of Moi's book, or as it might also be viewed, the dramatic denouement of an argument that reaches its high point in *The Lady from the Sea*. The important point is that the trajectory of this argument is only possible when one retrospectively fills the concept of the "everyday" with more positive potential than it seems to have in the metaphoric system of the play itself. Following the general trend of Ibsen's later plays and their denigration of the domestic, *The Lady from the Sea* seems more like the last gasp of a workable home idea in Ibsen's works than it does the high point or positive resolution of a theme.

This impression is reinforced by developments in *Hedda Gabler*, in which Ibsen returns to a negative domestic vision with a vengeance. When *Hedda Gabler* appeared in 1890, "home" seems once again to have become a thoroughly discredited position for Ibsen, represented only by the pathetic Jørgen Tesman and his aunts. As we watch Tesman's connections to ridiculous forms of domesticity proliferate throughout the play, beginning with the auntly *mise-en-scène* of the newlyweds' first home together, the tenuously positive compromise view of domesticity offered by Ibsen in *The Lady from the Sea* recedes quickly from view. Domesticity in *Hedda Gabler* is the love of lavender and hats left behind in the new home (note that Aunt Julle is co-owner of Tesman's new house, having signed the second mortgage). Tesman, the slipper enthusiast, is also an archival scholar of "domestic handicrafts in Brabant [*den brabantske husflid*] in the Middle Ages."[65] He is excited to get to work on the material he has gathered, "Especially now that I have my own comfortable house and home [*mit eget hyggelige hus og hjem*] to work in."[66] Knowing the trajectory of the play, it is difficult to imagine any home where Hedda lives as *hyggelig* in any positive sense of the term. The *hygge* in this play is instead a grotesquely empty remnant, existing only in the world of dying aunts and Tesman, their only heir. From Hedda's perspective, the association with the domestic makes her famously describe the whole situation to Judge Brack as "these meager circumstances [*tarvelige vilkår*] I have entered into."⁶⁷ Put another way, Hedda is the one character who can see the new space as *merely* a home. She had hoped for something more than that: as she says to Tesman earlier, she had hoped to "maintain a house [*føre hus*],"⁶⁸ which is to say, to entertain at a certain level of social elegance. "Meager circumstances" not only describes her dissatisfaction with the home that she has gotten instead, but it would be a good description of the domestic in many of the later Ibsen plays as well.

The idea of the "dream home" is raised briefly in the play only to be thoroughly debunked. In the same conversation with Brack, Hedda reveals that what everyone has taken to be the home she has always wanted, the villa formerly belonging to the widow of a cabinet minister named Falk, is nothing of the sort: "Do you also believe in that wishful story [*ønskehistorien*]?"⁶⁹ The word *ønskehistorien* carries a specific resonance here because of the closely related term *ønskehus*, which would be the Norwegian word for "dream house." Hedda tells Brack instead that her current occupancy of the supposed house of her dreams was all the result of a misunderstanding; when Tesman used to walk her home from social events before they were married, she explains, they would pass the old house. Tesman got so tongue-tied one evening that Hedda, showing uncharacteristic pity for once, simply made up something to get him out of his difficulties: "so then I happened to say, purely as a lark [*rent letsindigt*], that I would like to live in this villa."⁷⁰ This completely arbitrary small talk about the house, Hedda continues, was the entire basis for their relationship: "But it was in this infatuation with the Falk villa [*dette sværmeriet for statsrådinde Falks villa*] that Jørgen Tesman and I came to an understanding, you see!"⁷¹ Hedda continues to note that the personal consequences of this arbitrary utterance were severe and relentless in their interrelated logic: "engagement and marriage and honeymoon and everything else."

A common complaint about the plot of *Hedda Gabler* is that Hedda's choice of Tesman seems too unmotivated – many a reader or viewer has wondered along with Brack how this truly astonishing mismatch could ever have taken place. The passage just cited makes clear, however, that the utter architectural arbitrariness of the marriage is exactly the idea that interested Ibsen. What if it all simply started with a whim about a *house*? Hedda ends up in it because of a misunderstanding that nevertheless entails everything else in her situation. Seemingly married accidentally, she is also the accidental inhabitant of a house that everyone else thinks is her dream

Mere homes

home. As the play opens, she literally has no history there – although it is quite clear from the text that she has just returned from her honeymoon, it is easy to lose track of the fact that she has only slept there one night and will end up living in "Hedda's house" for just a couple more, the most temporary of the house's inhabitants, actually. The deflation and denigration of the founding myth of the Tesman marriage is completed with this exchange:

BRACK: Yes, but now? Now that we have arranged it to be a little homey [*hjemligt*] for you!
HEDDA: Ugh, – I think it smells like lavender and pressed roses in all of the rooms. – But maybe Aunt Julle left that smell behind her.
BRACK: (laughs) No, instead I think it was the dear, departed cabinet minister's widow who left it.
HEDDA: Yes, there is something dead about it. It reminds me of flowers from a ball – the day after.[72]

The whiff of domesticity that clings to this alien home is intolerable for Hedda. Without necessarily ascribing her "home allergies" to Ibsen himself, it still remains to point out that the equation of "hominess" with the odor of death is a radically different position from those that existed in the earlier plays.

The possibility for thinking of "mere" homes becomes even stronger in the following plays, in which all homes seem to be evacuated of true feeling. In a previous article, I have argued at length that the idea of home in *The Master Builder* is that of an empty copy of a lost original, with all of the building activity taking on an aspect of endless repetition.[73] Here, I might add a few brief comments that follow the thread through the final plays, such as the way the home in *Little Eyolf* is associated with the imagery of the Rat Woman who asks Allmers and Rita, "Do the master and mistress have anything gnawing here in the house?"[74] Despite their immediate denials, that does actually seem to be the case in a more figurative sense. The Rat Woman's decidedly *uhyggelig* image of rats scurrying throughout the walls of the house makes clear how far from true pillars and solid foundations Ibsen's housing imagery has come. In *John Gabriel Borkman*, it is not just Erhart who flees the Rentheim estate and its "parlor air [*stueluften*],"[75] its *Danse Macabre* soundtrack, its faded décor, its emotional chill, and its living-dead inhabitants. The smell of roses and lavender – that nice, homey touch – practically chokes Erhart as well, and Borkman himself speaks of the "prison air [*fængselsluften*]" in the home.[76] Eventually, all of the characters flee for the exits: the son and his traveling companions to the South, Borkman by making his own prison break into the wintry cold, and

Ella Rentheim and Gunhild Borkman by following him up the mountainside. As Borkman says definitively, "Never in my life will I set foot under that roof again!"[77] The entire house is evacuated at the end of the play.

Ibsen's final play, *When We Dead Awaken*, is a drama less often seen in architectural terms, since the sculptural metaphor clearly dominates. Rubek's masterpiece, *The Day of Resurrection*, lends the imagery for the play's title; sets its dominant themes and tone; and, as many scholars have argued, provides the key to its interpretation.[78] For these readings, the sculpture's several reported versions, both as described in dialogue and as reenacted visually on stage in the second act, contribute to a complexly ambivalent and ironic dramatic statement, a representational *mise-en-abîme* that precludes any possibility of secure grounding by the end of the play.[79]

For a play framed primarily by sculptural metaphors, however, there is certainly a lot of architectural discussion in the background as well. As might be expected from the overall theme of his study, Aarseth pays close attention to the setting in his analysis. He notes that the play supports his thesis about Ibsen's dramaturgy of confinement only in the sense that the bath and sanatorium spaces of the first and second acts seem devoted to the "living dead": guests who have come to the spot for health reasons. The key point for Aarseth is that these are spaces of diminished vitality, even if they are not as physically confining as the *glasskab* sets in previous plays.[80] Thus, he points out, the climb in altitude from act to act conveys a sense of life outside cages, a possibility of a freer and more dynamic existence.

For the present argument about diminished homes, however, it is the repetition of the domesticated animal theme that attracts attention. Animal imagery occurs in the beginning of the play, when Rubek and Maja have their tired initial conversation on the hotel veranda. Rubek confides that the portrait busts he has been sculpting on commission since he became famous actually have a hidden reality:

RUBEK: (decisively) Only *I* can see it. And it amuses me to no end. – Outwardly there is this "striking likeness," as it is often called, and which people stand and stare at with such surprise – (lowers his voice) – but deep down inside they are worthy, respectable horse faces and obstinate donkey snouts and drooping, low-browed dog skulls and engorged pig heads, – and slack, brutal steer images now and then –

MAJA: (apathetically) – all of the dear domestic animals [*alle de kære husdyr*], in other words.

RUBEK: Only the dear domestic animals, Maja. All of the animals that people have warped [*forkvaklet*] in their image. And which have warped people in return.[81]

The ferocity of Rubek's disdain is the most striking aspect of this passage; the adjectives pile up to create the effect of a grotesque menagerie. His contempt for his clients is about to reach its crescendo when Maja gathers his examples abruptly together under the rubric of "dear domestic animals." The resulting clash of terminology produces a scathing contamination of the domestic, since it is equated with both ugliness and a brutish lack of consciousness. Like *husdyr*, Rubek's patrons react ignorantly to his art, able only to enthuse about surface effects of realism without understanding the satire underpinning it. (One is reminded of the *Døgn-folk* attending the troll's church unawares, as was discussed in the Introduction.) This is the source of the "warping" or "deformity" of the busts. Thinking back on the loft residents in *The Wild Duck* and the *husfisk* in the carp pond in *The Lady from the Sea*, we see that the earlier pity for the tame has here developed into full-blown derision. In Ibsen's final play, the domestic has become a severely compromised category.

There is something further to note about this imagery in connection with the uncanny. I have previously noted Aarseth's argument about Darwin's contribution to the demotion of domestication.[82] Freud was interested in the uncanny potential of "tameness" as well. In his essay on the uncanny, he includes this example when evaluating available citations of the word *heimlich* in the Sanders dictionary:

> Of animals: tame, companionable to man. As opposed to wild, e.g. 'Animals which are neither wild nor *heimlich*,' etc. 'Wild animals . . . that are trained to be *heimlich* and accustomed to men.' 'If these young creatures are brought up from early days among men they become quite *heimlich*, friendly' etc. So also: 'It (the lamb) is so *heimlich* and eats out of my hand.' 'Nevertheless, the stork is a beautiful, *heimelich* bird.'[83]

Note the inherently positive aspect of the dictionary definition of *heimlich* as a synonym for "tame"; here it means friendly and "familiar" in a technical sense – an animal that can be included within the family or human circle. The implication in Freud's essay, however, is that *Heimlichkeit* in an animal could easily turn to its opposite, an eruption of the strange and wild within the familiar. Rubek's description of the sculpted animal faces would resonate with that view; as he tells Maja, the "dear domestic animals" actually have disturbing, atavistic qualities instead. Rubek's hidden animal faces are not those of the friendly, anthropomorphized "family" animals – they are not *husdyr* in that sense – but those showing trailing vestiges of their more primitive and beastly versions. The earlier layer, the brutishness supposedly repressed by the process of domestication, peeks through as a remnant making an *unheimlich* return. In addition, the fact that these animal faces are hidden to all but the artist, who alone can see them underneath the façade of familiarity ("striking likeness"), sets up this artistic vision as a superior, unhomely awareness or sensititivity.

A final example from *When We Dead Awaken* can underscore the degree to which the home has been evacuated of all positive content at the end of Ibsen's career. Throughout the play, Maja's flirtatious relationship with the hunter Ulfhejm forms a lively counterpoint to the brooding conversations about the past between Rubek and Irene. Frode Helland rightly cautions against seeing a simple endorsement of vitalism in this character-foil couple.[84] Although the contrast to Rubek's melancholic reflection and paralysis is clear, argues Helland, an overreliance on that schema can hide the levels of construction and role-playing that mark Maja's and Ulfhejm's supposed immediacy and action. Most relevant for my discussion here is the deflation that occurs at the beginning of Act Three when the two of them climb up to the "hunting castle" that Ulfhejm has promised Maja. Once again, the stage directions make available for the reader an impression that would be conveyed visually in a stage performance: the so-called hunting castle [*jagtslot*] is described at the outset of the act as "an old, half-dilapidated hut [*en gammel, halvt sammenfalden hytte*]" that Maja subsequently describes with disgust as "that old pig sty there [*den gamle svinestien der*]" when they come upon it.[85] The choice of the term *jagtslot* empties out the remaining architectural fantasies that might be left over from *The Master Builder*'s "castle in the air [*luftslot*]" by deploying the same root word as a euphemism for Ulfhejm's crass seduction locale. And just as the Master Builder's self-deceived ideal of the true "homes for people" was contradicted by the visual reality of disrepair in the "low, dilapidated row houses" at the beginning of that play's final act, the romantic fantasy of the hunting castle is here deflated by the physical decrepitude of the structure when it appears at a similar point in this play. One senses the final gasp of a certain kind of architectural imagination in this exchange, just before Maja and Ulfhejm begin their descent back down into society:

ULFHEJM: I have a castle to offer you –
MAJA: (pointing to the hut) Like that one *there*?
ULFHEJM: It hasn't fallen down yet.
MAJA: And all the glory of the world?
ULFHEJM: I'm telling you, a castle –
MAJA: Thanks! I've had enough of castles [*Slotte har jeg fåt nok af*].[86]

One might say that this ramshackle shelter that appears toward the end of Ibsen's final play is the last remnant of "Ibsen's houses." As the only house-like structure in *When We Dead Awaken* aside from the spa hotel, it is all that is left of the ideal at the end of Ibsen's career. Moreover, however one regards Maja's vitalism, it is clear that the existence she will seek in the future is a non-architectural mode of being: as she says, she has had quite enough of castles for the time being. She sings out that position at several points, including at the very end, in verses that constitute the last words in Ibsen's last play (even after the more famous "Pax vobiscum!"), which according to the stage directions are heard faintly in echo in the distance:

> I am free! I am free! I am free!
> My life of imprisonment is past!
> I am free as a bird! I am free![87]

Frode Helland has quite forcefully emphasized this point about Maja getting the last word, rebutting the many commentators who would prefer to latch onto the apparently redemptive "Pax vobiscum" uttered by the nun.[88] Helland's point is not to advocate for Maja, however; in his argument, her position is no more "redemptive" than the nun's (or that of Rubek and Irene who have just sacrificed themselves for art). Instead, he sees Maja's return down the mountainside as its own form of renunciation. Her "liberation" is also tinged by a loss that comes with her apparent embrace of "immediacy," namely the loss of the insight gained by art and an engaged intellectual life.

Marginal occupants

In their opening conversation on the veranda in the first act of *When We Dead Awaken*, Rubek and Maja have an extended conversation about home or, to put it more accurately, about what is left of the home. They are unsurprisingly estranged from the homeland they have not seen during their years abroad, and neither is particularly glad to be back. Rubek, who has been away longer, says it best: "I've just become so completely removed from all this here, – this hominess here [*dette her hjemlige*]."[89] Rubek's final term is not easy to translate into English, but *det hjemlige* is one of the Norwegian words that could substitute fairly accurately for *Heimlichkeit* in German. In essense, Rubek says in this scene that he has drifted away from everything *heimlich*, and even on returning finds that everything that was familiar is now strange. This leads to one of the most famous modernist images of the play, his experience of the local train stopping at every small station in the middle of the night, with two railway workers mumbling something "hushed and muffled and meaningless out into the night [*dæmpet og klangløst og intetsigende ud i natten*]."⁹⁰ It is a true stroke of unhomeliness to make one of the most rural and culturally interior places reported in the play the setting for the most striking image of estrangement. Ibsen locates the unhomeliest image of the play in the very heart of the familiar, the provincial, and the homey.

Lisbeth Wærp characterizes Rubek's and Maja's return to their homeland as "a homecoming to a place that is no longer at home, or to a place – at home – that no longer exists, a place that is not experienced as homey [*hjemlig*], but which only *resembles* in the way a corpse resembles the living person."⁹¹ Wærp's last image is especially intriguing and suggestive – that the experience of returning to find a place "like home" is for Rubek and Maja a grotesque, corpse-like sort of mimesis. Their thwarted expectation is that the place should *be* home, not just resemble it, but their shared boredom with the trip and each other gives their expectation much lower stakes than that of the lost Solness home, to choose a contrasting example. In this play, one senses that if home is not exactly what Rubek and Maja remembered – oh well.

The opening conversation circles constantly around this complete sense of apathetic homelessness. Professor Rubek and Maja have lived in a cosmopolitan city (which Georg Brandes identified confidently as Munich),⁹² where they have "an impressive home [*et prægtigt hjem*]," corrected immediately to an "elegant house [*et herskabeligt hus*]" and later referred to as "the palace in the capital [*palæet i hovedstaden*]."⁹³ They also have a villa on Lake Taunitz (Brandes claims this referred to the Starnberger See outside Munich) that has a complicated prehistory, if one pieces together the story from the clues strewn throughout the text. At one point, there was "the little rustic home [*det lille bondehuset*] on Lake Taunitz on this spot,"⁹⁴ and Rubek and Irene reportedly used to come out to that spot on weekends after the week's modeling work was finished. Irene calls it "our old house [*vort gamle hus*]" for that reason.⁹⁵ But like the statue they shared (their "child"), this old house no longer exists in its original form. Rubek explains in response that he has razed the original home and in its place has built "a large, magnificent, comfortable villa [*en stor, prægtig bekvem villa*] on the lot." This is where Rubek and Maja live in the summers when they are not traveling, and it is also the house Maja refers to as the "cold, dank cage [*koldt, klamt bur*], where there was neither sunlight or fresh air, ... but only gilding and great, petrified human ghosts around the walls" when she tells her life story to Ulfhejm in Act Three.⁹⁶

This housing prehistory helps us understand an odd exchange in the opening conversation of the play, one that comes so early in the scene that it initially has the effect of a puzzle. Maja tells Rubek that she is bored with their trip and wants to go back to their house on the continent:

MAJA: Why not leave right away? Just think, we who could be so cozy and comfortable [*ha' det så lunt og mageligt*] in our lovely, new house.
RUBEK: (smiles indulgently) Actually, one should probably say: our lovely new *home*.
MAJA: I prefer to say *house*. Let's just stick with that.[97]

Shortly thereafter, Rubek seems to give in to this way of seeing things when he catches himself saying "home" again, only to switch back to Maja's preferred term. These exchanges suggest that in spite of their shared unease with the return home, they still experience it from different positions that the play will spend its time sorting out.

This insistence on correct terminology for the domestic replays a scene from *The Master Builder* in which Halvard Solness shows similarly linguistic fussiness. When he and Hilde finish their conversation in the second act, she mentions that the wreath for the roofing ceremony will be laid "Over your new home, I guess," and Solness responds, "Over the new house. Which will never be *home* for me."[98] Solness's insistence on the word "house," however, comes from a position of disillusionment about the loss of a true home, so that his hypercorrection is the sign of disappointed ideals. He still clings to the idea of homes for others, but with bitterness insists on calling his own situation a house, not a home.

One senses that Maja's refusal of "home" must be different; there is no sense of loss, no obvious disillusionment on her part. She does not seem to be rooting around in the ashes looking for lost jewels – or even the lost key to a secret chest of creativity, as Rubek claims to be doing. She can even talk of being "cozy and comfortable" herself – but just not in a *home*. Perhaps it is the disciplined abstinence signaled by the word "house" that is so useful to her, since it does not necessarily entail any sly sense of obligatory belonging – not to a husband, not to a family, and not to a cultural context. Maja's idea of housing as a temporary, contingent arrangement is, in other words, a position beyond Peter Stockmann's "weak-tea" asceticism, or Rektor Kroll's dismay at his newly fractured home, or Solness's building of a seemingly endless series of houses-that-should-be-homes. Here, "house" seems to be the term for those who travel without regrets, for those who, like Maja, are confident that they will always be able to find a place to be that is adequate – the expectation is no higher than that. This makes her process of disentanglement from Rubek the most effortless of any relationship break depicted in an Ibsen play: "So then the two of us will simply avoid each other. Completely away. I'll always be able to find something new somewhere in the world. Something free! Free! Free! – There is no problem with *that*, Professor Rubek."[99] This simple, untroubled acceptance of a marriage breakup and loss of home suggests that for Maja the expectation of attachment was never very strong to begin with.

In general, when analyzing fictional characters without attachment to home, the overriding predilection is to cast this unhomeliness as a painful existential burden. Writing of homelessness in the medieval and Renaissance periods, Nicholas Howe observes,

> If home is problematic as both place and as idea, if it is at once a refuge against the world and also the site that must be fled to enter the world, homelessness arouses much less ambivalent response in us. To be homeless seems, in most of the cultures one knows anything about, to be a condition of hardship and often unendurable suffering. To be homeless is not, in conventional usage at least, to be free of home or well rid of its tyrannies.[100]

Ibsen's use of the concept of homelessness would in this sense be quite unconventional, because Maja's unperturbed itinerancy and rejection of home is precisely an effort to be "well rid of its tyrannies." The mere possibility of this attitude – the ability to leave home without regrets, with no expectation of return – seems to be a defining characteristic of modernity, one that would distinguish Maja's case from the older historical examples covered in Howe's anthology. Maja's attitude certainly comes closer to that advocated by Lukács in his Ibsen criticism when echoing Marx's call for a "cheerful parting from the past."[101] To be sure, Maja is no Marxist; my point is not to load up her character position with an exaggerated positive political potential. Instead, I simply suggest that she is as unburdened by debilitating notions of "original home" and "authenticity" as any good progressive person might be, even if her consciousness is not in any sense a sophisticated one. Her insistence on occupying the neutral ground of straightforward "housing" is at the very least the defense of a conceptual space unburdened by homes.

In other words, I would offer that it seems possible to make this observation about Maja without turning her into a housing heroine. She is after all not the main interest of *When We Dead Awaken*. While Joan Templeton treats her in basically positive terms in *Ibsen's Women* – as Rubek's "gregarious, simple wife"[102] – she ultimately sees her as representing a less ambitious life that has renounced all philosophical or aesthetic perspectives, making her final song an ironic one. For his part, Helland is reluctant to see in Maja an endorsed position of life-affirming vitalism, preferring instead to see the end of Ibsen's play as a clash of parallel positions that ends in an empty, ironic stalemate.[103] My interest in advancing the idea of "house" over "home" is not dampened by these observations; they are fair evaluations of Maja's subordinate role in the text. Instead, my curiosity is piqued by the realization that Maja's alternative housing stance is developed so incidentally, so much to the side of more central concerns with Rubek's lost creativity and its aftermath. Ibsen's main interest was indeed in the consequences of artistic consciousness, but the glimpse of an unburdened unhomeliness in the margins of his plays provides an intriguing second track of argumentation.

Casting one's eye back over the conceptual positions outlined in this chapter and the last, one can discern a genealogy of Maja's unhomeliness, beginning with Nora's tough negotiations with Torvald over acceptable vocabulary and future living arrangements ("Then I came into your house –").[104] Nora's eventual "stranded" position between Torvald's *dukkehjem* and her *hjemsted*, with uncertain prospects for the future, was one early example of the refusal of home in its extended meanings. Nora was willing to lose "home" to gain something else, something yet to be determined. One can see this "traveler" aspect of Nora depicted in her costume and demeanor from the world premiere performance in Copenhagen (Figure 12), where the actress Betty Hennings played the role. This is a stern traveler, but one who will clearly be viable outside Torvald's home.

Gina Ekdal's attentiveness to the practicalities of housekeeping was another reaction to the unhomely: amidst the male characters' tortured and destructive responses to the collapse of the home, she continues focusing on the necessities of living, unconcerned with the measure of a "true home." Hedda Gabler's seething rage at the hominess around her takes the form of a protest, but no habitable alternative positions seem to be available, hence the suicide in the farthest recesses of the house. In *John Gabriel Borkman*, Fanny Wilton and her fellow travelers also work out some alternative mode of dwelling at the literal margin, fleeing to the South outside the realm of the play.

The character that comes closest to Maja's marginal unhomeliness is Hilde Wangel. She too is a traveler, having come down to the Solness home from an extended hike in the mountains, and having left her childhood home for good with almost no possessions. Figure 13 is a studio actress portrait, again of Betty Hennings, that gives a strong sense of Hilde, the

Fru Hennings som Nora i „Et Dukkehjem".

Tegnet af **Erik Henningsen.**

Nora. — — Der maa være fuld Tillid paa begge Sider. Se, her har du din Ring tilbage. Giv mig min. (3. Akt.)

Figure 12: Betty Hennings as Nora, newly dressed as a traveler in Act Three. Production: Royal Theater (Copenhagen), prem. December 22, 1879.

Figure 13: Betty Hennings posed in a studio actress portrait as Hilde Wangel in hiking clothes, as described in Act Two of *The Master Builder*. Production: Royal Theater (Copenhagen), prem. March 8, 1893. Owner: Theater Collection, National Library of Norway.

more carefree traveler who is unburdened by the loss of home. When Solness asks her, "Did *you* have a cozy and happy home [*et lunt, lykkelig hjem*] – up there with your father, Hilde?" Hilde responds, "I only had a cage [*Bare et bur havde jeg*]," adding "The woodland bird will never return to the cage."[105] As we saw earlier, Maja's description of life with Rubek was that of life in a cage. Furthermore, Hilde can sleep soundly in a strange bed ("as in a cradle"), even in as haunted a room as one of the empty, useless, memorial nurseries in Solness's present house.[106] Maja reports the same to the supervisor at the spa: "I always sleep like a rock at night," and Rubek, by contrast, sleeps poorly.[107] The "robust conscience" that Hilde describes to her master builder could just as easily apply to Maja and would seem to be a prerequisite to a positive state of homelessness.[108]

Hilde's "castle in the air" is quite different from the matter-of-fact, more neutral relationship to houses that both Maja and Nora insist on maintaining, even when that castle is furnished with the "firm foundation" that Solness requires. Its defining characteristic is precisely that it is *not* inhabitable in any real sense, as Solness demonstrates in his fall from the tower. It becomes clear that the characters who are the least fit for living outside the home are most often male: Torvald, Hjalmar, Rosmer, Tesman, Solness, and Borkman all come to mind. There are exceptions, of course, but in general, Ibsen's men feel the loss of home more keenly, in a debilitating way. One might note with a bit of surprise that "homemaking" in Ibsen's plays is mostly a male concern, but it becomes more understandable if one takes that term to mean the defense of all of the extended meanings of "home": social stability, façade morality, personal comfort and *hygge*, and the ideology of patriarchal family life. To extend the sense of Templeton's term, "housekeeping" might be used as a contrast to help one think about a more pragmatic, careful relationship to the entanglements of shelter. And the achievement of this kind of positively "unhomely" position is generally of much greater interest to Ibsen's women.

The resilience of home

To this point, this chapter's argument has traced mainly a textual trajectory of decline for the notion of "home" throughout Ibsen's plays. The contemporary commentary on Ibsen's plays was keenly aware of this interest in house and home as well, especially after the architectural imagery of *The Master Builder* seemingly provided the critics of his day with a ready rubric for reading the totality of Ibsen's works. What becomes apparent from these reactions, however, is that recognizing the centrality of Ibsen's metaphors of house and home did not necessarily create consensus readings that supported the full force of Ibsen's critique, perhaps because metaphor always leaves a degree of interpretive wiggle room. Instead, it is possible to see in some of these reactions to Ibsen the stubborn resilience of existing conceptions of home: some commentators held tight to their domestic ideals in spite of Ibsen's deconstruction, even co-opting his positions of critique in what are easily seen as highly willful readings.

One of the best examples of this comes in a lengthy examination of *The Master Builder* in 1895 by Hanna Andresen Butenschøn (1851–1928), who wrote under the pen name Helene Dickmar. Butenschøn was a Norwegian writer who had participated in the morality debates of the 1880s on the conservative, idealistic side.[109] Interesting for the present argument is that this debate was also essentially about façades, namely what to do about the inevitable discrepancy between professed sexual ideals and actual social behavior. The answer on the political left throughout Scandinavia was to propose a liberation from outmoded sexual morals (to allow for free love), while the right argued that the disparity problem would be best solved by holding men to comparable ideals of chastity and monogamy as those imposed on women. In Norway, this debate about double standards was called the "gauntlet controversy," named after Bjørnstjerne Bjørnson's play *A Gauntlet* (*En Hanske*, 1883), which made Bjørnson the leading spokesman for the views of the conservative side, with Butenschøn supporting his position as a prominent female ally.

It is not surprising, then, to find Butenschøn a strong advocate of the ideals of home in her extended reading of *The Master Builder* a decade later. What is surprising, though, is the utter willfulness of her reading, which insists on seeing Ibsen as a *defender* of domestic ideals. She writes,

> In none of Ibsen's previous works does the thought strike one so clearly that perhaps the most central productive little seed in his entire production – as impressive, all-encompassing, and all-commanding as it is – might not still best find its expression in the one little, simple, bourgeois word: a home.[110]

This claim in itself is not difficult to accept, since as we have seen, many of Ibsen's cultural interlocutors focused in on the same theme. As she elaborates on this claim, however, an unfamiliar Ibsen comes into view:

> Throughout all of Ibsen's writing, ever since *Love's Comedy*, where in the midst of the bloodiest satire he nevertheless finds heartwarming and harmonious strings in order to sing the praise of "the home," and even more positively from *A Doll House* forward, it is as if he, as a wise, conscientious master builder, repeatedly and ruthlessly unveils and investigates the composition of

the *foundation*, which up to now has been laid under these homes that we call our own.¹¹¹

The image of Ibsen as a meticulous, protective master builder rather than a "dynamite specialist" is one striking aspect of this passage; another is the claim that a positive notion of home increasingly marks the plays from *A Doll House* forward. As should be quite clear, the opposite case has been presented throughout this chapter.

The more one examines Butenschøn's argument, the more one realizes how interpolative her reading actually is; her scene-by-scene account of *The Master Builder* consistently elaborates on the text by filling its gaps with the ready-made discourses of home that lie closest at hand. For Butenschøn, these are notions of the ideal, emotionally grounded and supported home, precisely the sort of true home discussed earlier. She does not see Aline and Halvard Solness as poking around in the rubble of that ideal; instead, she sees all their talk of lost homes as evidence of that ideal's continued importance. Butenschøn relentlessly recuperates the negativity of Ibsen's vision in the play as if it were solely restricted to a critique of society's failings:

> Shouldn't one actually be grateful to him because in his art he also takes up the fight against the *false* values, the *dead* things – the dolls, the old moth-eaten clothing, the empty, hollow shells, the melancholy, the irritability – which bit by bit have crept into the great truths! Which have confused and counterfeited words and concepts and require that we shall also pay to *them* our life-blood, and our happiness in life and our peace of mind?¹¹²

Butenschøn's frequent italicization of the word *hjem* throughout her fifty-one pages of commentary on the play makes clear that the concept she fears has been corrupted and misunderstood most is precisely a "true" notion of home. Ibsen's intent, according to her reading of the plays, is only to clean up misunderstandings about the term and re-establish the ideal by showing society's failings. In other words, she reads *The Master Builder* as if it were simply *The Pillars of Society*, Part Two.

Butenschøn's insistence on this interpretation, most would agree, distorts the structure and characterization in the play. In her version of things, Halvard Solness becomes a disappointed crusader for the ideal:

> But gently and firmly as never before resonates the *one* deep string that vibrates through his entire being: his unquenchable, glowing need and love for *the home*.
>
> The *ideal* home. The way it has built itself up in his imagination, richer, more beautiful, more attractive, in exactly the spot where every day's suffering and disappointment relentlessly broke down every stone he managed to lay for

the foundation! It has become a hallowed spot for him. Where *everything is shared*, and where everyone comes *who is not sufficient unto himself* [*som ikke er sig selv nok*]!"[113]

Butenschøn's Solness harbors the ideal of *hygge* deep in his heart. He is simply so uncompromising that he will only accept the authentic utopian version of home (the citation embedded in the last phrase makes clear that no Peer Gynts would be allowed there). This is not Hilde's (or Ibsen's) master builder; here Solness (*my* master builder, one can almost hear Butenschøn saying) dies a tragic death in defense of those core domestic ideals. Gone is the mix of the constructive king and the destructive troll in Ibsen's architectural imagination; with her Solness, there is only the king, trying in vain to lay the foundation stones for the ideal home, all the while they are being constantly broken down and carried away by everyday concerns.

Another obstinately idealist reading of Ibsen comes in a piece by a high school teacher in Christiania named Jon Sørensen, who published an appraisal of *When We Dead Awaken* in a Norwegian educational periodical in 1900. Given the pedagogical context of his writing, it is not surprising to find him working from within a persistently idealistic framework. This entails a rousing defense of Irene's virtue ("Irene is more pure than the dirt that some peculiar critics hurl at her in the name of morality") as well as a particularly disparaging account of Maja ("An inorganic being; she is what she is, can never become anything else. Good enough for a bear hunter, but when a sculptor chooses her, he deserves the punishment of having her").[114] Sørensen essentially takes all of the symbolic activity of this play to be a positive assertion of ideals of art, womanhood, and life.

He also calls the play an "architectonic masterpiece [*arkitektonisk mesterverk*]."[115] Like other commentators, he pursues a reading of the play that makes use of the building metaphors that Ibsen has put into play, but in his marked preference for Irene and the aesthetic idealism he thinks she represents, he constructs his own extended metaphor of two types of building:

> *Irene* is envisioned as the dream that rises from youth's distant lands and overtakes a man and hovers over his life as the dream of life. At times it sinks like a winged bird down on his breast, weighs down this breast like a nightmare; at times it rises like a castle in the air, a dream castle, a castle that glows. She lives in that castle, with the key to his burglar-proof picture chest. Down on earth he builds a house – that shines – and moves in with a woman he likes. She has the keys to the bedroom closet and the kitchen cupboard, but no key for a picture chest, – which has been jammed in any case. And then the dream castle begins to haunt his house, in the hallways

and rooms. And his house does not shine. All at once it has become so oppressively low, pinchingly narrow, and first one, then two go walking around in there freezing.[116]

In this recap of Ibsenian motifs from both *The Wild Duck* and *The Master Builder*, Sørensen reverts easily to the rhetoric of disappointed ideals, re-establishing the hierarchy of castles over houses. Interestingly, he too casts this highly sculptural play as an architectural tragedy. There is no hint in his reading of the strategic use of the house as a "place to stay" that I argue can be seen through several of the later, more itinerant characters. Instead, for Sørensen, a house is only a claustrophobic, disappointing reality, a terrible miscalculation on Rubek's part; only the ideal of true homes – castles – can shine.

Each of these idealist readings of Ibsen suggests a persistence of the home as a mental construct. However relentless and devastating Ibsen's critique of the home, these and other commentators seemed able to recast all of his deconstructive energy as a continuation of the simple reformer's zeal for the unrealized ideal, as if nothing had changed since *Pillars of Society*. The resulting readings seem overly cheerful, however, only if one imagines each play to have accomplished something, to have settled an issue once and for all – in other words, if one assumes Ibsen's gradual dismantling of home to have been immediately effective in changing social attitudes. Stubbornly idealistic responses like these, however, demonstrate the resilience and adaptability of the home ideal, which can seemingly absorb and recuperate even the most powerful unveilings and critiques and write admiringly of Ibsen's uncompromising commitment to domestic life.

The arbitrariness of this kind of response can be demonstrated by a contrastive example, a review of *The Master Builder* by Theodor Caspari in 1893. Caspari was a headmaster at the Cathedral School in Christiania at the time and was also a Norwegian poet and friend of Ibsen. Although his review appears in essentially the same cultural context as Butenschøn's, he comes to diametrically opposite conclusions about the issue of true homes: in his reading, the play is indeed another "marriage drama [*Ægteskabsdrama*]," but one that goes much further than the previous plays in its open criticism of the institution itself.[117] Caspari would agree with Butenschøn only on the most general of points, namely that Ibsen's *oeuvre* centers on the idea of home:

> From *The Doll House* [sic] forward, in play after play, Ibsen has worked "to build homes," "homes for people," tried to get "life together to become a marriage," by raising "towers" on the building of the home. *The Doll*

House – *Ghosts* – *The Wild Duck* – *The Lady from the Sea* – *Rosmersholm* – *Hedda Gabler* – all show how persistently but also how completely futilely he has worked for that cause.[118]

Caspari argues that the reason Ibsen's lifelong search for the true home and marriage (he conflates the two) has failed is that society's "marriage building [*Ægteskabsbygning*]" itself is flawed:

> Never before has Ibsen – and here I am providing his own view of the issue – managed to build a real home for people [*et virkeligt Hjem for Mennesker*], because the people, tied as they are to outdated views, by the "Rosmersholm view of life," "don't want any home," at least not a home after Ibsen's heart, no. In other words, marriage is so far from freeing itself from the old sour-faced religious view of life that it is actually a nursery, a hotbed [*Arnested*] for that view, the favorable soil for the old system's bacteria. Out from the homes – such as they presently are – these bacteria ooze out into all social relationships.[119]

The "home after Ibsen's heart" would presumably have to loosen its conflation with marriage, since that social institution is in Caspari's view the very source of the most crippling and narrow-minded attitudes. He locates marriage at the very center of the home metaphor when he identifies the *Arnested* as the source of contamination, mixing both architectural and negatively organic imagery. In Caspari, in other words, one finds an Ibsen commentator who is himself speaking from a position of inversion similar to Ibsen's on the question of home: Caspari shares Ibsen's disparaging view of home as the site of wounded ducks, carp ponds, and lavender-scented aunts and their old-fashioned hats; rather than imagining a "truer" architecture, he sees that form and what it represents as competely infected.

No matter how hard Ibsen might try to build a "home after his heart," Caspari argues, as long as that effort is built on marriage, it will be doomed to fail. Those who do not give up on the idea of the "marriage home [*Ægteskabshjemmet*]" are condemned to build and build and build in vain. He describes the futility of Ibsen's attempts in terms familiar to the present discussion:

> But what more could Ibsen possibly do to free marriage from the "dark demons"? Hasn't he already these many years exerted himself sufficiently? Hasn't he single-handedly set fire to the entire old system? Hasn't he in drama after drama opened all the windows for ventilation in order to once and for all get rid of that vile musk and lavender smell? What else should he do, the old master builder, for this recalcitrant "home" that absolutely refuses to rise at his hand?[120]

It is not difficult to see where this argument is leading: if the marriage-based home is so difficult to redirect toward more positive ends for the benefit of individuals, perhaps something is wrong with the basic architectural plan. Both the fires and housecleanings of Ibsen's previous domestic dramas were dogged attempts that proceeded from the wrong premise, Caspari claims, namely that homes should be built exclusively on the idea of marriage.

In *The Master Builder*, however, Caspari counters that Ibsen has finally "delivered the sketch of the social building of the future [*Fremtidens sociale Bygning*], which one day will be the sanctioned one."[121] In Hilde Wangel, Caspari sees the positive image of an unencumbered individual of the future who will be able to enter into open and free personal relationships outside the entire complex of home building. She is Rebekka West's "avenger," he says, a figure who would never be crushed by the Rosmersholm view of life:

> Because she strides in through the door, happily and confidently, openly and honestly, and demands: Away with marriage! This hotbed of old-fashioned views, this storeroom with its dolls and portraits, lacework and silk clothing, this nest for monomania and sickly consciences, this home that can never be a home, because inside us in our own sensual nature live "powers," "trolls," "devils" that require richer and more varied joy than that housed within the marriage-home. Away with marriage! This antiquated form, which modern life with its richer content must shatter.[122]

What does Hilde propose in its place? For Caspari, the answer is unequivocal: "*Free love*, 'the most delightful thing in the world,' 'the castle in the air with a foundation underneath,'" and he adds, "She is the *enfant terrible* of the coming modern society."[123] And although the old master builder falls in the attempt to climb the tower, Caspari nevertheless sees him as having shown youth the way into a future without marriage.

Caspari's vision of the future culminates by the end of his article, where he envisions his progressive view from the highest possible architectural vantage point:

> What will Henrik Ibsen – if I am right in my understanding – come out with next? With the most delightful thing in the world: An open relationship – two young people, who from the balcony up there in "the terribly tall tower" look down "on all those who build churches and homes for father and mother and for the flock of children." Two liberated young people, who sing along with Ibsen himself in "On the Heights," "the old house is merely burning, with the Christmas beer and the cat!" and who exult at the end: "now I exchange my last verse for a higher view of things."[124]

Since Caspari mentions "On the Heights," it is worth asking whether his views constitute a return to the callous position of the hunter-mentor and his hardened rejection of home. The modern position at the very top of a high tower – again, almost beyond the architectural principle altogether – looking down on all the futile home-building activity being carried out with mistaken blueprints, is reminiscent of the view from the plateau in that early poem. Despite Caspari's enthusiastic reference to the poem, however, the young couple he imagines at the top of the tower has nothing of the hunter's anaesthetic view, nothing of his grim willingness to aestheticize the death of a family member; instead, there is almost an equal idealization in the direction of liberalization.

While Caspari's reading of the play is a remarkable articulation that gets straight to the core of Ibsen's architectural imagination, his notion of the play as a polemic for free love ignores the complexity of the Hilde/Solness relationship. His article provoked a pointed response by one of those "resilient" commentators, Professor E. F. B. Horn, who calms his readers with reassurances that fictional dramatic characters like Hilde, no matter what they seem to be demanding, in practice stay confined to the stage. They are products of an artist's fantasy, intended only to provide a temporary imagination of a position of thought but are ultimately of no lasting consequence.[125] By setting up a firewall between art and reality, Horn ensures the deflection of Ibsen's architectural metaphorics into the realm of the imagination only.

Perhaps Caspari's insistence on a polemic social reading of the play made Horn's response inevitable, but his observation that Ibsen keeps pushing against the limitations of an architectural metaphoric system, even as he repeats the building and rebuilding of home after home on stage, is a useful one. Caspari seizes on the potential of that idea and tries to extend it into implications for the "social building of the future." His impatient, strong-arm reading nevertheless reveals the hidden direction of Ibsen's thinking. Caspari's elaboration allows us to see that a more radically open architectural vision would require of Ibsen a rejection of all notions of original and authentic homes, a more cheerful parting with the past.

CHAPTER 4

The tenacity of architecture

Judging from the material examined to this point, dissatisfaction with the architectural status quo for Ibsen's characters leads to two main alternatives. The first might be characterized as "cleaning house." This is the impulse to unmask, to open windows, to air out, and perhaps even to mop up (as much as Dr. Stockmann might debate its value). This is the position of the reformer, and the basic architectural expression of this position is in the idea of *renovation*. Existing social structures are understood to be fundamentally sound; in fact, a firm attachment to the enduring value of foundations despite the contingency of buildings themselves is a key characteristic of this position. It is the structures built on top of those foundations that are sometimes in question. If they are poorly designed, misused, or corrupted in any way, the reformer nevertheless sees no real threat to the idea of the social building itself, whose essence is understood to be in the foundation. Matters can be put right by adjusting what is above ground to bring it back in line with the more constant principles below. This position can work itself out entirely within a metaphorics of architecture.

Another possibility is to imagine demolishing the existing structure completely to build anew. The reigning metaphor here is *razing*. This stance takes renovation to be an unacceptable compromise with the past. It views all architectural structure – foundations included – as equally contingent. Since ruins can get in the way of the new, the argument goes, it is sometimes necessary to start completely from scratch. The assumption here is that the present and the past cannot easily coexist; there is something antagonistic and limiting about the past, so that even foundations must be cleared to make way for something entirely new.

Each of these positions implies a philosophy of time and history; each typifies a mode of modernity and a stance toward traditional social structures. Renovation allows for a coexistence with the past, a hybrid of past and present that posits temporal continuity and an overlapping model of change. It assumes that there is place for the old within new frameworks. In contrast, razing embraces the clean-break mentality of much modern thought and assumes that change happens in temporal ruptures that destroy the hold of the past on the present. This was the attitude expressed by the modernization (Haussmannization) of Paris in the 1860s, in which entire neighborhoods were demolished to make space for the modern boulevards.[1] Perhaps even more relevant here, it also happened in the modernization of Rome in the early 1870s, which took place between the times of Ibsen's two extended stays there.[2] If there is a utopian modern element to this kind of creative destruction, it is to be found in the assumption of an easily subdued past that cooperatively yields to the demands of the present and future.

On the more traditional side of the nineteenth-century modernity divide, one can find competing patterns of architectural thought that proceeded from entirely different assumptions about the past. In his book *Change Mummified*, Philip Rosen identifies these mainstream traditional positions as the alternatives of "restoration" and "preservation."[3] The former describes the activity of returning to a putative original unity of form at a previous point in time. Architectural restoration thus attempts to recreate an imagined pristine condition, even if the building never actually existed in reality as a completed, unified whole. The more general historical attitude that proceeds from this practice is a denial of the intervening difference between present and past. "Preservation" in Rosen's schema is by contrast an embrace of the "corrosiveness of the ever-continuing work of temporality,"[4] in that it allows for the rescue of a more hybrid architectural object that has developed over time in different styles and in different ways. It entails a respect for an unfolding historicity and for existing evidence of wear and decay – at least until the moment of preservation, at which point the object is again frozen in time.

Having now introduced no fewer than four competing architectural concepts – renovation, razing, restoration, and preservation – this discussion owes the reader some sorting and analytical distinctions when applying the terminology to Ibsen's plays. The main division seems to be this: though "renovation" and "razing" differ in intent (and Ibsen makes several important distinctions between them), they do at the very least share a forward-looking aspect. These activities are not in any way crippled by the *loss* of the past; that is not the central philosophical problem with which they engage. A shared orientation toward future building makes these terms quintessentially modern, a stance of basic appeal for Ibsen. The challenge for him was to reckon with the ways that the past can never quite be shaken off as much as one would like.

What both "restoration" and "preservation" share, on the other hand, is "a founding assertion or obsession with overcoming the breaks between the present and the past," as Rosen claims.[5] He continues, "Preserving remains, reviving vanished lifeways, replicating old artifacts – these share the ambition to have something of the past available to perception in the present and thereby to freeze time at the service of a beholder or spectator." There was a time when Ibsen participated in this other relationship to the past – namely, when he himself was writing historical plays earlier in his career. Many of these plays would fit Rosen's idea of "restoration" quite nicely, which is distinguished by a return to an origin that never actually existed as a unified whole. That is certainly a characteristic stance of these and other saga-historical plays in mid nineteenth-century Norway. When the more general national romanticism of the 1840s and 50s in Norway imagined the recovery of a medieval age of greatness, it attempted to ignore the "corrosive" intervening passage of time throughout the centuries of Danish rule.

Preservationism flourished in nineteenth-century Norway as well, although it did not achieve its fullest expression until later in the century, around the time Ibsen had moved on to his prose plays in the 1880s and 90s. These energies concentrated around material-culture collections that laid the groundwork for the invention of the living history museums. Rosen discusses this preservationist practice at length in its U.S. context,[6] and, in previously published work, I have examined the Norwegian (and broader Scandinavian) folk-museum movement as a contrastive context for Ibsen's prose.[7] What is worth reminding of here is that the moment of collection and preservation for these samples of rural architecture in Scandinavia in the 1880s and 90s was contemporaneous with Ibsen's own investigations of modern temporalities, and that the preservation practices became so culturally consequential that they formed the influential prototype for living history museums internationally. The Scandinavian museum founders were keenly interested in providing spectators with access to the past in the form of authentic buildings that showed all the signs of multi-generational inhabitation and the passage of time. The genuine (and positive) encounter with the past that these museums offered spectators respected the otherness of the past (distinguishing their main mode from that of restoration) and at the same time made it accessible to modern spectators who were invited to imagine themselves at home in the old environments. This was Scandinavian preservationism in its most potent expression.

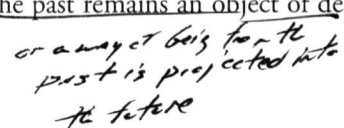

The most important commonality between restoration and preservation is that the past remains an object of desire. In the folk museums, visitors were provided with a preserved environment in which they could seemingly encounter a physical remnant of an edifying national past in a direct and material fashion. Similarly, in Ibsen's national-historical plays such as *The Vikings at Helgeland* (1857) and *The Pretenders* (1863), viewers were restored to an age of imagined national unity. In Ibsen's later plays, by contrast, the assumptions about the past could not have been more different. For him, the idea of the past had gradually become a disruptively uncanny force that prevented people from moving forward to embrace the new. A past that "ought to have remained secret and hidden but has come to light" (to return to Schelling's formulation, as cited by Freud)[8] was obviously no longer an object of desire for Ibsen in the latter part of his career; quite the opposite was the case. The theoretical point, however, is that the past can only be *unheimlich* once one intends to bury it, not resuscitate it.

One of Ibsen's poems captures his pivot between these two fundamental attitudes toward the past. Entitled "To the Accomplices" (*Til de Medskyldige*), it was included in the uncompleted preliminary version of *Brand* that Ibsen began writing in 1864, the version known as the "Epic Brand." The poem develops at length the striking image of Norway's heroic past as a corpse that has been artificially embalmed and made up to look alive by Ibsen and his "accomplices," namely the other Norwegian writers who like him have devoted national-romantic writings to "a burned-out lineage [*en udbrændt Slægt*]."[9] Here, the idea of restoration is cast in a macabre light; the joint nationalist search for a useable, living past is equated with the propping up of a corpse beyond its proper life-span. Instead, the poem's narrator states,

> That which is dead, can't be lied back to life.
> That which is dead, must go down into darkness.
> A dead thing has only one task: namely, to give
> itself over as nourishment for a newly planted seed.[10]

With this striking imagery, Ibsen urges his fellow poets to give the corpse of the national past a proper burial instead of artificially and grotesquely preserving it with the cosmetics and playacting of national-romantic writing. As the Norwegian literary historian Francis Bull put it, "He himself was an 'accomplice' in the worship of the dead; he had for many years established a personal and national memory cult, not only through his historical dramas, but even more so through his poetry."[11]

It is likely that Ibsen's fury at Norway's refusal to go to the aid of Denmark when it was invaded and defeated by Prussia in the spring of 1864 was the catalyst for his abandonment of the pursuit of the past. All the talk of Scandinavian greatness in former times rang hollow for him in the face of the cowardice he perceived in his countrymen. For Ibsen, the heroic past had not only proved to be unusable but distracting and directly deceptive as well. The narrator of "To the Accomplices" continues:

> Thus have I turned my view and my mind
> away from the soul-deadened saga of our past,
> away from our lying dream about a future dawning,
> and enter into the hazy world of the present.[12]

The turn to these indistinct perspectives of the present manifests itself in the writing activity immediately following 1864, with *Brand*'s fierce condemnation of cowardice and compromise, and *Peer Gynt*'s merciless attack on Norwegian nationalism. Although Ibsen would return to the topic of history in his mammoth world-historical play *Emperor and Galilean* (1873), which would occupy him for almost another decade, when he did finally settle on the contemporary prose play as a dramatic form in 1877, he did not turn back. In doing so, one might well say that he had not only engaged profoundly with the present moment, but that he had fundamentally shifted his valuation of the past. By arguing for its necessary burial, he had created the necessary preconditions for the past to return as an uncanny force, thereby adopting the more modern temporal model that would persist to the end of his career.

Ownership disputes

The notion expressed in "To the Accomplices" is that the duty of the dead is to give way to the living. Ibsen's appeal to this "natural" order and "proper" temporal sequence has such a commonsense aspect to it that one might not immediately notice the quintessential modernity of the logic, namely that it is the *right* of those in the present to assert their priority. The past is simply not justified in persisting, so when it does, it is understood as a grotesquely antagonistic force impeding progress. Modern ways of framing the past include these progressive biases almost invisibly in their rhetoric, but certain terms such as "leftovers," "vestiges," and "remnants" build them almost imperceptibly into the discourse. Only when that progressive world view grew in influence in the modernity of the late nineteenth century did it become possible to think of the past as unruly and uncooperative whenever it made claims on the present, and without the availability of that assumption, there could be no Freudian model of the uncanny.

Thus, in the first part of his career, Ibsen considered the past to be an object of desire; in the latter, it was an adversary. This shift goes far in explaining Ibsen's markedly increased interest in architectural metaphor in the latter half of his career because buildings provide a concentrated way of thinking through problems of an improperly persistent past. This derives from the simple fact that the life-span of a building generally exceeds that of its occupants. A building typically has both preceding and subsequent inhabitants, no matter how completely its current occupants might imagine their ownership of the space. One's feeling of being at home is thus always potentially threatened by the realization that the spaces one inhabits and makes one's own can never be completely and totally possessed. No matter how tightly one imagines an equation between inhabitation and ownership, in some basic sense every occupant is a squatter. This view of inhabitation would not always have counted as the baseline position or essential truth of inhabitation, but it increasingly did so in the strand of modern thought in which notions of belonging came to be seen as mere illusory effects distracting from a given existential homelessness.

The claims of prior occupants do not have to be threatening; as suggested earlier, a consciousness of the inhabited past, if one can call it that, inspires in antiquarians and preservationists a positive sense of historical awe and connection, and in cultures with strong traditions of ancestral worship, the past is moreover frequently considered a friendly force. For others, however, that same awareness can give rise to more unsettling anxieties. An acute consciousness of prior occupants can just as easily lead to imagining the traces of their continued presence as an alien and stubborn force, as leftover forms of inhabitation persisting beyond their proper time in uncanny ways. This threatens the idea that one can assume rightful control and full ownership of an architectural space, precisely because the prior inhabitants do not stay properly buried and out of one's way. By the same token, the projection of inhabitation into the future – imagining subsequent occupants of what is now one's own – might make one feel just as "possessive" in turn. One might dread giving way to those who are to come.

Even a superficial experience with Ibsen could produce ready examples of both of these attitudes – of the ghosts and white-horse ancestors who do not vacate the house when they properly should, or of youth knocking at the door, demanding too soon that the old make room for the young. Both are essentially different versions of the same ownership question, however: a competition for "place." Insecurity about one's place in the home leaves one open to attack on both temporal fronts, by the past that persists too long or the future that encroaches too soon. It is easy to see how a time of rapid social change (especially but not only in late nineteenth-century European modernity) could make the hold on one's present architectural niche suddenly seem quite precarious, as Helge Rønning has suggested in his discussion of *The Master Builder*.[13] If the untroubled perception "I am fully here now" is what makes a space *heimlich*, the sense that "someone was here before" or that "someone will follow," if allowed full rein, can easily make it *unheimlich*. This was precisely what Ibsen was interested in doing.

As hinted, anxieties of ownership have likely waxed and waned throughout history, motivated by particular social circumstances at any one point, but it is worth pointing out that they have deep roots in the Scandinavian cultural tradition, something alluded to quite directly by the title of Ibsen's 1881 play *Ghosts*. The title in Norwegian is *Gengangere*, a word that points to a notion of the living dead more than it does to spooky apparitions (that kind of ghost would be a *spøkelse* in modern Norwegian). Although no English translator to my knowledge has ever attempted to translate Ibsen's title as *Zombies*, that choice would capture an aspect of *gengangere* that gets blocked by other cultural associations with "ghosts." In Scandinavian tradition, a *genganger* is a dead person who "walks again," or perhaps more to the heart of the idea, "persists in walking." William Ian Miller explains the tradition this way:

> Given the very proprietary interests of Norse ghosts it should not be surprising to learn that Norse ghosts were not really ghosts at all. They were the living dead, characterized not by airy spirit but by the grossest matter and tons of it. Icelandic ghosts get heavy in death; they gain weight. Oxen flounder trying to drag them away. They seem to become the very earth itself merging with their sod home – their heaviness becoming paradoxically the way they make their spiritual claim to domicile – and claim a powerful deadhand control over the property they enjoyed in life.[14]

This is the tradition that Ibsen activates with his title. In that tradition, as Miller explains, there are many folkloric variants of ways to confuse a corpse so that it cannot find its way back home, implying that, at least in the deeper folk traditions, the underlying assumption is that conscious measures must be taken to ensure the rights of present inhabitants to their buildings. Only when protected from the claims of previous occupants can a proper ownership be asserted in the present.

When Ibsen uses the word *gengangere* for the title of his play, he draws on and transforms that tradition. What he borrows most directly is the idea of a contest between the living and the dead for possession of an architectural space, as a matter of intergenerational property rights: the dead assert their rights of prior occupancy, and the living insist in turn that the dead yield their claim on the space. He extends the folk tradition, however, by amplifying the problems inherent in the temporal continuity of the building itself. That is what makes this an intractable problem for modern thinking. Modernist thought might prefer each generation to build from scratch; buildings would then not work so potently as symbols of "overlap" and "leftover" ideas and attitudes. The multi-generational durability of architectural form presented a new kind of problem for modern thinking: buildings appeared "stubborn" in a new way. Houses and homes were useful for Ibsen and other nineteenth-century authors in thinking through the temporality of modernity precisely because they *last*, and by doing so they impose all the entanglements of familiarity – values, attitudes, beliefs – on those subsequent inhabitants who had no role in building the structure.

By calling this a modern problem, I mean to underscore once again that there is nothing inherently necessary about the way Ibsen uses architectural metaphor. Instead of fixating on the unreasonable duration and persistence of buildings, one might just as easily notice the potential for decay and ruin inherent in architecture, as the Romantic poets were inclined to do. Competing with the expectation that buildings will last is the possible recognition that many of them will tumble down instead. When seeing through that framework, that is, one might be inclined to emphasize the ways that an apparently solid structure does *not* persist, as much as one might want it to do. One could see in buildings a relentless and tragic struggle with weather, decay, and dilapidation, a view that would instead make them seem highly *vulnerable*, not persistent. Metaphors are always partial and strategic in their comparisons, and recognizing the full range of possibilities for architectural metaphor makes even clearer the particularity of Ibsen's choices. For him, the quality of architectural structure that was most useful for his writing was the imposition of past structure on present occupants, the stubbornly durative aspects of buildings.

A look at the reception material reveals that it was quite possible for Ibsen's contemporaries not to see the modern logic of the *genganger* motif: namely, the way the new application of an old folkloric figure addressed the problems of temporal overlap created by modernity's sudden transitions and rejection of cultural continuity. This early Norwegian review of the published version of *Ghosts*, for example, blends a (foreign) Gothic-Romantic view of ghosts with that of the *gengangere*:

> The Englishmen say that every home has its ghost [*Spøgelse*] hidden away some place or another that constantly threatens to burst forth and show itself. In Mrs. Alving's house there is a haunting in every corner and at all hours of the day, even in broad daylight at the dinner table and in midst of the clink of glasses and plates. Everyone who exits and enters the house has their own ghosts [*Gengangere*] at their heels, but the worst ones are those who are born and raised in the house itself, if one can use such an expression about ghosts [*Spøgelser*]. These are straight-out loathsome and there is no remedy to drive them out; on the contrary, they grow as the plot moves forward, with terrifying fertility until they storm forth, exercise their power, and lay everything waste.[15]

As is clear from the original Norwegian terms in this passage, this reviewer shows some indecision about whether the play primarily deals with phantoms (*Spøgelser*) or the living dead (*Gengangere*). The tug of the Gothic spectacular is clear in the rhetoric of the passage, betraying a preference for *spøgelser* over *gengangere*. If there is any further doubt on this point, one might also note the review's closing complaint that the play lacked "some kind of supernatural scene" showing the dead Captain Alving's torments in the other world, "in the manner of Dante's *Inferno*."[16] There is probably general agreement that such a scene would not have improved the play; more importantly, that kind of Gothic revenge scene would have made the play less modern in its logic.

The term *spøgelser* also does not provoke the same level of revulsion as the image of dead flesh walking. In this sense, the word *gengangere* gets much closer to the notion of the artificially preserved "cosmetic corpse" we have already identified as Ibsen's newly emerging modern view in the poem from "Epic Brand." This concept of an unnaturally revivified past is a much more appropriate expression than *spøgelser* for Ibsen's eventual intellectual stance toward the past, namely that these old things really ought to get buried away once and for all. One senses as well Ibsen saying that if it were not for all the continuing architectural support these *gengangere* receive (buildings are collaborators with the past), that might just be possible. Ibsen takes the instinctive sense of scandal one feels about the *gengangere*'s doggedly animated flesh and links it to the persistent materiality of an architectural structure living past its proper time.

The equation between flesh and bricks becomes especially potent in modern times when more substantial structures might carry the weight of several generations. As Miller points out, the Icelanders and their dead were basically fighting to possess nothing more than modest sod structures. In Ibsen's plays, the present occupants fight with entire picture galleries of ancestors to wrest away the possession of large manors and estates for the new purposes of the present. *Rosmersholm* is only the most obvious example, for the dead do not only cling to the Rosmersholm parsonage. They also refuse to give way at the Rosenvold estate in *Ghosts*, and in the Wangel home in *The Lady from the Sea*, and in the widow Falk's villa in *Hedda Gabler*. All of those structures retain the influence of the dead, not necessarily as a personified force, but instead almost as a vague, seemingly unbeatable material inertia. When one contrasts these dead zones with the home in *Pillars of Society*, the most striking difference is that there is no generational layer evident at all in that earlier fictional home – as far as the play is concerned, it is as if Karsten Bernick is the house's original occupant. It is tempting to conclude that it is the irrelevance of the dead for the Bernick household that makes their *glasskab* house a reformable structure in the first place – when the only tensions in the plot are those that play out among the living, there is much less to overcome. Once the rival owners include the dead, however, the architecture becomes much less malleable and more intellectually problematic.

The Rentheim property in *John Gabriel Borkman* poses special problems of ownership, given its configuration within the plot: Borkman, Gunhild, and Ella are all implied to be living-dead people competing for possession of the same house. The dramatic situation describes a house that belonged first to Borkman, but who can in the play's present no longer own anything legally because of the collapse of his finances. At the time of the scandal, his home was protected from bankruptcy when Ella Rentheim purchased it at auction; when the play begins, however, it is clear that she herself has not been living there. Instead, having returned it to her sister Gunhild and Borkman to rent, she lives elsewhere as a long-absentee owner. John Gabriel and Gunhild in turn have lived apart within the house, with she staking claim to the first-floor territory and he the upstairs. They have reportedly held to this impossibly hyperbolic, stalemated contest of possession for eight full years. So even though the stage directions call this "the Rentheim house [*det Rentheimske hus*],"[17] the proper inhabitation and ownership of the space are not at all clear. This exchange between Ella and Gunhild in Act One shows the complicated ambiguity the reported arrangement has produced:

ELLA RENTHEIM: I will be staying here for the rest of my days, if needs be.
MRS. BORKMAN: (composing herself) Well, of course, Ella – the estate is yours.
ELLA RENTHEIM: Oh, please –!
MRS. BORKMAN: After all, everything is yours. The chair I am sitting on is yours. The bed I lie awake tossing in belongs to you. The food we eat, we get through you.

ELLA RENTHEIM: Can't be arranged any other way. Borkman can't have his own property. For then someone would promptly come and take it away from him.
MRS. BORKMAN: I know that well enough. We just have to come to terms with living off your charity and mercy.
ELLA RENTHEIM: (coldly) I can't prevent you from seeing it from that point of view, Gunhild.
MRS. BORKMAN: No, you can't. – When do you want us to move out?
ELLA RENTHEIM: (looking at her) Move out?
MRS. BORKMAN: (with agitation) Well, you don't imagine that I would stay on living under the same roof as you! – No, I'd rather end up in the poor house or out wandering the roads.[18]

This is essentially a typical *genganger* property dispute in that it is a battle between predecessors and current occupants, but here played out between several of the living-but-dead characters in a kind of no man's land of ambiguity: the space is contested, and the competing claims on the property seem impossible to resolve given the financial situation as it is depicted in the play. The only truly "living" characters in the play (Erhart, Frida, Mrs. Wilton) all flee as far as possible from the property and the entire question of ownership.

Occupancy of a house is made even more precarious by the imagination of an animating presence in the structure itself that makes full inhabitation and possession impossible: that is the classic formula for a Gothic haunted house. From a more modern perspective, it is easy to see this flight of the imagination as a common response to anxieties about the basic fact that most houses outlive their occupants. In response, one imagines a kind of living agency in the building itself. Gothic-Romantic forms of haunting spring immediately to mind: the house façade that functions as a goulish face, interior doors that open of their own accord, noises with no apparent source, the active malevolence in the walls that seeks to crush interlopers and makes the space uninhabitable. The domestic structure in Edgar Allan Poe's "The Fall of the House of Usher" is a paradigmatic example, with its organic and animating decay. There, the façade is characterized by "vacant and eye-like windows," and even the bricks of that home are said to be alive with fungi.[19] The collapse of the house at the end of the tale seems to be as much an act of some super-architectural will as it does the consequence of natural processes of decay.

Although this form of active malevolence was more typical of Gothic Romanticism, remnants of it appear in Ibsen's "modern unhomely" as well. The 1888 play *Rosmersholm* provides the best example of a house positioned between traditional forms of haunting and more modern forms of unhomeliness. In the only Ibsen play to be named after its architectural setting, the agency of the house is a matter of overt but permanently suspended discussion. In the opening conversation between Rebekka West and Mrs. Helseth, the housekeeper, one finds two opposing views of inhabitation represented. Watching from a distance as John Rosmer takes his habitual daily walk, they note that as always he avoids crossing the footbridge from which his wife Beate committed suicide in the mill race:

REBEKKA: (gathering her crocheting) They hang onto the dead for a long time here at Rosmersholm.
MADAM HELSETH: I think that instead, Miss, it is the dead who hang so long onto Rosmersholm.
REBEKKA: (looks at her) The dead?
MADAM HELSETH: Well, that is to say, it is as if they can't quite manage to get away from the ones who are left behind [*dem, som sidder igen*].[20]

Upon further questioning, Mrs. Helseth links the return of the dead to the coming of the "white horses," thus introducing the main symbol (and working draft title) of the play. This deceptively simple opening exchange is apparently intended to stage a clash between a folk-superstitious and an enlightened attitude toward the dead and their power over the living (Rebekka does not appear to believe in the white horses, just as she does not initially imagine any significant impediments to her own entry into the house). The initial conversation also contrasts several views of ownership: is the best explanation for Rosmer's traumatized behavior that Rosmersholm's emotionally crippled inhabitants simply have problems shaking off the memory of the dead (Rebekka's modern view), or is it that the dead themselves cling to the place and the occupants whom they left behind (Helseth's folk-traditional view)? Or does the house itself, by outliving the entire family line, exist as an architectural idea above the level of human fate and agency? The dramatic action of the play gets its power as much from the stand-off these explanations represent as it does from the personal conflicts depicted there.

This ambiguity about where the power resides – with the current occupants, with the living dead, or with the house itself and its white horses – is left unresolved for much of the play, which remains poised between traditional and modern models of haunting and inhabitation. The fact that the traditional viewpoint seems to get the last word after the final suicide scene (since we depend on Mrs. Helseth to report the conclusion: "The dead wife took them [*Salig fruen tog dem*]"[21]) led some commentators to frame the entire drama in more Gothic terms, and more than one of them referred to Rosmersholm as "the ghost manor [*spøgelsesgaarden*]."²² Especially when confronted with the materiality of the house on stage, it was tempting for some early spectators to see in Rosmersholm's architecture the vestiges of a Gothic malevolence. Take this response to the stage production at Kristiania Theater in April 1887, for instance. After criticizing a perceived weakness in the fourth act, the reviewer writes,

> The ending has the opposite effect, with wild, genuine Ibsenian eeriness [*Uhygge*]. The other doors, which stand there grimacing at the ones who have been dragged away, and then Mrs. Helseth's final lines about what is happening on the footbridge over the millrace, make the spectator feel chills down the spine. It is an ending that in its unsettling [*uhyggelig*] effect does not lag at all behind *Ghosts* and *The Wild Duck*.²³

The image conveyed here – of the house witnessing the suicides as if gloating in triumph, of "wild, genuine Ibsenian *Uhygge*," and of chills running up and down the spectator's back – all combine to make Ibsen into a would-be Edgar Allan Poe. This viewer clearly read Ibsen through an older, available Gothic framework – as if Mrs. Helseth herself had not only had the last word but had also written the review of the play.

In the text, it is Mrs. Helseth's idea of the white horses and Rosmersholm's effects on the surrounding society that perpetuates the notion of an independent architectural agency or will in the house itself. She claims that the Rosmersholm way of life is the reason that nobody under its influence ever laughs: "It began at Rosmersholm, people say. And then it has probably spread out like a kind of infection [*et slags smitte*]."²⁴ Although it is only with condescension that Rebekka entertains these ideas of an active architectural infection at the start of the play, by the end she has moved closer to that logic herself: "Because Rosmersholm has paralyzed [*magtstjålet*] me. My own courageous will has been squelched. And bungled! For me, the time is past when I would dare almost anything. I have lost the ability to act, Rosmer."²⁵ By using the word *magtstjålet* (literally, power-stolen) to describe the effect of Rosmersholm on Rebekka, Ibsen gives full rein to the Helseth view of an all-powerful house crushing the wills of its inhabitants.

If the figuration of the house as a fictional antagonist expresses the leftover anxieties of older models of inhabitation, what then is unhomely in the modern sense about the play *Rosmersholm*? One might point to Rebekka's attempted strategic inhabitation of the space as one example. Her initial position in the house worked the ambiguous margin between "housekeeping" (in Gina Ekdahl's sense) and something more intimate in the home. Her project was in essence a fine-line strategy to occupy the house without being occupied in return, or perhaps to occupy it only enough to gain access to Rosmer without being pulled under by the power of the tradition the house represents. At one point in their opening conversation, Rebekka says to Kroll, "I have after all gotten so used to the house [*så husvant*] now, that I almost think I belong here [*næsten synes jeg hører til her*], I too."[26] The word *husvant* is some distance from a deep sense of rootedness – it is a well-chosen term that describes becoming accustomed to a place with just enough "belonging" to provide some strategic room to maneuver.

When Kroll mentions that she was really the one in charge of the house near the end of Beate's illness, Rebekka corrects him: "It was more like a kind of regency [*et slags regentskab*] in the name of the house mistress."[27] This kind of proxy position suited Rebekka perfectly because mastery of the house (and possibly, the house's mastery of her) would not be an issue as long as she could stay at the margins, using the position without fully inhabiting it, wielding the power without becoming enmeshed with it. Another way of putting this is that she intended an enlightened, modern model of inhabitation, one that assumes that one could make use of the home without activating all of its entrapping aspects. One might even compare her intentions to Hilde Wangel's unperturbed stay in the Solness home – with the difference being that Rebekka's project fails and Rosmersholm prevails. The two characters' strategies of occupation are similar enough, however, that Theodor Caspari would see the "avenger [*Hevnerske*]" of Rebekka West's downfall return in the character of Hilde.[28]

Perhaps one way to regard Rebekka West's failed conquest of the home is that when she is on the verge of succeeding in fully replacing Beate, she sees that she would become fully entangled in the home in a decidedly non-strategic way. Freud's famous reading is that Rebekka is caught in the vise of an unwitting family romance, which is still the generally accepted reading.[29] But that, one might say, is in itself simply a more extreme version of the kind of "entanglements" of home that I outlined in the preceding chapter. If Ibsen were overseeing a gradual evacuation and denigration of the domestic in these later plays, nothing would speed up the process of de-*familiar*ization like placing an incest taboo at the very hearth. Thus, the moment when Rosmer proposes is when Rebekka both succeeds and fails because she realizes that to join with him in marriage inextricably requires that she assume what we might call an "architectural" position in the *house* as well:

ROSMER: But do you know what I am thinking of? Don't you? Don't you see how I best can achieve liberation from all nagging memories, – from all of the dreary bygone matters?
REBEKKA: Tell me!
ROSMER: By juxtaposing to it a new, a living reality.
REBEKKA: (grasping for the back of the chair) A living –? What is – this?
ROSMER: (coming nearer) Rebekka, – if I asked you now, – will you be my second wife?
REBEKKA: (speechless for a moment, exclaims with joy). Your wife! Your –! Me!
ROSMER: Fine. Let us give it a try. We two shall become *one*. Here there must no longer be an empty spot left behind after the dead.
REBEKKA: I – in Beate's place –!³⁰

A detail that is sometimes left untranslated in English versions of the play is that Rosmer is so gallant as to propose explicitly that Rebecca be his *second* wife.³¹ Ibsen's careful phrasing makes it clear that what Rebekka is actually being offered is to repeat a role that Beate has already played, not the chance to make "a new, a living reality," as Rosmer so hopefully puts it. Second, the emphasis on her filling the "empty space" left behind by the dead makes clear that the proposal entails accepting an existing position within an existing structure. Her second-wave reaction ("I – in Beate's place!"), more conflicted than her first spontaneous exclamation, shows that she sees that there is more at stake here than her initially wished-for union with Rosmer. As Atle Kittang has discussed, she suddenly grasps the inescapably triangular geometry of the arrangement.³² My reading would put more emphasis on the idea of Beate's *place*, however, which seems to me to refer to Rosmersholm as a preexisting structure as much as it does the interference the empty slot creates in a triangle of personal relationships. In short, what Rebekka realizes when offered "Beate's place" is that Rosmer's proposal has architectural implications. She sees that she is being offered a spot in a *genganger* house, with only an opportunity to repeat, not create.

Rebekka's ambiguous relationship to the Rosmersholm house was clearly sensed by the reviewer of the initial Christiania theater production of the play, cited earlier. He writes,

> Rebekka is the driving force in the piece. She is the one who brings the old house at Rosmersholm into disrepute, but who also awakens the possibilities in Rosmer. She does not believe in the white beasts of death [*de hvide Dødningsbæste*], but even so she herself becomes the smothering and half-smothered monster in this low-ceilinged, quiet, ghost-like house [*spøgelsesagtige Hus*], which she wants to make into a fortress, – at the same time that this house is her nest and shelter.³³

One senses in this response the difficulty the reviewer has in making sense of Rebekka's position in the house. She both ruins reputations and awakens possibilities; she is a smothering (or "choking," "strangling") monster, even as she herself is half-smothered, choked, or strangled in return; she wants to use the house as a fortress, as a strategic command center, even as it functions as a more traditional home (a nest and a shelter). All of the impressions circulating in this review are justified by the text's own ambiguities; Rebekka's position *is* strange, a kind of pseudo-inhabitation, and the fictional place itself is one of the most complicated architectural imaginings of Ibsen's entire *ouevre*. It confronts directly the question of ownership, the potential hybridity of architectural space, and the difficulties that present themselves in matching subjectivity to an existing built structure.

Because the ending of the play takes place offstage, it is useful to see how commentators elaborated on something the text leaves essentially undepicted. It is clear that the Rosmersholm manor does not fall in on itself and bury its cursed inhabitants, as does the House of Usher in Poe's tale, even though the Rosmer and Usher family lines ultimately suffer the similar fate of extinction, with Rosmersholm also emptied of its last rightful inhabitant. For one later critic, writing in 1910, however, the end of the Rosmer way of life was imagined as the destruction of the building itself. Writing in 1910 of the itinerant Ulrik Brendel's role in inciting the double suicide at the end of the play, the Danish author and academic Poul Levin stated,

> But before [Brendel] sinks into "the mere [sic] nothing," he still has the energy to topple Rosmer and Rebekka, his own unfinished work, down to death. With a final effort he drags himself to Rosmersholm and blasts it in the air. After Rosmer's and Rebekka's death there is no longer any Rosmersholm. *Rosmersholm* is thus a completely anarchistic drama.[34]

Levin goes on to claim Brendel as Ibsen's direct counterpart, joining the interpretive tradition that saw Ibsen as the dynamite specialist, even though there is not really any textual basis for anything more than a figurative demolition of the Rosmersholm concept in the extinction of the family's last surviving member; only when the building is understood as synonymous with a world view is that reading possible. But even then, it could be argued that the Rosmersholm way of life – the devotion to the weighty past – does not seem the least bit weakened at the end of the play; rather, it is strengthened by the elimination of Rebekka, the play's only potentially progressive force.

Other commentators on *Rosmersholm* sensed that beliefs might outlive the actual walls of the manor. Closer to Ibsen's own conception of the tenacity of architectural form would be the view of Theodor Caspari, whose review of *The Master Builder* and advocacy of free love were discussed at length at the end of the last chapter. In that piece, he makes a comparison with *Rosmersholm* that is motivated by his profound distrust of all built structures, precisely because of the tight connection he sees between buildings and habits of thought:

> To be sure, Mrs. Rosmer threw herself in the millrace long ago, and Mrs. Aline Solness's family home, the old tumble-down shack – the storeroom with the portraits, the nine dolls, and all the other junk, just as long ago has gone up in flames; but what has been gained from it? Aren't "the white horses" at Rosmersholm immortal? And while the master builder Solness's children – on whom the happiness of the home depended – are dead due to the fire, haven't the dolls and all the other clutter – alias all the miserable, old-fashioned notions – survived the fire? Don't they continue their empty zombie activity [*sit tomme Gjengangerspil*] in the dutiful Aline's limited mind?[35]

In Caspari's view, old attitudes are unfortunately both fire and dynamite resistant – even after the buildings are destroyed, the attitudes they embodied persist in something approximating the "immortality" of the walking dead.

Brand's church

In this book's Introduction, the 1864 poem "A Church [*En Kirke*]" served as an entry point for understanding Ibsen's twin interests in building and demolition. The poem seems especially intriguing for its discussion of the "double style" that results from the simultaneous activities of the king and the troll. The argument laid out so far in this chapter gives that idea a different inflection; seen from Ibsen's most modern vantage point, the challenge is not actually how to get something built despite the trollish forces, but instead how to clear the ground completely of useless buildings and foundations that refuse to give way. That is to say: the modern architectural problem is that in spite of one's best efforts at demolishing and replacing traditional society's leftover structures, they persist in exerting their influence.

The best remedy against the living dead would clearly be to raze structures to the ground, since that would leave no architectural foothold for the dead in the present. This is also the purest sort of architectural modernism and was the preferred solution of urban modernizers from Haussmann to Le Corbusier: to clear the ground and build everything new. Henrik Jæger identified this as Ibsen's basic stance in his comprehensive treatment of the plays in 1892 as well. Writing about *Ghosts*, Jæger says of Ibsen's view of conventional morality:

> He did not, however, believe that this conception was alive any longer. Like so many other respectable remnants of the past [*ærværdige fortidslevninger*] it existed only as ruins. The common people's tendency to compromise sought to preserve that which was crumbling away and patch it with modern scraps; Ibsen on the other hand wanted to tear the ruins down to rubble [*rive ruinerne i grus*] and build a unified and modern concept on the vacant lot. In *A Doll House* he had sketched the plans for the new building; in *Ghosts* he went about cleaning up in the ruins.[36]

Jæger goes on immediately to call Pastor Manders "a full-blooded man of the ruins [*et fullblods ruin-menneske*]" because it is in him that the *genganger* ideas and attitudes are given full play. Jæger's depiction of the renovation alternative as the "tendency to compromise" that one finds in "common" people makes clear that his sympathies lie with the razing that he sees as Ibsen's true calling.

Around the time *A Doll House* was first published, Ibsen expressed a similar view himself in a letter to his friend Lorentz Dietrichson, the art and literature historian he attached himself to when he first came to Rome in 1864:

> But it strikes me as highly doubtful how much it would succeed to get our good Norwegian population shaken up and reformed bit by bit [*stykkevis*]; it strikes me as doubtful that it is doable for us to get better artistic conditions in place, unless the intellectual soil in all directions is cleared out and cleaned up and drained of all the swampiness [*grundigt opryddes og renskes og skaffes afløb for alt det sumpede*] ... My opinion is: in the short term there is no point in using one's weapons *for* the sake of art, but instead *against* the enemies of art. Get this cleared away first, then we can build.[37]

Ibsen estimates Norwegian society to be perfectly resistant to "piecemeal reform," echoing with the word *stykkevis* one of Brand's famous condemnations of the same: "That which you are, be fully and completely, / and not piecemeal and divided [*Det, som du er, vær fuldt og helt, / og ikke stykkevis og delt*]."[38] Ibsen links social transformation to a more radical form of building – a razing and overhaul of the very land on which the social building lies.

The first drama in which the issues of razing and renovation get sustained attention is *Brand*, and before turning to a discussion of this issue in the prose plays, it will be helpful to backtrack temporarily and take a careful look at this earlier verse drama from 1866. Increasingly, it should be clear from the arguments I have presented that architectural issues seem to have been especially lively for Ibsen in the time immediately after his departure from Norway in 1864, when the break from his homeland inspired a range of new thinking about the home. The immediate fruits of that experience were the poem "A Church," the poem "To the Accomplices" in "Epic Brand," and the play *Brand* itself. Taken together, these might be considered a joint architectural manifesto about the necessity of creative destruction and razing. Like all manifestos, however, the initial statement is complicated by subsequent practice, and in this case the stance toward razing and renovation shifts with the dramatic context of each subsequent play. *Brand*, however, is the crucial place to start the discussion. In its range of architectural vision, it is a thoroughly modernist play that anticipates most of the issues raised in Ibsen's later "housing dramas."

The key scene for these purposes is the discussion in Act Four between the local taxman/bailiff (*Fogden*) and Brand about their respective building plans for the district.[39] The two men have been in conflict for much of the play, but the Bailiff comes to Brand to capitulate in this scene; Brand has clearly won a more popular following, and as a purely political opportunist, the Bailiff sees which way the winds are blowing. In a heavily satirical passage, Ibsen depicts him confiding to Brand that he has ambitious building plans that will restore his standing with the public. The first subsection he has planned for his building is a quarantine (*Pesthus*) for the poor, which the Bailiff says can easily be combined with an actual jail (*Arresthus*). Yet another wing could contain a political meeting hall (*politisk Festhus*). He has considered adding an insane asylum (*Daarekiste*) as well, but estimates that with the likely surge in potential patients in modern times, they could probably not make the building large enough to house them all.[40] Besides, he adds, the other parts of the building could do double duty if necessary:

> If the building plan will hold
> we'll get an asylum for free,
> we'll have gathered under one roof,
> protected by a single flag,
> the most crucial elements
> from which our town gets its color.[41]

The imagined civic structure the Bailiff proposes is nothing if not a bastard building, if we might borrow the evocative term Henrik Jæger later used for the Ekdal home. The Bailiff imagines a building full of compromises, mixed use, and calculation, united only by the superficial rhyme of its member parts (*Pesthus/Arresthus/Festhus*). It is a hybrid space befitting a highly juxtapositional age, a "modern" building project in a highly perjorative sense.

Brand, it turns out, has building plans of his own, namely to tear down the old village church and build a much bigger one in its place, one that can house the expansive souls that he imagines to be the fruit of his religious efforts. The opposite of the Bailiff's civic center, this church would be built from a single, uncompromising vision and would be a building of perfect architectural integrity. The Bailiff bristles immediately at this news of a competing building project just as he himself is ready to proceed, so he grabs the only defensible position he can see, namely to become a devout preservationist:

> Let the church stand, that's what I would advise;
> in a way it could be called
> a piece of refined heirloom gold.
> It *is* a refined heirloom; –
> it should not come down on a whim![42]

One can practically hear the Bailiff talking himself into the preservationist role in these lines as he continues, "I'll step forward as the champion / for the relic on our shores! [*Jeg træder opp som Riddersmand / for Mindesmærket på vår Strand*!]." In his enthusiasm for the idea, he decides on the spur of the moment that the church must (why not?) come from King Bele's time, a reference to the mythological saga material that was the basis for Esaias Tegnér's *Frithiofs saga*.[43] In other words, the Bailiff builds his preservationist argument on an invented historicity.

As the commentary in the new critical edition of *Brand* points out, the Bailiff's adopted position is most likely a commentary on the contemporary movement to preserve Norway's stave churches in the 1840s and 50s in the face of a sudden population growth that necessitated larger meeting spaces.[44] In actuality, the Association for the Preservation of Norwegian Relics of the Past (*Foreningen til Norske Fortidsminnemerkers Bevarelse*) was founded in 1844 with this stated purpose: "to track down, investigate, and preserve Norwegian relics of the past, especially those that illustrate the artistic abilities and sensibilities of the people, as well as to make these objects known to the public through depictions and descriptions."[45] This is an early forerunner of the folk-museum movement and is exactly the sort of activity that Ibsen describes himself abandoning in "To the Accomplices": according to that poem written in the draft process for *Brand*, the remnants of the past, along with all other similar attachments, should be allowed to decay and "go down into darkness" to make way for the new. In the final version of *Brand*, a conversation in Act Five is almost a direct incorporation of this material from "Epic Brand," when the schoolmaster says, "The moldy must go down into the dust; / the rotten is nourishment for the fresh − [*Det muggne maa i Muldet ned; / det raadne er det færskes Næring, −*]."[46]

Brand argues the same point: he tells the Bailiff that whatever the actual historical status of the church, none of the church's former glory is now evident in its present form anyway. This only makes the Bailiff more adamant:

> So I therefore have to say straight out
> that the razing of the Church is impossible; −
> it would be shameful, an awful
> barbaric action without equal![47]

Besides, why tear it down, argues the Bailiff, when a bit of superficial repair would do the trick, at least as far as the present generation is concerned: "When with a tiny bit of care, / one can shore up the old just *enough* / that it won't fall down in *our* time?"[48] With that, the satire of both the preservation and renovation positions is under way. The one is shown to be based in arbitrary historical fantasy, and the other in short-sighted compromise.

The Bailiff turns on a dime, however, when he hears that Brand will be using his own inheritance money to pay for the church. Brand will not be competing with the Bailiff for public funds and donations, as he intends to rid himself of his mother's doubtful legacy by spending every cent of his inheritance on the project. At the same time, he hopes that the church will express his own ideals and vision (more later on the parallels with Mrs. Alving's project in *Ghosts*). As in everything else, Brand throws himself into this project completely and refuses to make compromises. The Bailiff, on the contrary, quickly sees the advantage in tagging along:

> You go first, and I'll follow.
> You are in the forefront; you can do the work [*virke*],
> and I can coax my way forward [*lirke*] step by step. −
> Brand, *together* we will build a church![49]

The rhyming pair the Bailiff uses here (*virke/lirke*) is the same as in Ibsen's poem about the king and the troll ("but the king's work / and the troll's prying / produced a double style [*men kongens virken / og troldets lirken / gav dobbelt stil*]"), as discussed earlier in the Introduction. The recurrence of the word pair may simply be a convenience of rhyme, but it is interesting given the roughly simultaneous composition dates to see the slightly different take here, because there is no hint here that this might be an interestingly subversive *lirken*, as there was with the troll. Here, to work (*virke*) is to take

Brand's church

the direct and unbending route, as Brand does, and to coax (*lirke*) is to go roundabout as an unprincipled opportunist. The "double style" that comes from this joint church-building project does not give the church an intriguing appearance or interesting complexity; instead, it undermines the project and dooms the church to be exactly the kind of compromise object that Brand detests. The *lirke* element is only contamination for Brand.

The Bailiff is the ultimate perspectival man, so his suddenly enthusiastic shift over to Brand's razing project leads to his own scathing disparagement of the preservationist position he had so recently embraced. The very church whose cause he was going to champion now *clearly* needs tearing down, as it looks entirely different from his new position:

> And where is style, architecture,
> when one actually examines the ceiling and wall?
> What should one call arches like that?
> An expert would call them horrid; –
> And I would have to say the same!
> And the roof's moss-covered tufts, –
> I swear they're not from King Bele.
> No, piety can go too far!
> Everyone must surely be able to see and understand
> that this rotten old shack
> is in every respect a piece of trash![50]

The sudden reversals in architectural convictions have the effect of painting preservationism as a kind of humbug, to be sure, but the Bailiff's nimble switch back to Brand's position undermines the legitimacy of razing as well, since the Bailiff clearly inhabits every position equally fervently, depending on the perceived advantage. This rhetorically deconstructive effect of inhabiting all possible positions to evacuate their authority is reinforced by the fact that when the church is finished, even Brand himself wonders about the value of his project. There is a distinct sense of anti climax, even when Brand proclaims:

> The house of God will be built large;
> that is what I boldly promised;
> clearing out, leveling, sweeping away,
> tearing down was easy enough to venture; –
> now the work is all finished.[51]

But even though the razing proceeded without regrets and the new church seems big in a relative sense – bigger than any other in the area, for example – Brand now begins to wonder if it is big in an *absolute* sense.

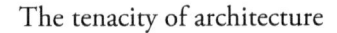

He had imagined instead an "image of a temple [*Tempelbilled*],"⁵² that could house every flight of the soul, so he wonders if "big" is big enough to do that. Perhaps it is *merely* "big," still too limited and material for his aspirations: "*Is* it big? Is this house / fully and completely, what I wanted? [Er *den stor? Er dette Hus / fuldt og helt, hvad jeg har villet?*]"⁵³ He wonders if they have simply traded "an old lie for a new one" or gone "from the musty shelter of a relic / to a modern spire beneath the sky [*fra Mindesmærkets muggne ly / till Nutidsspiret under Sky*]."⁵⁴ In other words, he suddenly sees that no matter how big the church might get in a physical and architectural sense, as long as it takes the form of a built structure, it may still be using the wrong materials:

> You have to want the new *completely*, –
> the clearing away of *all* rotten buildings, –
> before the great temple hall
> can be raised as it ought to be!⁵⁵

With that, Brand locks the main door to the new church, throws the keys in the river, and tells the crowd that they will have to break in through the musty cellar if they want to use the building. In other words, Brand's motto ("All or nothing!") applies to his architectural vision as well, with paradoxical implications. It is clear that he calls for the complete razing of existing structures because they are all shot through with the spirit of compromise. Nothing is worth saving from the past precisely because it is *past*. But what kind of future building could possibly house Brand's spirit in the future? Doesn't architecture by definition entail a compromise with the material world? And no matter how completely new, big, and unified a structure might be at the moment of its building, won't the passage of time immediately begin to eat away at its perfection? Time itself is a compromise; architecture's persistence means that no matter what the structure, there will always be a point at which it appears old and ready for razing once again. It is constantly possible that other buildings will replace it as bigger and more perfect.

Brand seems to realize this in a moment of architectural disillusionment when he throws away the keys at the very moment of the church's inauguration; with that gesture, he assumes a position of profound skepticism about any possible fit between architecture and occupant. He has come to see the architectural as a trap, as a lure, and his project as misguided. Throwing away the keys, Brand tries vaulting beyond the architectural to something more – the totality that can never be a building. He wanted a church that would not only house a limited Sunday faith but also everything in life. That, however, exceeds the very notion of "housing" as a kind of containment. He thus urges the crowd to see beyond the limits of a church that only ends up reflecting their own mediocrity:

> Away with the work [*Væk med Værket*] accomplished here!
> Only as a lie is it great;
> everything is ramshackle in spirit,
> worthy of your paltry wills.[56]

Væk med Værket might also be translated as "away with the building," a turn of phrase that reminds us of Caspari's later discussion of the "marriage building" ("away with marriage!"). In Ibsen's first extended architectural play in 1864, then, we already find the most extreme form of architectural critique, a disillusionment driven by a demand for absolute integrity that literally cannot be housed.

Renovation and razing

If Brand's assessment of architecture as an unacceptable material compromise had been Ibsen's final dramatic word on the subject, the shape and theme of the subsequent prose plays would have been quite different. A philosophical rejection of all architectural limits would not leave much to do on stage. Instead, when a decade had passed since *Brand*, Ibsen began the prose-play cycle in which one might say that the house had become the very medium of his dramatic craft. After having Brand toss the keys to the building in the river, Ibsen seems to have gone fishing to retrieve them in domestic form, because he goes on testing the resilience of structures from both the interior and exterior perspectives in the subsequent plays. Like the troll, he keeps poking and prodding at the walls but now is focused on the bourgeois home.

One can see this in the way his dramatic characters return repeatedly to ideas of razing and renovation throughout the prose plays: those are some of the most common architectural images. Some of his dramatic characters remain in the metaphorical register; Lona Hessel, for example, is a renovator in spirit, with her abstract talk of substituting new pillars for old. Others, however, enact the issues more directly by engaging in literal building projects of their own. The more one considers this, the clearer it becomes that Ibsen has other master builders besides Halvard Solness in his aggregate cast of characters. The fictionalized architectural projects they undertake demonstrate the limits of both renovation and razing and ultimately call into question the efficacy of both building and housing as ways of conceptualizing an individual's relationship to the past.

The most underappreciated of Halvard Solness's construction-industry colleagues is undoubtedly Helene Alving in *Ghosts*. Her development of the orphanage project memorializing her late husband is her best-known work, but less conspicuous is the fact that she has been a long-term home renovator as well. When one pieces together Helene Alving's building history from clues in the text, one sees that she has worked through several alternative stances toward the limits of built structure. She began her married life with Captain Alving living in town, close enough to Pastor Manders that she could flee to his house after her first year of marital misery, when it had become obvious to her that the "rumors" of the captain's dissipated behavior were true. When Manders convinced her to return to her husband, the couple moved out to the Rosenvold estate in their second year of marriage. Shortly thereafter, their son Osvald was born. Over the next few years, Rosenvold then became a kind of private tavern, with Helene serving as the captain's drinking partner to keep an eye on him at home. This did not prevent him from seducing the maid, however, around the time that Osvald was seven years old. Helene describes it as an invasion of the home: "But when the offence came inside our own four walls – [*Men da så forargelsen kom indenfor vore egne fire vægge –*]."[57]

Reconstructing the time line from clues in the text, it is clear that about nine years into the nineteen-year-long Alving marriage, Helene felt compelled to send Osvald away to keep him from becoming contaminated by the now sexually polluted home. From then on, Helene Alving took control: "then I swore to myself: there has to be an end to this! And then I assumed power in the house – complete power – both over him and everything else."[58] During the next ten years of fictional time, Osvald was apparently never allowed to set foot in the house, and the captain himself seems to have been in serious decline; Helene claims that for the most part, he lay about on the sofa reading old government yearbooks.

It was also during that ten-year period, however, that Helene Alving became a master renovator. As she explains to Manders:

> I would never have been able to bear it if I hadn't had my work. Yes, for I dare say I have worked! All of these expansions of the property, all of the improvements, all of the useful innovations that won Alving so much praise and renown, do you really think that *he* had that kind of initiative?[59]

The point of all this renovation activity was to create a public reputation that would take on a life of its own, a story that Manders and others had for years accepted at face value: that Alving had reformed and become a "benefactor" with Helene as his "competent co-worker [*dygtig medarbejder*]."[60] The

Rosenvold estate renovations and improvements are thus in essence the equivalent of this false story about Alving. Their main purpose is to cover over the truth of the captain's decline; as Manders puts it (using rhetoric cited many times already in this study): "Your entire marriage, – your entire life together these many years with your husband was in other words nothing more than a covered abyss! [*en overdækket afgrund*]"[61]

The orphanage is thus Mrs. Alving's *second* big building project, since it was not begun until after the captain's death. It continued for yet another ten-year period, to be rounded off by the scheduled dedication of the building on the exact anniversary of his death. The reader is told that the orphanage construction has been funded by the remainder of the captain's original fortune, the money that made him "a good match" at the time Helene married him. In retrospect, she now sees that sum as her "purchase price" and is building the orphanage to make sure that Osvald inherits absolutely none of it. She tries in essence to bury both the captain's money and influence at once in the new building. Since she insists that she has calculated the captain's share of the wealth exactly, the implication is that everything that is now left in the original Rosenvold house after the completion of the orphanage is the result of her own hard effort during the years of renovation work on the estate. These renovations are not *all* theatrical façades; they are not the exact conceptual equivalent of the superficial patching of the ship in *Pillars of Society*. As the play develops, however, it becomes clear that despite the inherent value of Mrs. Alving's work at Rosenvold, those improvements are still not enough to keep the captain's influence at bay. Even the purified and improved Rosenvold, that is, the imagined future home for mother and son alone, does not play out as planned since the seeds of decline are already within Osvald as well. In the world of this play, the new elements of a renovated building are no match for the *gengangere* that are resident in its leftover, unmodified parts.

The resulting mixed aspect of the current version of Rosenvold presented in the present time of the play has not been immediately apparent to all readers, although it seems to have been a major design element in August Lindberg's renowned traveling production of *Ghosts* in 1883. Edvard Brandes was not at all enthusiastic about this set, though it seemed to pick up perceptively on the building's fictional past as presented in the text:

> The exterior *mise-en-scène* has been the object of much praise. But is it deserved? It was difficult to reconcile oneself to this restless room [*denne urolige Stue*], with its embarrassing Gothic ornamentation and its half

elegant and modern furnishings. Rosenvold is an old estate, where the furniture should be kept in strictly consistent style, and the overall impression should have been dark, "without joy of life, full of duty."[62]

Brandes's criticism is interesting because one can see his expectation of aesthetic unity colliding with the text's own information about Rosenvold, namely that by the time we encounter it in the play, there has been a ten-year renovation project that without doubt would have introduced modern elements among the old and produced a mixed style. It is easy to miss that point, given that the stage directions at the beginning of the play are silent on the period details of Rosenvold's style;[63] Ibsen is asking both readers and scenographers to look beyond the stated stage directions and infer something extra about the look of the house from stray comments strewn throughout the dialogue. Lindberg actually seems to have gotten it exactly right by presenting a room on stage in mixed Gothic and modern styles. When Brandes reads Lindberg's version of the room against an aesthetic norm of unified style, he finds it "restless," but if Helene's home has constantly been in transition, a hybrid appearance is an extremely effective and economical way of conveying the mix of innovations and architectural leftovers that have reportedly marked her building activity during the time Captain Alving was alive. Edvard Brandes may have wanted a consistently old décor to sharpen the disparity between old structures and new inhabitants, but the fact is that Mrs. Alving's renovation activity in the main Rosenvold house has instead created an architectural monument to the idea of partial reform and mixed style.

Conservative commentators in Ibsen's day who would have been alarmed at the idea of revolution could nevertheless sense the potential for upheaval at stake in these architectural models, so they clearly preferred the idea of renovation to that of razing. One contemporary Swedish commentator on the published text of *Ghosts* summarized what he took to be Ibsen's position:

> Partial reforms thus mean almost nothing: everything must be fundamentally recast [*omstöpas*]. Hasn't Ibsen himself said at one time,
> I want nothing to do with rearranging the pieces;
> To knock over the playing board: that is more like me.[64]

The cited verses in this Swedish review come from the 1869 poem "To My Friend the Revolutionary Speaker [*Til min Ven Revolutions-Taleren!*]," in which Ibsen suggests his famous improvement on the Noah story, namely to repeat the flood but this time to torpedo the ark.[65] That way, none of the old world's vestigial traces would be left over to contaminate the resulting new order. Now *that* is revolution, Ibsen seems to be saying, unlike the rhetorical poses one most often hears from would-be revolutionaries. This kind of rhetoric led another conservative Swedish reviewer cited earlier to prefer Ibsen's compatriot Bjørnson. He warned, "It is the difference between *revolution* and *reform!*"[66]

In *Ghosts*, the equivalent of the Biblical flood is the fire that destroys the orphanage. Ross Shideler's treatment of *Ghosts* makes an interesting point about the separation of the Rosenvold estate from the new orphanage project built on the same property: "From one point of view, the orphanage is Mrs. Alving's attempt to kill the heritage of the dead father, an attempt quite literally to get him out of her house and into his own."[67] The fire has burned this structure completely to the ground,[68] so if the captain had been "externalized" in the other structure, one might think that there could not have been a more complete destruction of his legacy. But Ibsen's main point with *Ghosts* is not really to clear ground for the new. Instead, it is implied that the income from the investment that was intended for operation of the orphanage will now be redirected to Engstrand's brothel. The captain's legacy thus lives on architecturally in spite of the razing of the orphanage itself, as if it had a will of its own. Similarly, the Rosenvold estate, which Helene Alving had imagined as a purified haven for mother and son alone, will apparently continue its mixed *genganger* legacy: Osvald's rapid decline at the end of the play, at the moment he should finally be able to see this idealized home, makes clear that Mrs. Alving's renovations were insufficient to banish the captain's influence on the present. Perhaps if Rosenvold, that eleborate renovation experiment, had also burned to the ground along with the orphanage and Osvald himself, there might be the chance of an unsullied future.

Razing and renovating make an oblique appearance in *Enemy of the People* as well, this time in response to the news that the town baths may be polluted. This would be an obvious case for drastic measures, precisely the sort of drainage and hygiene project that Ibsen had described in his letter to Lorentz Dietrichson three years earlier, with its reference to Norway's "swampy" intellectual terrain. Dr. Stockmann is originally dismissive of such extreme solutions, however, reassuring those around him instead that the situation is not so serious that a complete razing of the baths would be necessary:

HOVSTAD:	Four to five articles, you said? On the same topic?
DOCTOR STOCKMANN:	No, far from it, my friend. They will be about quite different things. But everything stems from the water plant and from the sewer. The one thing entails the other, you see. It is like when one begins tearing down an old building, – exactly like that.
BILLING:	That is so true, God help me; one can never seem to finish until one has torn down the whole junkheap [*revet ned hele skramlet*].
ASLAKSEN:	(from the print shop) Torn down! I hope the doctor isn't thinking of tearing down the bathhouse?
HOVSTAD:	Far from it; don't you worry.
DOCTOR STOCKMANN:	No, this concerns completely different things.[69]

This exchange comes in Act Three, before the town meeting radicalizes Stockmann's position, so his reassurances here are premature; in fact, when he lays out his argument at the meeting, one gets exactly the impression of an initially limited renovation that has gone out of control. As his critique escalates recklessly up the level of abstraction from the pollution in the baths to the lies and corruption in individual houses, in the entire town, in society, and in the entire country, one gets the distinct impression that he cannot stop the process of social demolition once it has started.

One is reminded of a similar concept in *Ghosts*, where Mrs. Alving describes the unraveling of her old belief system. She says to Manders that the forced return to her husband in the name of "duty" led her to begin examining all of Manders's conventional views:

> It was at that time that I began to examine the seams in your teachings. I only meant to pick at a single knot; but when I had untied that one, it unraveled altogether. And then I understood that they were flimsy seams.[70]

Both of these rhetorical images – the demolition and the unraveling that cannot be stopped once they have been started – seem to aspire to the status of natural law in the characters' minds, but there is nothing inviolable about Ibsen's idea of an irresistible deconstructive momentum. It is worth observing, just to contain the metaphors a bit, that in real life, renovating and mending often seem to be perfectly adequate as purely pragmatic solutions. Only when one shares Ibsen's assumptions about the essential flimsiness of the social building (or the social fabric) do these metaphors persuade powerfully of the inefficacy of reform.

Ibsen's best-known master builder, Halvard Solness, has a complicated housing history of his own that can only be reconstructed from references in the text. First, one might note that the original church-building project in Lysanger that began his strange relationship with Hilde was not a project like Brand's. There was no razing of old churches, no vacant lot, but a new tower on an old church, as Solness reveals when he first refers to "the summer when I was there building a tower on the old church."[71] The fact that he later distinguishes between building churches and building church towers as separate activities further indicates that the confrontation between the master builder and God on the high tower was not the crowning moment of an uncompromising construction project like Brand's, even though he later describes his earliest church-building phase as "the most worthy thing I could choose."[72] Instead, by the time he was working on the Lysanger church tower, he was already engaged in something more composite: a new tower on an old building. That combination of new and old never bodes well in Ibsen's architectural world; when Solness defies God at the top of the tower by saying that he is now going into business for himself by building only "homes for people,"[73] it can be seen as a rejection of composite building activities. The imagined consistency of the simple, single-minded task of homes for people replaces the complications of church building for another master, or to put it another way, of building one's own structures on someone else's leftover foundation – which, it should be noted, is the actual position of every person born into the world.

It has already been noted that this new home-building activity is just as shot through with contradictions and disappointment as the church-building activity. He tells himself that he builds happy homes for others, even though we discover that those homes have become dilapidated after ten short years. He is in the midst of building yet another, a new home for himself, although he intuits that it is pointless to expect happiness and *hygge* in the new setting. Furthermore, he has now returned to a mixed style – a home, but with a tower that is "much too high. For a home at least."[74] Even Hilde's imaginary castle in the air gets a hybrid characteristic in Solness's hands, namely the firm foundation that he adds nervously to the conversation whenever she mentions it.[75]

One might also point out that none of Solness's recent building activity seems to have been "unmixed" or free of the influence of the past. The limits of existing architectural structures exert a constant drag on his work, as does the limited ambition of building "mere" homes. Perhaps those first churches, built when he was still pious and humble, would qualify as buildings of perfect and unmixed structural integrity:

SOLNESS: And I dare say that I built these small, poor churches with such an honest and warm and sincere attitude [*et så ærligt og varmt og inderligt sind*] that – that –
HILDE: That –? What?
SOLNESS: That I thought he ought to be satisfied with me.[76]

But this naïve approach has been out of reach for some time, if it ever existed at all for Solness other than in memory. It is in any case clear that Solness's more recent building history is marked by the instability of competing styles of transitional architecture.

A second observation about this play concerns the failure of razing to produce something new and lasting in its place. The fire that destroyed the Solness home, like the fire that destroyed the Alving orphanage, burned everything to the ground. The new aspect Ibsen introduces with this motif is that the razing seems to have had two parallel effects at once: that of debilitating loss on the one hand, and an apparent liberation from the past on the other. We find both meanings represented in this conversation between Doctor Herdal and Solness in Act One:

DOCTOR HERDAL: First that ugly old robber's fortress [*den gamle fæle røverborgen*] burned down for you. And that was truly a lucky thing.
SOLNESS: That was Aline's ancestral home [*familjehjem*] that burned. Remember that.
DOCTOR HERDAL: Yes, for *her* it must have been a heavy sorrow.
SOLNESS: She hasn't gotten over it to this very day. Not in all these twelve-thirteen years.
DOCTOR HERDAL: What happened afterwards, that must have been the worst for her.
SOLNESS: Both that and other things.
DOCTOR HERDAL: But *you* – you yourself – *you* got a boost up from it. Began as a poor boy from the countryside, – and now you stand here as the most prominent man in your profession. Oh yes, Mr. Solness, *you* have been a lucky man.[77]

The contrastive emphasized pronouns in the original dialogue make clear that assessing the outcome of the fire depends completely on one's perspective: for Aline, it meant a trauma with no recovery in sight; for Halvard, it was the golden business opportunity that made his career. This fire, like the one observed in "On the Heights," thus generates only competing perspectives, not secure meaning. The more Solness broods on his career, the more hollow his success seems to him. He sees only futility in all of this building activity. His self-assessment in Act Three could in some sense be seen as the negative end point of all of Ibsen's architectural explorations:

SOLNESS: Yes, for now I see it. People don't have any use for these homes of theirs. Not in order to be happy, anyway. And I would not have had any use for such a *home*, either. If I had owned one. (with a quiet, bitter laugh) You see, *that* is the entire reckoning, as far, far back as I can see. Nothing built after all. And nothing sacrificed to *get* something built either. Nothing, nothing – all of it.[78]

Solness clearly realizes that his limited equation of homes and happiness was a mistake, but until this point it does not seem to have occurred to him that people could seek happiness outside the home. Although the idea of people no longer "having any use" for their homes is here cast in the negative light of a despairing master builder who imagines himself put out of work, these young people with new tastes and needs hint at a more positive potential as well. Imagine, that is, if people like Ragnar Brovik truly had no use for the kinds of homes we encounter as readers of the other plays, the homes advocated by Rørlund, Helmer, Manders, Peter Stockmann, Kroll, and Aunt Julle. From a youthful, forward-looking perspective, the cumulative effect of that composite home is something of a nightmare. Just picturing it suggests great reasons to give homelessness a try, or at the very least, to work out a new kind of architectural plan.

Also interesting in this passage is Solness's realization that in his case, the accidental razing provided by the fire seems to have been pointless, in spite of the career opening it provided. Even when the ground is completely cleared in the way that Solness imagined so often earlier in his career, the old structures seem to persist in ghostly architectural ways. One sees evidence of that in Solness's design for the new house that is about to be dedicated. The inappropriate and distinctive tower is the house's most noticeable feature,[79] the one that would set it apart from the old "robber's fortress" and "wooden crate [*trækasse*]"[80] of an ancestral home that it is replacing. Yet, a quality of repetition and empty mimesis is even more striking, if less obvious. Not only is Solness building the new home on the same spot as the one lost in the fire, but he has also insisted that it share a useless architectural feature with the old house: three empty nursery rooms. Just as Solness has built for a feeling of *hygge* that he knows will elude them, he has also built for the children who will never come. Since this house is a completely new construction on a razed lot, it could have been designed exactly to suit its inhabitants' future needs. The nurseries are thus vestigial in the purest sense of the word: the needs of the past continue to haunt the new structure.

Although Ibsen's contemporary Helene Butenschøn saw in the architectural repetition of the nursery an undying idealism and Solness as heroically optimistic in the way he holds tenaciously to the failing ideal of the home and builds the new nurseries against all reason,[81] Frode Helland's reading is the more reasonable one. Helland frames the inexplicable building plans and their inclusion of an unnecessary nursery as a melancholic reaction to loss, a reading that allows us to perceive the inherently negative potential Ibsen saw resident in architectural structure itself: even when given the chance to build fresh, Solness repeats.[82] To add to that argument, though, it can be pointed out that the repetition of the nurseries might be more than a personal symptom of Solness's (or Aline's) melancholic condition; the persistence of the nurseries might convey a central point about architecture's durative features more generally. Using Helland's productive framework, that is, one might extrapolate and claim that Ibsen's architectural imagination is itself essentially melancholic. We see that in the tendency of built structures to repeat and rigidly outlast their original functions, in the difficulties they have accommodating the changing needs of future inhabitants, and in their overwhelming inertia.

The impression of an empty mimetic pattern accumulates when one realizes that there is a second house with three nurseries in between the old and the new, namely the one in which the Solnesses currently live, and where the couple has presumably been living since the fire occurred eleven to twelve years before. We know little about this house beyond what we see of it (or read of it in the stage directions), since it does not attract as much overt discussion in the dialogue as do the Solnesses' past and future homes. We can readily see that it is another "bastard home," in the sense that like the Ekdal apartment, it combines workplace and living quarters. We are not told whether Solness built it himself, although it seems to be situated on the same general property as Aline's original home, as it too adjoins the family garden. Halvard and Aline may or may not have lived in it for the entire time of their displacement from the original home – again, the text is silent on this point. It is likely, however, that the construction of the third house with the tower was a later idea that came up after Solness had built many of his "homes for [other] people" and achieved his career success.[83]

The nurseries in the present home shown on stage are described both as empty spaces and "fully prepared [*fuldt færdige*],"[84] so that when Hilde arrives she is able to move immediately into one of them and use it as a guest room. Helland mentions that although the twin boys might have motivated the existence of nurseries in the present house, there is clearly no reason for the rooms in the new one.[85] However, since we are told that the twin boys had just been born before the fire occured, and barely lasted " a score of days" afterward,[86] it seems fictionally inconsistent that the nurseries described in the current Solness dwelling could have ever logically served a practical function, no matter how they ended up in the present house. They were certainly not constructed with those particular children in mind, because Halvard and Aline came to the house only as a result of the accident. In the eleven years that have passed since the twins' deaths, though, it seems that the rooms have remained fully furnished, as if still awaiting future occupancy, and they have been repeated as a set of three without explanation in the new house as well. Note that the sign of repetition is not the nurseries themselves, since all houses might logically contain *one*; instead, it is the excess of the number three (one more than the number of Solness children), repeated three times, that makes the presence of the rooms unusual. The nurseries simply seem to have a logic of their own, as if no matter where Solness might move, there will always be three unused children's rooms. This seeming independence of vestigial architectural structures like the nurseries is what ultimately makes razing pointless and ineffective at wiping out the past in *The Master Builder*. That is also the sense in which the actual cause of the fire is beside the point.

A few final examples of razing in the subsequent plays reinforce the impression of the futility of imagined fresh starts. The first example comes from a scene near the end of *Little Eyolf* (1894). There the context is a discussion of the run-down poor area near the wharf where Eyolf has drowned. His father, Alfred Allmers, bitter about the lack of response from the area's inhabitants to Eyolf's distress in the water, declares that everything at the waterfront should be totally torn down as a kind of payback. His mental image of these improverished families, a caricature of drunken fathers beating their children while their mothers cry for help, shows that he does not really care where the families might end up after his imagined demolition. Rita Allmers has a different suggestion: not to demolish the ramshackle housing, but instead to take the poor children into her own wealthy home to fill the empty place that Eyolf's death has left behind: "They will be allowed to live in Eyolf's rooms. Allowed to read his books. To play with his toys. They will take turns sitting on his chair at the table."[87]

Most would agree with her husband about the craziness of this plan: neither Alfred nor Rita seems particularly well suited to be a foster parent. If, however, one insists on reading sincerity in their eventual reconciliation as he accepts her plan, as many critics have, one is still left to explain a sharp departure from positions that have been developed fairly consistently in previous plays. The substitution of poor children in Eyolf's place, for example, calls up echoes of Rebekka at Rosmersholm ("I – in Beate's place"). There is good reason to be pessimistic about this kind of architectural slot substitution in Ibsen's later plays, if only because he has developed a cumulative argument against the possibility of meaningful repetition that has not really been answered or solved in *Little Eyolf*. Of course, there is no need for all of Ibsen's plays to be consistent in their architectural vision; as has already been noted, *Lady from the Sea* hints at some sort of reconciliation within the home and thus poses a challenge to claiming a clear trajectory throughout the plays. Helland's reading of the final scene of *Little Eyolf* as melancholic-ironic, however, seems more persuasive when thinking contextually about the prospects for Rita's planned adoption project.[88] If *Little Eyolf* was intended indirectly as a breakthrough vision of an authentic inhabitation of the house by an alternative family of choice, it is a singularly unconvincing one. The children involved seem too much like pawns in a game of forced restitution, serving only the emotional needs of Rita and Alfred Allmers.

One senses Ibsen trying out another architectural alternative in the next play with the frozen house of *John Gabriel Borkman*. If there ever were a structure that could use a good razing, this would be it. Instead, we get what amounts to razing's negative image here: we see what happens in Ibsen's world when characters abandon the impulse to struggle against the inherent inertia of architecture, but become one with it instead. The stage directions describe a downstairs living room marked by "old-fashioned faded splendor [*gammeldags falmet pragt*]," and upstairs, a "formerly splendid hall [*fordums pragtsal*]" with tapestries in "faded, bleached-out colors [*falmede, afblegede farver*]."[89] Empire-style furnishings in and of themselves would not have been particularly anachronistic in late nineteenth-century Norway or Sweden, since royal interest in the style extended its longevity in the North. Combined with Borkman's self-consciously Napoleonic posing, however, the faded décor conveys the sense of a house frozen in time, not lovingly preserved – it is something closer to the cosmetically augmented corpse kept alive past its proper lifespan. In short, this is a building suffering from a severe case of lag time, one in which the living dead refuse the realities of their present situations, replaying instead the traumas, mistakes, and wounds of the past.

This also a household dominated by hopes of restoration. Rosen's terminology is again relevant here. To remind us of the way he uses the idea: restoration entails the recovery of an imagined perfection, unmarked by the passage of time, rescued out of the clutches of the past. Architectural restoration is the historical mode that attempts to make something old appear in the present as it is imagined to have looked when it was new. When Borkman and Gunhild use the term "restoration" (*oprejsning*), they mean something very similar. For Borkman, it means a complete rewinding of the clock, a return to the height of his previous fame and influence. For Gunhild, it is the restoration of her reputation and her son's family name. When the "hour of restoration" strikes, they imagine that a lost perfection from the past will be retrieved and made fully present, as if no trouble had ever intervened.

The visual evidence from the Rentheim estate, however, constantly contradicts the viability of these restoration fantasies because the corrosion of time is so apparent. With all colors and fabrics faded, the testimony of loss is all around them. There has been no renovation here at all, no attempt to update the furnishings or keep the house moving forward into the present and future. It simply persists as a perfectly inert object, looking exactly as it did at the moment of catastrophe. In this regard, it is interesting that one reviewer of an early stage production in Christiania complained that the set design there made everything seem too *new*:

> Inside we should be met everywhere by a former, faded splendor. But the gilding on the furniture in Mrs. Borkman's living room shines too brightly at the Kristiania Theater, just as the colors on the murals in Borkman's great hall are too fresh and lively. They do not show the blanching of life [*Livets Afblegethed*], they do not proclaim the decline of life.[90]

The reviewer then goes on to protest that the actors' performances are too fresh and vital as well – the emotional life of the characters, like the set itself, is supposed to be "faded" but in this production was too present and passionate. In other words, the Christiania Theater seems to have performed precisely the kind of restoration that the characters fantasize about. Instead of a powerful discrepancy between fantasies of the past and the visual realities of the present, the spectator in that performance was given access to a past that seemed all too new, without the noticeable wear of time called for in the text. It is not an insurmountable challenge for theaters to create new sets with a distressed look, so it would have been possible, and the play's text clearly describes visual discrepancy as a central feature of the setting, so this seems like a missed opportunity in that production.

For these reasons, we might say that the Rentheim estate is an extreme example of persistent architecture. It is not a house that conceals its living dead until moments of sudden, uncanny revelation; the *gengangere* are instead the play's main characters, pacing about in the open. Although the house itself is stylistically unmixed, frozen in a single lost style of the past, that does not give it any advantage over the unstable "bastard rooms" we have seen in the other plays. This is not a naïve return to the modes of restoration and preservation; unlike the attractively modeled past of Ibsen's earlier history plays, here at <u>the end of his career we find a past</u> that is a grotesquely accessible cosmetic corpse, at least <u>when seen from the</u> position of <u>modernist bias that makes it uncanny</u>. (As a thought exercise, one might imagine a preservationist stumbling into the world of the play and enthusing about the house's authentic time-capsule detail.)

A final encounter with the notions of razing and renovation occurs in *When We Dead Awaken*. Although it is not common to treat Ibsen's last play as an architectural treatise, at least one commentator at the time, the Danish literary critic Valdemar Vedel, saw strong lines of continuity with *John Gabriel Borkman*'s acute architectural sensibilities:

> Ibsen's new play proceeds directly from its predecessor and takes up the thread where we left it three years ago. That was in the Rentheim family estate, with icy mausoleum air in all the rooms, where the "Death Dance" was played and three "corpses" walked around in hopes of awakening each other to life again, but it ended with two shadows offering each other a hand over a corpse.[91]

The most obvious link to the previous play may well be that between Irene and the Borkmans as members of the same living-dead extended family, but there are other affinities as well. One of them is less obvious, namely that Professor Rubek seems to have been something of a master builder himself, to the side of his more obvious career as a sculptor (a German review from 1900 reached even further back with its title, "Professor Rubek's Doll House [*Professor Rubeks Puppenheim*]").[92] Rubek's building project can again be assembled analytically through clues, beginning with "the little farmhouse by Lake Taunitz [*det lille bondehuset ved Taunitzer See*]."[93] Irene calls this "our old house" because it was where the two of them would go after the week's work of sculpting and posing when they were first working on the statue together.[94] In other words, the sculptural and architectural activities alternated during that time, with the artistic modeling taking place during the week and the playing house on the weekends. For it was at that country house that Rubek and Irene repeatedly played the game of metaphor by the creek, imagining the leaves in the water as white swans and Lohengrin's boat.

The fact that this idyllic memory was limited as an "episode," as Rubek describes it coldly, is clear from the fact that he later purchased both the property and the house, as he had yearned to do back then, but then had the old house razed:

IRENE: (glancing at him from the corner of her eye) Do you live out there now, then – in our old house?
PROFESSOR RUBEK: No, I've had that torn down long ago. And then I've built myself a large, splendidly comfortable villa [*en stor, prægtig bekvem villa*] on the lot, – with a park all around. *That* is where we usually – (pauses and changes the wording) – *that* is where I usually stay [*holde til*] in the summers –
IRENE: (restraining herself) So you and – that other one stay out there now?
PROFESSOR RUBEK: (a bit defiantly) Yes. When my wife and I are not traveling, – as we are this year.
IRENE: (gazing in the distance) Lovely, lovely was life on Lake Taunitz.[95]

Irene clearly has precisely the kind of problems with subsequent occupants described earlier – she does not easily yield her spot in that house to her successor. The fact that Maja now lives in Irene's place as if she were the second wife – echoing Rebekka West's position – is further proof that Irene was "just an episode" for Rubek. The idea that the shared memory of "our old house" is permanently out of reach is underscored by the complete razing of the old structure. Irene reacts to this news by "restraining herself," indicating that the destruction of the old house may be as big an ethical breach in her mind as Rubek's constant renovation of the sculpture ("our old house" being the match for "our child") after she left. In this way, too, the architectural shadows the sculptural theme in the play.

One senses in Rubek as well the idea that the new modern, comfortable villa has not actually offered him the fresh start he likely imagined. When he catches himself to change the wording in the cited passage, it appears that he cannot quite bring himself to say the words "we" and "live" together to describe his life in the house with Maja. Instead, he corrects himself to link "I" to the weaker expression *holde til*, which gives more of an impression of a temporary stay than a rooted dwelling. This is in keeping with his earlier discussion of the villa in the play's first scene with Maja, when Rubek says, "Yes, for it is elegant and splendid all of it, Maja, I dare say. And spacious also. We don't need to be always hovering over each other –."[96] Even in that early expository conversation one senses that although the villa is big and luxurious, it is a structure without meaning or real emotional attachments. Most significant is that for Rubek, the combination of temporariness and extreme regrets does not add to an unencumbered, modern form of inhabitation, but a crippled one instead. There is nothing even close to a liberating, "cheerful parting with the past" when Rubek razes the old farmhouse at Lake Taunitz. In effect, he lives there in the old house still, as does Irene, even though the structure itself no longer exists and is out of reach – like the old couple in Ibsen's poem, they are searching in the ashes for lost jewels. The last example of razing in Ibsen's plays thus remains an exercise in futility.

An architecture of forgetting

Inheritance is a potent form of persistence, one that potentially might express the range of varied attitudes toward the past outlined in this chapter. It can be a gift from one generation to another, a prized legacy, but it can also be a particularly coercive form of memory, as if forced by older generations onto the young, whether one speaks of inherited traits, wealth, or property. Legacy can be both a boon and a curse. In Ibsen's dramatic world, it is most often the latter, a burden on the free individual that must be outwitted by a variety of ironic, marginal strategies.

One can find an early inkling of this already in Act Two of *Brand*, in the scene in which Brand confronts his mother about her fortune. Her ferocious greed has helped her amass a tidy sum in money and property to pass on as an inheritance to Brand; she appears in the scene as a grotesque, grasping figure with stuffed pockets; according to Brand, she had earlier even ransacked the corpse of her husband looking for money. She imagines the continuation of her property in the family lineage to be a kind of immortality and stipulates the only condition of the inheritance to be that Brand pass on the property and wealth within the family alone. She insists on a lasting architectural legacy of unbroken property ownership.

Brand, however, sees only temptation and earthbound thinking in this kind of coerced inheritance: "And if I instead had in mind / to scatter it to the winds? [*Og hvis jeg tvertom fik isinde / at strø den ud for alle Vinde?*]"[97] Nothing horrifies his mother more than the thought of that dispersal of her legacy fortune, but Brand sets as the requirement for his adminstration of her last rites that she voluntarily give up her hold on all earthly possessions. As she lies dying, she offers first half, then nine-tenths of her possessions but ultimately dies without his blessing: he had demanded that she give up everything and refuses to compromise when she does not.

What this means is that Brand inherits it all. To rid himself of the taint of his mother's money, he decides to pour all of the resources into the building of his church:

> I will build with my own resources; –
> All of my inheritance, down to the last mite
> shall be given over to this task.[98]

Intended to sever the chain of inheritance, Brand's building project thus becomes a form of forgetting, and the church a building of double purpose. Of course, Brand's church never pretends to be a memorial site – in fact, as we might recall, it replaced one. The historical church that the Bailiff was initially so eager to preserve was called a *mindesmærke*, which translated literally would be "memory-marker." That is also the word used for "monument." That was the church that was razed, however, so the new church is intended to aid forgetting in two ways: to forget the site's own long architectural history by building an entirely new structure and to sever the line of inheritance from Brand's mother by diverting the money away from her family and into the church. The church is not named in memory of Brand's mother, and when Brand throws the keys into the river, he disowns the building. Building a church is not exactly scattering the fortune to the winds, but it is also not memorial architecture in the traditional sense of the word, since it functions as a deceptive façade for its true purpose.

By contrast, Mrs. Alving's orphanage project clearly claims memorial status. Its official name, as mentioned earlier, is "The Captain Alving Memorial [*Kaptejn Alvings minde*],"[99] Like Brand's church, the Alving orphanage has been financed by inheritance money precisely to use it up, to prevent all continuity from one generation to the next. In addition to the many instabilities in nomenclature discussed previously, however, there is also this central irony about the Alving orphanage: it is a memorial structure that is designed to make people forget. Or rather, by memorializing the "benefactor" version of Alving, the structure forces a forgetfulness of the other Captain Alving, the drunken lecher. Mrs. Alving is counting on the decoy effects of her memorial project to "squelch all rumors" and to make it as if "the dead [man] had never lived in this house."[100] Her memorial orphanage is intended to be like a cairn of rocks that nails the *genganger* to the earth outside the house, never to walk or cross the threshold again.

What is not often noted about Mrs. Alving's orphanage project, however, is its obsessive aspect: it is not just a single building. When Manders reads from the official papers, we are told that an entire section of the

Rosenvold estate, the Solvik farm, has been the construction site for an entire complex of buildings connected to the new orphanage: "dormitories, a schoolhouse, a teacher's residence, and a chapel."[101] It is easy to lose track of how many buildings are involved, especially when the orphanage burns at the end of Act Two. Of six consulted English translations, all of them speak of the orphanage in the singular and translate Regine's line at the beginning of Act Three as if a solitary building were burning – Fjelde renders it as "it's burning still in the basement."[102] This choice obscures the fact that all of the buildings in this large complex have apparently burned to the ground, for in the Norwegian original the word "basements" is plural: *Det brænder endnu i kælderne.*[103]

It is worth dwelling on this picture of a devastating fire destroying an entire complex of buildings because the scope of the blaze gives a better picture of Mrs. Alving's sprawling architectural project. To spend every penny of the captain's fortune and clear the inheritance ledger for good, she has been erecting building after building for ten full years, spending until the money was gone. On the eve of the dedication, she has ended up with an extensive, fully functional orphanage complex with all the necessary interrelated parts. Even so, one senses that what she truly cares about is not the orphanage itself, but the corollary rededication of the main Rosenvold house as a newly purified home for herself and Osvald. When she says that she had "to fight with a vengeance [*kæmpe på liv og død*]" to keep the truth from coming out,[104] we might as well substitute "to *build* with a vengeance [*at bygge på liv og død*]," for that is how her desperate attempt to deceive the public has expressed itself: as one long, compulsive building project.

The eventual collapse of Mrs. Alving's housing complex, however, brings into focus a central characteristic of Ibsen's architectural imagination: buildings can be just as narrowly rhetorical as any narrative story. Mrs. Alving's orphanage is theatrical in the sense that she not only creates an elaborate stage set, but she also creates a fictional character to inhabit it, namely the deceased philanthropist, renovator, and innovator Captain Alving. It is around that imagined character that the orphanage is ostensibly built. If the building complex had actually been dedicated and opened on schedule, an ongoing future performance would have been set in motion around this fictional deceased protagonist as well, with Regine playing a supporting role as one of the staff. Mrs. Alving would have known that all of the participants would have simply been "playing" orphanage; no matter how realistically convincing the scene, she would always have known the backstage view and true purpose of the buildings, namely to forget the captain as he really was.

An architecture of forgetting

Although Mrs. Alving thus starts the play as a master builder, her motivations for building have always been deceptive in nature, whether when carrying out the renovations in the captain's name or building the memorial to a false memory. The dramatic action of the play concerns the collapse of this elaborate façade structure. The architectural decoy fails, the buildings burn to the ground, and Mrs. Alving loses all interest in the building projects that have occupied her for the previous twenty years of fictional dramatic time. Manders, who through the end of the play continues to live in the world where real estate still matters, speculates to the very end on how to sell the remaining land and what to do with the proceeds. Mrs. Alving, by contrast, has left her building days behind. She responds to Manders's suggestions of how to dispose of the property by saying listlessly, "Do what you will. The whole thing doesn't matter to me at all now."[105]

Given the irresistible force of the past in Ibsen's dramatic world, given its power to force its way through both façades and surfaces, it is probably not surprising that Mrs. Alving's memorial project failed. As a matter of fact, given how disastrous the suppression of past truths usually is in Ibsen's plays, it is hard to think of anything less likely to turn out well than a memorial. The partial, idealized version of past lives and events that characterizes most memorials puts them in the same company as all the other deceptive stories Ibsen's characters tell about themselves and their past, but with a memorial the story is set in stone.

A culminating example of the architecture of forgetting comes from *John Gabriel Borkman*. There the memorial takes a strikingly different form, yet it is so functionally similar to Mrs. Alving's memorial project that it is difficult not to read them side by side. In the earlier play, one of the terms for the Alving memorial was *hædersmindet*;[106] translated literally, this would be "memory of honor." Here in this late play from 1896, the word in question is *mindesmærke*. It shows up in Act Three of the text, after Borkman has finally come down from his upstairs confinement of eight years. His wife Gunhild, in her first conversation with him in the same number of years, describes her attempt to wipe out all memory of him and his actions:

GUNHILD: (without listening to her) I'll raise the monument [*mindesmærket*] over your grave.
BORKMAN: The pillar of shame [*Skamstøtten*], I suppose you mean?[107]

The word *skamstøtten* ("the pillar of shame") is an uncommon word in Norwegian – it is not in the current dictionary of *bokmål* and is in the older

Norsk Riksmålsordbok only in reference to this same line in *John Gabriel Borkman*.[108] It should not be considered an Ibsenian neologism, however, as it is by contrast a quite common word in modern Danish. The main reason for the difference is historical, namely that a famous pillar of shame was erected in Copenhagen in 1663 to disgrace the Danish traitor Corfitz Ulfeldt, who was accused of plotting against Frederik III while abroad in Germany. Since he was sentenced *in absentia*, an effigy was mock-executed in his place, his house was razed to the ground, and a monument to his shame was erected on the spot with the inscription on four sides: "Corfitz WF Ulfeldt / The Traitor / For Eternal Derision / Shame and Infamy [*Corfitz WF (Ulfeldt) / Forræderen / Til ævig Spott / Skam og Skændsel*]." In the years 1664 to 1842, the square called Ulfeldts Plads in Copenhagen featured this pillar of shame, which, in keeping with its intended task of "eternal derision," was even reconstructed once after it was destroyed in the Copenhagen fire of 1728. It was eventually moved to the courtyard of the National Museum (Figures 14–15), and its former location is now called Gråbrødretorv, the renaming ironically contradicting the previous nomenclature's intended "eternal" memorial intentions.[109]

Ibsen may have seen the Ulfeldt pillar of shame at the National Museum in Copenhagen in the late nineteenth century; he may also have encountered the idea in Germany, where the *Schandsäule* was known from the seventeenth century forward, or in Italy, where a *colonna infame* from the early 1600s received a famous depiction at the pen of the Italian author Alessandro Manzoni in 1840.[110] Whatever the source, elements of the cultural practice resonate well with Borkman's situation as a disgraced embezzler. He imagines Gunhild constructing a pillar of shame that would demand something like the "eternal derision" of the Ulfeldt *skamstøtte*. He asks if her idea is to create a marker of stone (Ulfeldt's is made of granite) that would memorialize his shame and ensure his infamy throughout future generations. In addition, since the pillar of shame generally stood in for a house that had been razed as a warning, never to be built up again, it has a certain substitute architectural logic in addition to its more obvious sculptural qualities. Moreover, Borkman's dispossessed, voluntary incarceration for eight years in the upstairs apartment of what is now Ella Rentheim's house and the impossibility of his owning property again echo the kind of "unhousing" implicit in the practice of constructing pillars of shame. Were Gunhild to follow through on the kind of project that Borkman imagines, she too could be a master builder of the Helene Alving variety, though clearly not with the decoy intent of preserving a false

Figure 14: The Pillar of Shame erected for Corfitz Ulfeldt (1664/1728). Located at The National Museum of Denmark (Copenhagen).

Figure 15: Close-up of the base of the Pillar of Shame.
Source: National Museum of Denmark (Copenhagen).

memory of her husband. Instead, she simply wants all memory of him to disappear, to be eclipsed by the reputation of Borkman's rehabilitated son.

Gunhild refuses that kind of project, however. The monument she imagines is not a pillar of shame; instead, it will be of a more curious sort, a *mindesmærke* designed for forgetting:

> GUNHILD: Oh no, it won't be a monument of stone or metal. And nobody will be allowed to scratch some derogatory inscription into the monument I will raise. There will be planted something like a cluster of living hedge, of trees and bushes so tight, tight around your gravelife. All the darkness that once *was* will be covered over. Hidden in forgetfulness [*Skjules i glemsel*] for the eyes of all people, John Gabriel Borkman![III]

There are several intriguing revisions here of the earlier notion of memorial we saw in *Ghosts*. First of all, Gunhild's comments convey an understanding of the limitations of permanent materials for a memorial. Suppose that she, like Mrs. Alving, were to create an idealized version of the financier Borkman and immortalize it in stone to counteract his current shame (if one were to match the false image of the benefactor Captain Alving, one can even imagine an appropriate Napoleonic pose of Borkman caught at the height of his wealth and influence, since he models that himself in Act Two). Even if she did that, however, there would be nothing to stop someone else from coming along with an alternative, negative memory and using the same permanent materials to immortalize a parallel "derogatory inscription." Similarly, even a monument to shame made of "permanent" materials could shift meaning with new cultural contexts (one pillar of shame erected to a Protestant heretic in Germany actually turned into an honorific memorial when the Reformation finally arrived in that area).[112] The permanence of the stone or metal itself cannot control shifts in contextual meaning or future rhetorical juxtapositions.

Instead, Gunhild imagines that Borkman's "grave-life" will be covered over by a "living hedge," a tangled mass of vegetation that will grow so fast and luxuriantly that it will soon overwhelm all traces of the dead man. This is a new and bold assault on the power of the past: the line reads, "All the darkness that once *was* will be covered over," with emphasis on the past tense of the verb. Gunhild Borkman's memorial is not even ostensibly designed to remember, but instead to forget the dead completely and utterly: an "architecture of forgetting," indeed, and with a vengeance. But her project has noticeably also substituted natural means for the more straightforwardly architectural; her plan seems to indicate that to truly forget, one actually has to leave the idea of built structure completely behind, that is, to forget architecture. In this gesture, we sense Ibsen's own reckoning with the limits of built structure in this, his last play to feature a house as its setting.

Conclusion

Ibsen the Architect: as it should now be clear, there is more to that idea than the (sometimes begrudging) admiration of Ibsen's workmanlike playwriting skills or his technical mastery of the stage. Instead, this study has shown how Ibsen transformed the consensus architectural metaphors of his day to unsettle his readers and viewers and to dislodge them from habits of thought. He created a cumulative drama of architectural unease. His unhomely plays depict characters in various stages of detachment from their formerly secure dwellings, some who mourn their loss, some who renovate and rebuild, and others who imagine existence beyond architectural limits. Taken together, however, Ibsen's contemporary prose dramas constitute a sustained and meticulous argument against the notion that domestic comfort and security are the highest human aspirations. The fact that he argues this point so painstakingly should be taken as an indication of both the dominance and pervasive invisibility of that cultural assumption.

Using the house as his main artistic medium, Ibsen turned ideal homes into "mere homes." Or to state his accomplishment even more dramatically, he made it possible for his readers and viewers to think of catastrophic fires as "merely catastrophic fires," and to think of the loss of home as a liberation from the past. "It's just the old house burning down – now turn to the future," he seems to urge his readers and viewers. As these propositions play out in his entire series of fictional houses, however, he seems to arrive at the impasse that the "old home" – the structures of *Ghosts*, *Rosmersholm*, and *The Master Builder*, for instance – is not shaken off so easily. In play after play, those who would liberate themselves from architectural constraint realize most often that the emotional tug of home does not yield unproblematically to forward-looking human plans. His dramatic characters might throw open curtains and windows, slam doors, renovate, tear down, or even wish for castastrophe, but somehow the home as a psychosocial structure keeps on returning to them in *unheimlich* ways. For his characters, homelike thinking proves to be strangely resilient, outliving the various breaks with the domestic that they experience. Even those characters who would rather leave home completely behind often remain in crucial ways marked by home: home-*less* rather than home-*free*.

Nevertheless, Ibsen's dramatic world forced into existence a cultural space for thinking about alternative modes of inhabitation: about the competing varieties of homes; about the architectural impediments to individual freedom; about how to detach from and (perhaps) reattach to domestic space; and about new, as yet unbuilt structures and what they might look like. He was more than willing to entertain the possibility that behind the façade or underneath the apparently solid foundations, there was only "the great nothing," as his character Ulrik Brendel put it in *Rosmersholm*.[1] Or as several of Ibsen's commentators noted repeatedly, Ibsen seemed to be claiming that underneath all might be one giant sinkhole. At the same time, however, Ibsen kept returning to the idea of built structure, as if to test whether there might not after all be some strategy that does not house the individual in a subordinating or confining way, and by extension, whether there might not be some room for the individual in given social structures and institutions, a way of inhabiting the house strategically. This repeated thematic return to architectural thinking might be proof of Ibsen's intellectual tenacity, of his desire to exhaust an entire range of dramatic permutations of the same basic question; conversely, it might be seen as an empty or compulsive repetition, more a symptom of Ibsen's own personal homelessness than an intellectual virtue. To understand Ibsen's architectural imagination is to give full play to both explanations. Clearly, all of this takes one considerably beyond the view of Ibsen as a simple technician of banal domestic realism. House and home, as Ibsen depicts them, are much more complex issues that resonate in multiple ways with the complex experience of mobility and belonging in the world, even today.

Ibsen's thoroughgoing strategy of architectural "unsettling" was in many ways a central intellectual precondition for the culture of modernity. His attack on the central values of nineteenth-century domesticity – the invisible but consensus priority given to notions of shelter, safety, comfort, patriarchy, tradition, historical continuity, and rootedness – called into question the conceptual foundations of home and family. By questioning the typically unquestioned cultural authority of the hearth, he loosened the automatic connection between home and happiness and facilitated the imagination of new ways of "taking place" that were no longer so ensconced in the home and its various ideological entanglements. The fact that these ideas were put forward in the conditional mode of drama on stage, precisely as character *positions* in a fictional architectural space, should not lead one to underestimate their cultural influence. At the height of Ibsen's fame in the 1880s and 90s, members of the European literary public read each new Ibsen play in a remarkably coordinated and simultaneous act of reception. Especially in the Nordic region, they formed a shared literary culture that for a time collectively devoted its attention to thinking through the problems of Ibsen's imaginary buildings and their inhabitants. Many of those housing scenarios, such as the idea of the inauthentic gender relations of the "dollhouse" or of the "master builder" tragically exceeding his natural limits, have left deep tracks in Western culture and beyond.

Architectural metaphor was an accepted *lingua franca* of Ibsen's day, even if the metaphoric domains were debated. In a time of rapid social transitions and the accelerating transformation of urban environments, the participants in late nineteenth-century social debates saw in architectural imagery the condensation of many contradictory aspects of their own experience: the appealing security of middle-class material comfort, regrets about imagined lost origins, the exhilaration of the new, the claustrophobia of rigidly supervised interiors, the liberated mobility of cities, and the rapidly shifting boundaries between public and private. From the entire range of possible metaphors that might help interpret that social transformation, late nineteenth-century writers and cultural commentators turned frequently to building metaphors to articulate that experience. Foundations, façades, pillars, and doors were all active components in the metaphoric currency of the day. This shared metaphoric system was used as a means to persuade, cajole, defend, and object. No matter how fierce the cultural conflicts of the day, there was little questioning of the architectural basis of the discussion. Most agreed that such a concept as "the social building" indeed existed; what was debated were its qualities and its future.

Ibsen both shaped and was shaped by this discourse. He accepted the assumption that built structure was a key site of conflict for his age, and he spent his later career pushing and prodding, demolishing and burning, renovating and testing the limits of the social building in his dramatic writing. If he did not depict in detail the trajectories of those characters who left that structural haven in search of other alternatives, that omission was simply an indication that part of him remained ensconced in those same social structures and assumptions. At the same time, however, he pushed the discourse of architectural metaphor beyond its conventional limits. He asked his readers and viewers to accept the idea that ideals of homey *hygge* might be deceptively confining. He created vantage points from which to see model homes as museums of hypocrisy, to see the most confident defenders of hearth and home as deceived and stunted. He asked readers to see the intellectual value of being lost, or of leaving, or of traveling. He described impossible, contradictory structures – castles in the air – that might replace the newly evacuated homes. And he wondered vicariously, through characters such as Hilde and Maja, whether there might be ways to conceive of ironic, strategic forms of inhabitation.

The idea that Ibsen both used and was used by the thought structures of his day comes through in perhaps the most extended architectural metaphor in all of Ibsen criticism, a summation in 1960 by the renowned Ibsen scholar James McFarlane:

> As an architect of drama, Ibsen built with the materials of his age; he displays to view a great deal of grey, massive, solid masonry; but at the same time he appears to be doing astonishing things with his conventional material, to be reaching heights of sublime humdrum, to be performing abnormal feats of normality, to be operating within a style of extravagant sobriety. At times his drama seems tremendously firm and monumental, at other times recklessly audacious and top-heavy; it is only on closer inspection, when one has worked out the hidden architecture, that one realizes how extraordinarily steely it all is, how spendthrift even in its strength. When one looks at the plans, sees from the drafts and sketches (especially of some of the later plays) the meticulous process of re-designing that went on, one realizes that behind and within the outer cladding there is concealed a frame of invention of the highest tensile strength; one discovers not only the pillars of load-bearing realism but also a steel skeleton of poetic imagination. One sees how he shored up the fabric with further devices; buttresses of precise and meaningful stage-direction, scaffoldings of symbolism, motifs that appear decorative but which on examination are discovered also to be taking part of the strain, until the whole thing is braced and strutted into complete rigidity. Only thus was Ibsen to use so imaginatively such unimaginative language, to compose dialogue that is so unnaturally natural, to make such a vivid impression with creations so uncompromisingly monochrome.[2]

Because the dominant metaphor worth discussing for Ibsen and his contemporaries was "society is a building," this subsidiary metaphor of "Ibsen's plays are buildings" had easy currency in Ibsen's day, as was suggested earlier in this book's Introduction. When Ibsen's contemporaries assessed his dramaturgy, the "used" part of the building metaphor domain was the idea of careful design and solidity, suggesting that when the plays were put under pressure by readers and viewers, hidden structures of considerable ingenuity would reveal themselves. Mixed in with those qualities in the use of the play-as-building metaphor by Ibsen's contemporaries were architectural values such as imposing scale, beauty, and verticality that linked to the more abstract ideas of Ibsen's fame and renown at the time.

In the passage just quoted, McFarlane pursues the same play-as-building metaphor, but in a way that makes clear the later twentieth-century shifts in Ibsen's reputation. McFarlane's admiration for Ibsen here is expressed with a great deal of the double-voicing representing a different view that had consolidated after the passage of later, more daring experiments in twentieth-century modern drama, namely that Ibsen was a workmanly and skillful playwright, but that his plays were too tied to nineteenth-century form to be of much enduring modern interest. The terms in McFarlane's passage representing that position pile up in this way: "grey," "massive," "solid," "conventional," "humdrum," "normality," "sobriety," "unimaginative," and "monochrome." Using the play-as-building metaphor, McFarlane uses the familiar rhetorical contrast between façade and interior to claim that once invited inside the play by a skillful critic, the reader or viewer will discover an architectonic excitement in the construction design. Although McFarlane concedes the exterior appearance, namely that Ibsen *seems* boring, stodgy, and uninteresting when seen from more modern perspectives, he asserts that the view behind the surface of an Ibsen play, the critic's view from inside the structure, reveals the intellectual rigor behind a seemingly ordinary surface.

The Introduction noted that linguistic theories of metaphor typically make distinctions between the "used" and "unused" qualities of the source domain, which in the society-as-building metaphor would concern the possible features of a building. Ibsen's contribution to a larger discourse of the social building in late nineteenth-century Scandinavia was incomplete in the sense that his use of this conceptual metaphor was inevitably limited by the partial metaphoric utilization that characterizes all figurative speech. The analysis of the preceding chapters has made it possible to suggest more precisely what Ibsen meant when he told the painter Erik Werenskiold that architecture was his "profession." Rather than simply accepting Ibsen's statement as a clever paradox, it is worth pushing further by asking what kind "architecture" Ibsen practiced. Since he was obviously speaking metaphorically, what was the subset of the potential meanings that attracted Ibsen to thinking so consistently about buildings?

First of all, when Ibsen foregrounded an architectural consciousness, it was domestic architecture that interested him most, that is, homes and the challenges they present to the development of free individuals. Although Brand's church was not a domestic structure, there too the central question was one of fit between the size of the soul and the shape of the structure, so questions of inhabitation were front and center. That question only intensified in Ibsen's later prose plays when fit was measured not in terms of souls, but of increasingly complex modern personalities instead. Of all the available architectural expressions – civic buildings, commercial structures, religious edifices, and so on – it was the home that interested Ibsen most consistently because domestic architecture forces to the forefront questions of dwelling, inhabitation, and fit between subject and space.

Ibsen's interrogation of the home was dominated by a deep distrust of *hygge*. It was not so much a simple question of a pessimistic temperament as it was his belief that homey values often fronted for other less admirable attitudes, such as deception, mediocrity, fear-driven provincialism, patriarchal control, and conformity of thought. The creation of comfort always requires the delineation of protective boundaries, a sharp distinction between inside and outside. Ibsen's own experience between home and abroad for twenty-seven years left him suspicious of the insider thinking that *hygge* required. Some of the most ardent fictional defenders of homey comfort in his plays (Helmer in *A Doll House* and Kroll in *Rosmersholm* are only two examples) are thus portrayed as a kind of purity police protecting the home from the polluting spirit of discord. *Hygge* emerges as an obliquely coercive form of power in many of the plays.

Ibsen also found *hygge* to be falsely theatrical, an effect of staging every bit as contrived as the family tableau Rummel prepares in *Pillars of Society*. *Hygge* for Ibsen was a family game, an illusionist performance that could be halted at any moment by the breaking of the spell. Whether that rupture comes from a glance in the mirror, as it did in the poem "From My Domestic Life," or from the intrusion of an outsider like Gregers, as in *The Wild Duck*, it is clear that Ibsenian *hygge* depends for its effects on a tenuous suspension of disbelief by all involved. *Hygge* is not fully *real* for Ibsen, but something that can only be performed under certain conditions. The fact that it distracts from a clear-eyed view of the house's actual circumstances is its greatest drawback.

Ibsen also saw in domestic architecture the means to examine the "givenness" of social structures. As he emphasized in his autobiographical fragment, he was born into the world as an always-already "architectural" subject surrounded by built structures. For Ibsen's emerging sense of self, the architectural environment defined the parameters of what *was* much more strongly than it did what *could be*. One senses even in that account of his earliest memories a nascent protest against the fact that existence in some basic sense defines itself as an architectural predicament: one becomes conscious within a structure not of one's own making. Buildings in this way became for him the perfect expression of the social limits of the "found" world; they presented him with a structure to push against.

Taking this line of thought further, we can see that architecture for Ibsen was pure persistence. Rapidly evolving individuals in his plays, members of society's "advance troops" such as Nora, Mrs. Alving, Stockmann, Rebekka West, and others, necessarily outgrow the structures that house them. Ibsen's prose dramas, in fact, showcase an entire series of ill-fitting houses that have not adapted appropriately to the changes experienced by their occupants. The architecture itself repeatedly proves to be resistant to renovation and change; Ibsen's houses are rigid, ungiving structures that outlast the needs of their inhabitants. Since Ibsen does not view architecture as pliant and adaptable (coming as he did before the period of modular modernism), it can serve evocatively in his dramas as the emblem of an overly persistent past.

The famous "ghosts" of Ibsen's dramas are in this sense not simply dead characters who will not give up their place in life, but they are inherent in the very idea of persistent structure itself. When Mrs. Alving generalizes from the problems of family repetition to society at large, she is talking about the social building, about the way that all kinds of "structures of thought" (itself an inescapably architectural metaphor) persist rigidly despite dramatic changes in those who are left thinking them. Ibsen's houses are simply the most intimate and familiar of those structures of thought.

Ibsen was also quick to emphasize the rhetorical status of built structure. Despite the size and scale of the imagined objects in question, Ibsen understood the ways in which buildings could be enlisted for a partial and strategic form of storytelling. The deceptive façades of the Bernick, Helmer, and Alving homes are prime examples of this, as is the polluted health spa in *An Enemy of the People*, but the sheer size of these projects magnifies the effects of the deception. A project such as Brand's church, or Mrs. Alving's twenty-year expansion of the Rosenvold property, or Halvard Solness's never-ending series of "homes for people," cannot be undertaken casually. Because these characters' described architectural projects are imagined to have been played out on a large public stage using weighty and extensive materials, when the projects are unmasked, one is left amazed at the scale of the decoy and the determined, obsessive effort of the deception. That is the figural advantage of architecture over writing as an activity for a fictional character.

One might also refine the specific sense of Ibsen's architecture by asking what it is not. Looking for Ibsen's architectural opposite in the plays yields many answers. This is only to be expected in theatrical texts, for Ibsen's whole point in dramatizing the architectural dilemmas of modernity is to enact different scenarios and character temperaments on stage to see where they might plausibly lead. So for Brand, architecture's opposite is a sense of the absolute, untinged by material compromise. For Nora Helmer, it is a free space in which individuals can develop an authentic individualism. For Mrs. Alving, it is a future family existence uncontaminated by the past. Dr. Stockmann, who seems as much an enemy of architecture as he is of the people, apparently comes to see all built structure as a cover-up for the truth. Dr. Relling, for whom architecture is the necessary deception that shelters the weak from reality, sees only vulnerability and destruction for the Ekdals of the world who venture outside the home. Ulrik Brendel sees only "the great nothing" in life outside the house. Rosmer and Rebekka West find exactly that in their own rejection of Rosmersholm's "shelter" – beyond that house lies their mystical death. For a time, Ellida Wangel thinks she sees a radical freedom beyond architecture, out in the open sea, but she eventually finds the means to reconcile herself to the limits of built structure, while Hedda Gabler does not even entertain the thought of life on the outside, no matter how extreme her entrapment. Hilde and Solness stretch the limits of architectural structure, but ultimately he, at least, cannot leave it behind. For Maja and Rubek in *When We Dead Awaken*, architecture's opposite is the restless, mobile life we see on stage, far from their reported homes down in Europe.

Although forcing together these summaries in this simplified way reduces the complexity of each individual play, the juxtaposition nevertheless helps point to a cumulative answer to the question of what lies beyond architecture – for Ibsen, that is. The next step, however, would be to leave behind Ibsen's particular assumptions and to recover a wider, contrastive sense of possibility for thinking about built structure. The goal of the present study has primarily been to examine the dynamics of the Ibsenian discourse and to define the "architectural imagination" he put into play within his cultural context, but it will be helpful in closing to point suggestively to other trajectories leading out of the late nineteenth-century discussions of house and home, to think of aspects of the source domain of "architectural experience" that were suppressed or neglected in Ibsen's particular formulations.

The first would concern the resilient position that absorbed Ibsen's critique without accepting its extreme suspicion of architecture. There were many in this position – probably even the majority of Ibsen's contemporaries, as we have seen in the responses documented in this study.

For many of these participants in the cultural discourse of the day, nothing in the discussion of imaginary architectural structures necessarily entailed a real-life rejection of house and home. Ibsen's exploration of scenarios pushed their thinking and possibly dislodged the concepts of house and home from their previously natural status, but this was rarely accepted as inevitable in all of its pessimistic conclusions.

One might choose from any number of examples to illustrate this point, but it might be most instructive to follow a particular metaphoric image out from an Ibsen play into the surrounding discourse. The idea of "homes for people" in *The Master Builder* is a particularly rich intersection of competing architectural imaginations set in motion by Ibsen's writing and for the purposes of this conclusion can stand in for broader patterns. One that comes directly from the discussion of the day within theatrical circles is a play written by Ågot Gjems Selmer, a feminist writer who began her career on the stage at the Christiania Theater in the mid-1870s (she even played the role of Petra there in a production of *An Enemy of the People* in 1883). She married and moved to North Norway that same year and subsequently became a playwright and author of children's books as she raised her family. Obviously fluent in the Ibsenian discourse of homes and houses, she wrote a play called *A Home for People* (*Et Hjem for Mennesker*) in 1901.

The title takes Halvard Solness's empty slogan and refills it with more positive content. The action concerns a woman, Edle Halmrast, who has given up a promising singing career in the city to marry and move to a remote rural district where her husband is a well-to-do farmer. The more the life suits him there, the less it suits her, and the play explores the conflict that arises when she realizes that she must recover her lost artistic outlet in the larger world. During the final confrontation scene (which in its arrangement strongly echoes that of *A Doll House*), Edle offers up this definition of "homes for people":

> No – a *home for people*, where personalities can grow up straight and cheerful, must open up all windows to the sunny side of its own being, there where the individual life's sunshine streams in and radiates. *Only then* will the rooms be warmed by the sun, [only then] will there be strength in the roots of character – and in such spiritually lively homes for people [*slige aandelig vaagne menneskehjem*], where women are allowed to live *their own* lives, *they also*, there you can be sure that both young people and husbands would rather be than in any other place on earth.³

Like Helene Butenschøn, Selmer was a devotee of italics, so it is not difficult to locate the privileged terms in this passage. She offers up a view in which architectural constraint is completely reconcilable to individual growth. The home is imagined as a much more pliable structure that can be spiritually awakened when it is turned toward the sun (one might note that this was not equally helpful in Ibsen's *Ghosts*). Furthermore, this house is imagined as a structure in which individuals can grow up straight and true, as long as they are given a degree of free choice.

This seems close to the position Nora or Ellida might take; but all the talk of spiritual awakening strikes one as foreign to the Ibsenian world. Indeed, after husband and wife are reconciled in a flexible arrangement that allows Edle to travel and return at will, the idea of "homes for people" takes on a positively visionary status, here described to her daughter Else near the end of the play:

> I – can't explain it – Else – everything all at once has become so bright and beautiful – so new – amazing – a reflection of something far off – it is something I *see* almost rising up far down in the south – in the sunlight, a *home for people* [*et* hjem for mennesker] in the garden of happiness, where two personalities are free to grow straight upwards in freedom – to a delicious tree of life with only goodness.[4]

Seeing something so lofty emerge from a phrase that Ibsen himself put into play in the cultural discourse of the day as an ironic sign of disillusionment and self-deception almost makes one do a double take. Didn't Ibsen empty out that concept completely? For those who would overestimate the efficacy of Ibsen's deconstruction and evacuation of the home, this play from 1901, at the dawn of the post-Ibsenian era, provides one kind of counterexample. Selmer's response to Ibsen has absorbed his vocabulary, his plot devices, and his critical impulse, but it proceeds from quite different intellectual assumptions and application of architectural metaphor. Her ideology of the home bends without breaking.

Obviously, however, there are reasons why Ibsen is read today and Selmer is not. My point is simply to emphasize the value in reading a contemporaneous piece of drama that positions itself so consciously *adjacent* to Ibsen's housing metaphor without reaching the same conclusions. Selmer's sentimental articulation of house and home is not as complex, or as deconstructive, or ultimately as resonant as Ibsen's is for modern thinking, but this kind of play gives one a useful sense of the pockets of resistance to Ibsen's thought and the modernity it represents, a sense of one world that continued on apparently unperturbed outside his particular (and more intellectually influential) architectural imagination. The source domain of architectural experience of the day also made room for competing articulations of the "homes for people" metaphor.

A second example provides a fascinating interart example in the case of the Frenchman Henry Provensal's relationship to Ibsen's architectural imagination because he follows a trajectory almost entirely the reverse of Ibsen's. Provensal was trained as an architect but also considered himself a painter, a watercolorist, a sculptor, and an author. Working just after the turn of the twentieth century, Provensal imagined synesthetic, fantastic structures in poster paint and watercolor, such as *Dream Project* or *A Tomb for a Poet* from 1901.[5] Many of his art nouveau–inspired, oneiric ideas were gathered in a theoretical treatise published in French in 1904, *L'Art de Demain: Vers l'Harmonie Intégrale* (The Art of Tomorrow: Towards Integrated Harmony).[6] During this period in his career, in 1902 (a year after Selmer's play was published), he painted a piece that reflects his similar fascination with Ibsen's 1892 play *The Master Builder*. The title of the painting is *La Maison de Solness le Constructeur* (The Home of Solness, the Master Builder), and it was exhibited at the Société Nationale des Beaux-Arts exhibition in 1903 (Figure 16).

Provensal clearly recognized in Ibsen's play the same kind of oneiric building that he had been imagining in his previous work – a structure that would combine the idea of a "home for people," as Solness keeps saying in the play, with a church and a "castle in the air with a firm foundation," as Solness and Hilde imagine it together. Provensal's "home of Solness" contains elements of each. The depicted structure emerges directly from the rock beneath it yet seems to hover in the air. Hilde Wangel would be pleased – it is as if Provensal delivered in his painting what Solness did not in the play: "Castle on the table!" [*slottet på bordet!*].[7] And further, like the many churches the master builder is described as having built in the play, the "home of Solness" depicted here has a front portal, rows of what look like stained-glass windows, and a church tower, which cannot help but give the painting an ominous feel when one knows the ending of the play. But in what sense is this the *home* of Solness as well, as the title suggests? The smoke curling from a chimney, an incongruous element for a church, carries the whole visual weight of inhabitation in the painting, the only indication that people are also dwelling inside. (This smoke is the main contrast with his "The Tomb of a Poet" painted the year before, which showed an entirely vacant structure, even though it shares a general style with the master builder painting.) The way the chimney competes with the church tower for attention in Provensal's imagination of the Solness home conveys the unresolved hybridity of the structure: it is both church and home at the same time. The dark palette Provensal employs further creates a murky embodiment of the epistemological uncertainty of the architectural figures Solness and Hilde call into being in their conversations.

Figure 16: Henry Provensal, *La Maison de Solness le Constructeur* (1902). (RF 2005 6)

This is an extremely apt representation of the implied composite structure that develops throughout the cumulative discussion between Solness and Hilde in Ibsen's play, a fusion of the master builder's past, present, and future building activity. It shows that Provensal thought deeply about the described architecture of the play, perhaps because he recognized in Ibsen a fellow practitioner of the architectural arts. He clearly understood and to some extent shared the architectural imagination of this late Ibsen play, because he managed to depict the impossible structure that emerges in conversation there. It is the most striking representation of *The Master Builder*'s architecture that I have seen.

The turn Provensal's career subsequently took, however, seems like Solness's life in reverse; in 1905, he got an appointment in Paris as adjunct architect to the Rothschild Foundation, a health organization created to promote good vision through hygiene. In its fight against tuberculosis, it sponsored the design of clean and affordable housing for the working classes, and Provensal responded to the call. In 1907, he even assumed leadership of the foundation and in 1908 published a new, very different kind of architectural treatise, *Clean and Affordable Housing (L'Habitation Salubre et à Bon Marché)*.[8] This work indicates a new direction of Provensal's architectural imagination, namely a view that was politically progressive and pragmatic at the same time. In other words, Provensal turned in reality to the activity Ibsen's master builder claimed to have pursued earlier in his career, building "homes for people," but here in a more straightforward, positive sense, without Ibsen's equivocation. An illustration for the frontispiece of the 1908 book shows traces of Provensal's earlier art nouveau dreaminess in the ornamentation along the front of the building, but with ample windows all the way around the building signaling the access to light and air that hygienic housing would require. Curling smoke from the chimney seems once again to be the sign of inhabitation, a carry-over from the *The Master Builder* painting, but with the difference that it no longer signals paradoxical hybridity, but instead the practical project of comfortable, clean, and affordable housing.

The juxtaposition of Ibsen and Provensal underscores the importance of seeing "imagination" as a collective dynamic. When Ibsen's architectural imagination is taken as an isolated authorial phenomenon, his implicit metaphors carry a logic of inevitability, an effect amplified by his subsequent literary reputation. His growing architectural skepticism might even come to be seen as a natural and necessary progression of thought. Widening the idea of architectural imagination to the level of shared discourse, however, in which many metaphoric systems interact and collectively show the variety of experiences that are possible, demonstrates the rhetorical nature of any particular imagination of the architectural. At one point, the late Ibsen and early Provensal converged, but then the Frenchman moved on to a successful career actually building homes for people, so Ibsen's play apparently did not convince him in any permanent or fundamental way. Thus, one can see the ways in which the contest of metaphors implicit in a shared cultural imagination pits experience against experience, with neither inherently more legitimate than the other.

A further example from architectural modernism in the late 1920s, when architecture and design had returned to the forefront of Scandinavian avant-garde intellectual life, can extend this perspective. During this period of radical ferment, Scandinavian writers, architects, and designers imagined the reshaping of society through innovations in housing and building design. Their exhibitions, novels, manifestos, and designs laid the foundation for a new, confident application of architectural metaphor in the social democratic governments of the 1930s. This was after all the time of the "people's home [*folkhemmet*]" in Sweden, when the idea of a society built on rational design and collective values dominated intellectual as well as political life throughout the region. Once again, the architectural metaphor "society is a building" saturated the cultural discussion, but now driven by very different assumptions, with different qualities of the source domain ("building") going used and unused in the construction of the metaphor. Although these cultural radicals saw themselves as the direct heirs of the Modern Breakthrough writers and critics in Ibsen's day, their utter confidence in their ability to build for the future could not differ more sharply from the architectural pessimism of their predecessors.

These new cultural radicals assumed that built environments could not only house already existing modern personalities but could also actually train and produce them as well. Here is Edvard Heiberg, writing in the most important Danish design journal, *Kritisk Revy*, in 1927: "If the things that surround us in our homes are clear and logical, they will in turn help to create a truly modern culture in place of the current bastard culture. That will in turn entail more consistent people [*helstøbte Mennesker*]."[9] It is instructive that Heiberg finds nothing particularly *unheimlich* about a home that contains a mixture of furniture styles and contents from different, overlapping periods; it simply offends his sense of rational function. He has supreme modernist confidence in the ability of the present to master the past. This is quite some distance from Henrik Jæger's intense feeling of *Uhygge* when he encountered the "repulsive bastard room" at the Ekdal home on stage. It is also far removed from Ibsen's own assumptions about the inherent *genganger* aspects of architecture. Moreover, Heiberg's notion of rationally consistent (*helstøbte*) people is fundamentally different from Ibsen's view of the complex, overlapping layers of the human personality: as Rebekka West says in *Rosmersholm*, "But there is always something or other lingering on [*hængende*] inside that you can't free yourself from. That's the way we are."[10]

Heiberg's housing philosophy, like that of his modern-design colleagues, is by contrast confident and rational, a stance that allows the rhetoric of the home to take on new social functions. The "home" has clearly not been left behind simply because Ibsen had critiqued the idea so thoroughly; his metaphor use simply moved the discussion away from a naïve, instinctive use of the term. By 1927, thirty-five years after the fictional Halvard Solness was depicted reaching his creative degree zero of "nothing built, nothing at all," Heiberg could write:

> The home is a pedagogical cultural factor of the highest order. Healthy, rational, natural homes [*Sunde, fornuftige, naturlige Hjem*] will perhaps more than anything else have a hand in shaping our own culture today, in our own time. It is of the highest importance to have lived in a home that is a whole, not a collection of bits and pieces from all times and from all corners.[11]

What we find here is a culturally radical social philosophy that is entirely based in promoting the idea of home. It was a far different "home" than the one Ibsen critiqued, but it is remarkable to see just how robust the concept remains, beyond the time when Ibsen thought he had buried it once and for all. It is almost uncanny.

Notes

INTRODUCTION

1. Arne Garborg, "*Samfundets Støtter*," *Fedraheimen* (Christiania), October 27, 1877. All translations, unless otherwise referenced, are my own.
2. Arthur Bendixson, "Några Ord om Ibsens *Gengangere*," *Ny Svensk Tidskrift* (1881), 455.
3. Fedor Mamroth, *Aus der Frankfurter Theaterchronik (1889–1907)*, 2 vols. (Berlin: Egon Fleischel & Co., 1908), vol. 2, p. 330.
4. Karl Warburg, "Ibsens Nya Stycke," *Göteborgs Handels- och Sjöfartstidning* (Gothenburg), December 15, 1881.
5. S–e., "Hvad är Ibsens Mening i *Rosmersholm*? Ett Tolkningsförsöck," *Aftonbladet* (Stockholm), January 11, 1887.
6. Henrik Ibsen, "[Barndomsminner]," *HIS*, vol. 16.1, p. 496.
7. *HIS*, vol. 11.1, pp. 559–60. The image comes from Ibsen's poem "Til min Ven Revolutions-Taleren!" ("To my Friend, the Revolutionary Speaker," 1869), in which the poetic "I" proposes redoing the world's only true revolution – the Biblical flood – in a far more radical way by torpedoing the ark to ensure that no vestige of the old world remains.
8. Retrospective interview with Werenskiold in *Dagbladet* (Christiania), March 20, 1928, cited in Michael Meyer, *Ibsen: A Biography* (Garden City, NY: Doubleday & Co., Inc., 1971), p. 697.
9. Georg Brandes, "Henrik Ibsens *Digte*," *Illustreret Tidende* (October 22, 1871), 32.
10. *HIS*, vol. 11.1, p. 537. "Kongen han bygged / dagen lang. / Når natten skygged, / kom troldet og rygged / med spid og stang. // Så rejstes kirken / til spirets pil; / men kongens virken / og troldets lirken / gav dobbelt stil. // Døgn-folk flytted / dog ind i tro; / thi dags-udbyttet, / til nattens knyttet, / er *døgnets* jo."
11. "Døgnfolk," in Trygve Knudsen and Alf Sommerfelt (eds.), *Norsk Riksmålsordbok* (Oslo: Aschehoug, 1937), p. 798. Norwegian: "folk som bare lever i, har sans for nuets, hverdagens små begivenheder."
12. My thanks go to Vigdis Ystad for help in identifying the likely resonances of the term. There may be resonance with the term for "May fly" (*Døgnflue*) as

well, especially in the idea of living for the day, though here without the positive connotation of being carefree or happy-go-lucky.
13. In the Nordic countries, many legends address the problems that arise in the process of church building, such as the day's work being undone at night. Sometimes that is a sign that the wrong site has been chosen; at other times, the supernatural forces represented by trolls simply resist the building of a church. One common variant depicts the troll being tricked into building a church higher than would be humanly possible, only to be killed by the king speaking the troll's name out loud. See Henning Sehmsdorff, "Two Legends about St. Olaf, The Master Builder: A Clue to the Dramatic Structure of Henrik Ibsen's *Bygmester Solness*," *Edda* 54.4 (1967), 263–71; and Evald Tang Kristensen, *Danske Sagn som De har Lydt i Folkemunde*, 7 vols. (Copenhagen: Woels Forlag, 1931), vol. 3, pp. 112–39. My thanks also go to the participants in the Wildcat Canyon Advanced Seminar in Folklore and Cultural Studies for their lively interest in this poem and its sources.
14. Nina S. Alnæs offers a sustained reading of this poem and connects it to the themes and concerns of *The Master Builder* in her study of folkloric elements in Ibsen's writing, *Varulv om Natten: Folketro og Folkediktning hos Ibsen* (Oslo: Gyldendal Norsk Forlag, 2003), p. 360.
15. "A.," "Henrik Ibsens Drama *Rosmersholm*," *Aftenposten* (Christiania), November 24, 1886.
16. "Kristiania Theater. *Vildanden*," *Aftenposten* (Christiania), September 24, 1893.
17. Nils Kjær, "Ibsens Bog," *Dagbladet* (Christiania), December 12, 1894.
18. Nils Vogt, "*John Gabriel Borkman*," *Morgenbladet* (Christiania), December 24, 1896.
19. Bert O. States, *Great Reckonings in Little Rooms: On the Phenomenology of Theater* (Berkeley: University of California Press, 1992).
20. George Lakoff and Mark Johnson, *Metaphors We Live By* (University of Chicago Press, 1980), p. 52.
21. Ibid., pp. 10–13; Zoltán Kövecses, *Metaphor: A Practical Introduction*, Second Edition (Oxford University Press, 2010), pp. 91–106.
22. Ibid., pp. 121–33.
23. Lakoff and Johnson, *Metaphors We Live By*, pp. 52–53.
24. Astrid Sæther, *Suzannah: Fru Ibsen* (Oslo: Gyldendal Norsk Forlag, 2008).
25. See Halvdan Koht, *The Life of Ibsen*, 2 vols. (New York: W. W. Norton & Co., 1931), vol. 2, pp. 151–53; Mette Borg, "Her Tales ikke Dukkehjem: Omkring Urpremieren på Ibsens *Et Dukkehjem*," *Norsk Dramatisk Årbok* (1997), 16; and Tom Lerdrup Hansen, *Kampen omkring Nora: Et Dukkehjems Tilblivelse og det Modtagelse 1879–80* (Copenhagen: Gyldendal, 1988).
26. The review that set off the debate was a team review done in haste as soon as the newly published copies of the play hit the bookstores in Norway on November

11, 1884. The one-day turnaround time required a team review, with Ludvig Eriksen and Henrik Jæger combining efforts on reading and relaying the plot of the play before others could beat them to the punch: Ludvig Eriksen and Henrik Jæger, "Seneste Efterretniger," *Christiania Intelligenssedler* (Christiania), November 11, 1884. In response, Johan Irgens-Hansen, the Norwegian theater critic and director, came to the defense of more measured literary analysis in an article the following weekend that criticized the trend toward journalistic speed in reviews of Ibsen's plays, comparing the practice to "simultaneous impressions on a bicycle ride." Johan Irgens-Hansen, "Henrik Ibsen: *Vildanden*," *Dagbladet* (Christiania), November 16, 1884.

27. For a discussion of metonymic (vs. metaphoric) staging principles, see Freddie Rokem, *Theatrical Space in Ibsen, Chekhov, and Strindberg: Public Forms of Privacy*, Theater and Dramatic Studies 32 (Ann Arbor, MI: UMI Research Press, 1986), pp. 1–12.
28. "*Byggmester Solness* i Kjøbenhavn," *Bergens Tidende* (Bergen), March 13, 1893.
29. S–e., "Hvad är Ibsens Mening i *Rosmersholm*?" Original emphasis.
30. "Korrespondance til *Aftenposten*," *Aftenposten* (Christiania), December 24, 1879.
31. Ibid.
32. Sophie Adlersparre, *Gengangere ur Etisk Synpunkt: Föredrag Hållet i Stockholm Våren 1882* (Stockholm: Jos. Seligmann & Comp., 1882), pp. 2, 4–5, 8.
33. See, for example, Amalie Skram, "En Betragtning over *Et Dukkehjem*," *Dagbladet* (Christiania), January 19, 1880 and "Mere om *Gengangere*," *Dagbladet* (Christiania), April 27, 1882; for a more conservative female voice, see Helene Dickmar, "Henrik Ibsen: Bygmester Solness," *To Litterære Studier* (Christiania: H. Aschehoug &Co., 1895), pp. 24–75.
34. Ibsen's comment in the originally sketched notes for *A Doll House* in October 1878 was "A woman cannot be herself in today's society, which is an exclusively masculine society, with laws written by men and with prosecutors and judges who evaluate feminine behavior from a male standpoint." *HIS* 7.2, p. 191.
35. For the best discussion of the gender issues related to metaphor use in *The Wild Duck*, see Joan Templeton, *Ibsen's Women* (Cambridge University Press, 1997), pp. 166–80.
36. Margareta Wirmark, *Noras Systrar: Nordisk Dramatik och Teater 1879–99* (Stockholm: Carlssons Bokförlag, 2000).
37. Rebecca Cameron, "Ibsen and British Women's Drama," *Ibsen Studies* 4.1 (2004), 92–102.
38. To make that point, Wirmark sketches a quick comparison of a series of rooms on stage taken from the dramatic production of male and female Nordic dramatists in the 1880s and 90s. This section, entitled "Ett Eget

Rum" (A Room of One's Own), tests the connection between character and fictional rooms and demonstrates another way in which Ibsen's architectural sensibility might resonate further throughout a discourse of theater production and writing. Wirmark, *Noras Systrar*, pp. 116–24.

1 IBSEN'S UNCANNY

1. Nicholas Royle, *The Uncanny* (Manchester University Press, 2003), pp. 1–2.
2. Ibid., pp. 3–8.
3. Ibid., pp. 12–17. See also Sigmund Freud, "The 'Uncanny' (1919)," in James Strachey (ed.), *The Standard Edition of the Complete Psychological Works of Sigmund Freud*, 24 vols. (London: Hogarth Press, 1953–74), vol. 17, pp. 217–56.
4. Ibid., p. 347.
5. Ibid., p. 342.
6. Anthony Vidler, *The Architectural Uncanny: Essays in the Modern Unhomely* (Cambridge, MA: The MIT Press, 1992), pp. 3–10.
7. See, for example, Jo Collins and John Jervis (eds.), *Uncanny Modernity: Cultural Theories, Modern Anxieties* (New York: Palgrave Macmillan, 2008). Interestingly, a contemporary collection of short stories written in uncanny style has also found resonance in the recent literary market: Sarah Eyre and Ra Page (eds.), *The New Uncanny: Tales of Unease* ([Manchester]: Comma Press, 2008).
8. Vidler, *The Architectural Uncanny*, p. 9.
9. Sigmund Freud, "Some Character-Types Met with in Psychoanalytic Work (1916)," in Strachey (ed.), *Standard Edition*, vol. 14, pp. 308–16.
10. Unni Langås, "Fascinasjon og Uhygge: Kunsten og Døden som Kvinne i Ibsens Drama *Når vi døde vågner*," *Tidskrift för Litteraturvetenskap* 31.1 (2002), 28–50. For a critical assessment of the relation between Ibsen and Freud, see also Lis Møller, "The Analytic Theater: Freud and Ibsen," *The Scandinavian Psychoanalytic Review* 13 (1990), 112–28.
11. Freud, "The 'Uncanny,'" p. 225.
12. Vidler, *The Architectural Uncanny*, p. 26.
13. *HIS*, vol. 7.1, p. 453.
14. Collins and Jervis, *Uncanny Modernity*, p. 2.
15. Martin Jay, "The Uncanny Nineties," in *Cultural Semantics: Keywords of Our Time* (London: Athlone, 1998), pp. 157–64.
16. Collins and Jervis, *Uncanny Modernity*, p. 6.
17. Ibid., p. 3.
18. George Lukács, "Marx and the Problem of Ideological Decay," excerpted in Charles Lyons, ed., *Critical Essays on Henrik Ibsen* (Boston: G. K. Hall & Co., 1987), p. 98.

19. Ibsen expressed at least twice that he felt absolutely compelled to write *Ghosts*. First, there is a letter to Sophie Adlersparre on June 24, 1882: "But *Ghosts had* to be written; I couldn't stop with *The Doll House*; after Nora, Mrs. Alving had to come." See Henrik Ibsen, Letter to Sophie Adlersparre, June 24, 1882, *HIS*, vol. 14.1, p. 136.
20. Helge Rønning, *Den Umulige Friheten* (Oslo: Gyldendal, 2006), pp. 26–27.
21. Ibid., p. 22.
22. Ibid., p. 25.
23. Walter Benjamin, *Charles Baudelaire: A Lyric Poet in the Era of High Capitalism*, trans. Harry Zohn (London: NLB, 1973), p. 36.
24. Sigmund Freud, *Det Uhyggelige*, trans. Hans Christian Fink, afterword Nils Otto Steen and Steen Visholm, Rævens Sort Bibliotek 43 (Copenhagen: Forlaget Politisk Revy, 1998).
25. Arne Garborg, "Henrik Ibsen: *Gengangere*," *Dagbladet* (Christiania), December 14, 1881.
26. Georg Brandes, "Henrik Ibsen: *Gengangere*," *Morgenbladet* (Copenhagen), December 28, 1881.
27. Odd Brochmann, "Fra Kolde Hvide Vægge til Tegl og Træ," in *Om Hygge: Ti Kroniker* (Copenhagen: Politiken, 1965), p. 70.
28. *HIS*, vol. 7.1, p. 213: "En hyggeligt og smagfuldt men ikke kostbart indrettet stue."
29. *HIS*, vol. 8.1, p. 51: "Ateleriet er tarveligt men hyggeligt indrettet og udstyret."
30. *HIS*, vol. 8.1, p. 327: "Dagligstuen på Rosmersholm; rummelig, gammeldags og hyggelig."
31. Of the remaining seven plays that begin indoors, here are the central descriptions of each main dwelling space: *Pillars of Society*: "A spacious garden room in Consul Bernick's house" (*HIS*, vol. 7.1, p. 11: "En rummelig havesal i konsul Bernicks hus"); *Ghosts*: "A spacious garden room" (*HIS*, vol. 7.1, p. 385: "En rummelig havestue"); *An Enemy of the People*: "Evening in the doctor's living room, which is modestly but nicely equipped and furnished" (*HIS*, vol. 7.1, p. 531: "Aften i doktorens dagligstue, der er tarveligt men net udstyret og møbleret"); *Hedda Gabler*: "A spacious, attractive, and tastefully furnished drawing room, decorated in dark colors" (*HIS*, vol. 9.1, p. 11: "Et rummeligt, smukt og smagfuldt udstyret selskabsværelse, dekorert i mørke farver"); *The Master Builder*: "An attractively furnished, smaller room in Master Builder Solness's house" (*HIS*, vol. 9.1, p. 279: "En smukt udstyret, mindre salon hos bygmester Solness"); *Little Eyolf*: "An attractive and richly furnished garden room. Many furnishings, flowers, and plants" (*HIS*, vol. 9.1, p. 395: "En smukt og rigt udstyret havestue. Mange møbler, blomster og planter"); and *John Gabriel Borkman*: "Mrs. Borkman's living room, furnished in old-fashioned, faded splendor" (*HIS*, vol. 10.1, p. 11: "Fru Borkmans dagligstue,

udstyret med gammeldags falmet pragt"). Of these, only the last interior description lacks positive, extenuating value.
32. *HIS*, vol. 7.1, p. 46.
33. Ibid., p. 238.
34. Ibid., p. 470.
35. Ibid., p. 547.
36. *HIS*, vol. 8.1, p. 202.
37. Ibid., p. 331.
38. Ibid., p. 364.
39. "Din gamle Ven," "Fra Tilskuerbænken (Brev til en Udenbys)," *Aftenbladet* (Christiania), January 28, 1880; *Aftenposten* (Christiania), December 22, 1879; "Korrespondance til *Aftenposten*."
40. Erik Vullum, "Literatur-Tidende," *Dagbladet* (Christiania), December 6, 1879.
41. M. V. Brun, "Det Kongelige Theater: *Et Dukkehjem*, Skuespil i 3 Akter af Henrik Ibsen," *Folkets Avis* (Copenhagen), December 24, 1879.
42. Carl Thrane, "Det Kongelige Theater: *Et Dukkehjem*, Skuespil i Tre Acter af Henrik Ibsen," *Illustreret Tidende* 21:1057 (December 28, 1879), 145.
43. Peter Nansen, "Den Første Opførelse," *Vor Tid* (Copenhagen), August 26, 1883, reproduced in Hans Holmberg, "August Lindberg, Herman Bang, och en Historisk Teaterpremiäre i Helsingborg," *Kring Kärnan* 16 (1986), 150.
44. Peter Egge, "Ibsen i Italia," *Minner fra Nord og Syd* (Oslo: Gyldendal Norsk Forlag, 1952), p. 62.
45. "H. H.," "Kristiania Theater," *Dagbladet* (Christiania), January 20, 1885.
46. H. C. Andersen, "Studenten," *Andersens Samlede Værker*, Klaus P. Mortensen (ed.), 15 vols. (Copenhagen: Det Danske Sprog– og Litteraturselskab/Gyldendal, 2003–), vol. 7, p. 101. My thanks to my colleague Karin Sanders for providing the source and contextual information about this reference.
47. Thrane, "*Et Dukkehjem*," 145.
48. Edmund Gosse, "Ibsen's New Drama," *The Fortnightly Review* 49 (new series) (January–June, 1891), 4–5.
49. Francis Bull, *Samlede Verker*, vol. 9, p. 27.
50. "*Gengangere*," *Morgenbladet* (Christiania), December 18, 1881.
51. "*Gengangere*," *Throndhjems Stiftsavis* (Trondheim), February 6, 1882.
52. Karl Warburg, "Ibsens Nya Stycke," *Göteborgs Handels- och Sjöfartstidning* (Gothenburg), December 15, 1881. Alexander Kielland, Ibsen's compatriot and fellow Modern Breakthrough realist, was also well known throughout the Nordic region and Europe at the time and treats in *Else* the theme of the sexual exploitation of women.
53. Adlersparre, *Gengangere ur Etisk Synpunkt*, pp. 37–38. Original emphases.
54. Alfred Sinding-Larsen, *Om Henrik Ibsen: Fruen fra Havet og Personerne deri* (Kristiania: Albert Cammermeyer, 1889), p. 1.

55. Nils Vogt, "John Gabriel Borkman."
56. First published in *Illustreret Nyhedsblads Nytaarsgave for 1860*, 57–70, the poem was later included without changes in Ibsen's main poetry collection: *Digte* (Copenhagen: Gyldendal, 1871). In the *Henrik Ibsens Skrifter* edition, it appears in vol. 11.1, pp. 540–54.
57. Brandes, "Henrik Ibsens *Digte*," p. 33.
58. Toril Moi, *Henrik Ibsen and the Birth of Modernism: Art, Theater, Philosophy* (Oxford: Oxford University Press, 2006), pp. 173–74.
59. *HIS*, vol. 11.1, p. 550: "De ringede julens højtid ind / med de gamle hjemlige klokker. / Det lyser bagved min grandes grind, / fra min moders stue går ud et skin, / som sælsomt mig maner og lokker. // Hjemmet med alt sit fattige liv / blev en saga med billeder rige! / Heroppe lå fjeldvidden stor og stiv, / dernede havde jeg mor og viv, – / til dem jeg måtte vel hige."
60. Ibid., p. 551: "'mig synes min unge ven er rørt, – / ak ja, den hjemlige hytte!'"
61. Ibid.: "Og atter jeg stod med stålsat arm, / og kendte jeg var den stærke; / viddernes luftning kølte min barm, / aldrig den mere skal banke sig varm / for et vinkende julemærke!"
62. Ibid.: "men skytten trøsted: 'hvi så konfus? / Det brænder jo bare, det gamle hus, / med juleøllet og katten!'"
63. Ibid., p. 552.
64. Ibid.: "men det kan ikke nægtes, der *var* effekt / i den dobbelte natbelysning!"
65. Ibid., p. 546: "Gråden leger i hans latter, / læben taler, når den tier."
66. The range of early research commentary on this biographical element is summarized in Herleiv Dahl, *Bergmannen og Byggmesteren: Henrik Ibsen som Lyriker* (Oslo: Gyldendal Norsk Forlag, 1958), p. 135. See also *HIS*, vol. 11.2, pp. 49–51.
67. *HIS*, vol. 5.1, p. 212.
68. Ibid., p. 372.
69. Moi, *Birth of Modernism*, p. 49.
70. *HIS*, vol. 5.1, p. 224.
71. Ibid., p. 256.
72. Ibid., p. 367.
73. For some, this has been seen as Ibsen's ultimate rejection of Kierkegaard's "teleological suspension of the ethical," although several articles have tried to re-emphasize the positive ambivalence in *Brand* as well. See, for example, William Banks, "Ibsen and Kierkegaard Revisited: The Dialectics of Despair in *Brand*," *Ibsen Studies* 4:2 (2004), 176–90; and Helje Kringlebotn Sødal, "Henrik Ibsens *Brand*: Illustrasjon på en Teologisk Suspensjon av det Etiske?" *Edda* (1999), 63–70.
74. *HIS*, vol. 5.1, p. 450.
75. Ibid., p. 217. In the much later play *Hedda Gabler* from 1890, Jørgen Tesman, Hedda Gabler's husband, is characterized by his twin devotions to his slippers

and his aunts, suggesting that Brand's contemptible "Family God" has reemerged on a more human but still ridicule-worthy level.
76. Freud, "The 'Uncanny,'" p. 226.
77. Brun, "*Et Dukkehjem.*"
78. *Dagbladet* (Christiania), January 21, 1880, accessed at http://ibsen.nb.no/id/11157764.0.
79. F., "Opførelsen af *Et Dukkehjem*," *Aftenbladet* (Christiania), January 26, 1880.
80. *Fædrelandet* (Copenhagen), December 22, 1879, accessed at http://ibsen.nb.no/id/19567.0.
81. P. Hansen, "*Et Dukkehjem* og Recensenterne: Kritiske Betragtninger," *Kristiansands Stiftsavis* (Kristiansand), February 12, 1880.
82. Erik Bøgh, "Dit og Dat," *Dagens Nyheder* (Copenhagen), December 24, 1879, cited in Hansen, *Kampen omkring Nora*, p. 73.
83. "Din gamle Ven," "Fra Tilskuerbænken."
84. Cited in Hansen, *Kampen omkring Nora*, p. 72.
85. (Anon.), "Henrik Ibsen og Kristiania Teater," *Dagbladet* (Christiania), December 22, 1881.
86. Adolf Falkman, "Henrik Ibsens *Gengangere* paa Scenen," *Aftenposten* (Christiania), August 25, 1883.
87. Herman Bang, "*Gengangere*," *Vor Tid* (Copenhagen), August 26, 1883.
88. Cited in Holmberg, "August Lindberg," p. 153.
89. "F–n," "Henrik Ibsens *Gengangere* paa Scenen," *Aftenposten* (Christiania), August 25, 1883.
90. Jæger reversed his opinion of *Ghosts* between 1881 and 1883, publishing a reconsideration of the play in *Dagbladet* (Christiania), October 31, 1883, a short time before this account of *The Wild Duck*, which continues his begrudging admiration of Ibsen that soon would become more unequivocal. For an overview of Jæger's journalism on Ibsen's plays, see Narve Fulsås (ed.), *Biografisk Leksikon til Ibsens Brev – Med Tidstavle* (Oslo: Senter for Ibsen-Studier, 2013), pp. 228–29.
91. Henrik Jæger, "Kristiania Theater," *Christiania Intelligenssedler* (Christiania), January 13, 1885.
92. Ibid.
93. Two examples will suffice, the first from a review of *Ghosts*: "We won't say anything more about the play's subject and themes than that they provoke the most unpleasant and repulsive impression [*det uhyggeligste og modbydeligste Indtryk*]," in "*Gengangere,*" *Aftenposten* (Christiania), December 14, 1881. The second describes a performance of *Rosmersholm*: "When the curtain falls on all this gloom [*Naar Tæppet gaar ned over al denne Uhygge*] it is as if one cannot breathe, as if a crushing weight has laid itself on one's chest, as if we feel some

of the curse that lies over the old house inside that dark Western fjord," in "Theatret: *Rosmersholm*," *Bergens Tidende* (Bergen), January 20, 1887.
94. "c.," "Kristiania Theater," *Aftenposten* (Christiania), January 13, 1885.
95. In addition to his joint article with Ludvig Eriksen on November 11, 1884, follow-up pieces touch on the written version of the play as part of his responses to the criticisms of "bicycle journalism," or as we might put it today, "drive-by journalism." See Ludvig Eriksen and Henrik Jæger, "Et Tilsvar," *Christiania Intelligenssedler* (Christiania), November 18, 1884; and Ludvig Eriksen and Henrik Jæger, "Journalistik og Søndagskritik," *Christiania Intelligenssedler* (Christiania), November 20, 1884.
96. Jæger, "Kristiania Theater."
97. The date of this review is uncertain since it mentions only Hennings by name in the performance description and she performed that same role in repertory at the Royal Theater from 1885 to 1907. The date of Rothenburg-Mens's publication was 1906, but it may have been anthologized from an earlier newspaper publication date.
98. Arthur Rothenburg-Mens, "En Dansk Ibsenopførelse," *Kunst og Dilettantisme paa det Nordiske Teater: Nogle Bemærkninger om Drama og Skuespilkunst* (Copenhagen: Holger Ferlovs Forlag, 1906), p. 78.

2 FAÇADES UNMASKED

1. *HIS*, vol. 11.1, pp. 536–37. The dating of the first draft version of the poem to 1864 comes from Jens Bragge Halvorsen, *Bibliografiske Oplysninger til Henrik Ibsens Samlede Værker* (Copenhagen: Gyldendal, 1901), p. 43, but it was first published in the 1871 collection *Digte*. See also commentary to the poem in *HIS*, vol. 11.2, p. 747.
2. Dahl, *Bergmannen og Byggmesteren*, pp. 183–84.
3. *Samlede Verker*, vol. 14, p. 31.
4. I should note that the original unpublished version of the poem bore the title "From House-Life [*Fra Huslivet*]" without the personal possessive pronoun; the revision of the poem for Ibsen's first published poetry collection in 1871 personalized the title and removed some of the ambiguity about the equation of the stranger with the self.
5. *HIS*, vol. 7.1, pp. 253, 255.
6. *HIS*, vol. 8.1, p. 150.
7. Heinrich von Kleist, "Über das Marionettentheater," *Berliner Abendblätter*, December 12–15, 1810; for a recent English translation, see Heinrich von Kleist, "The Puppet Theater," *Selected Writings*, ed. and trans. David Constantine (Indianapolis, IN: Hackett Publishing Co., 1997), pp. 411–16.

8. Michael Fried, *Absorption and Theatricality: Painting and Beholder in the Age of Diderot* (Chicago: University of Chicago Press, 1980).
9. *HIS*, vol. 14.1, p. 551.
10. *HIS*, vol. 7.1, p. 20.
11. Ibid., p. 56.
12. Ibid., p. 14.
13. Moi, *Birth of Modernism*, p. 218.
14. *HIS*, vol. 7.1, p. 15.
15. Ibid., p. 17.
16. Ibid.
17. Ibid., p. 108.
18. This is the version of the title cited by Tore Rem in his anthology of British Ibsen reception documents, *Henry Gibson/Henrik Ibsen: Den Provinsielle Verdensdikteren* (Oslo: J. W. Cappelens Forlag, 2006), pp. 54–55, 325. A Danish review of the British premiere reports the title as *Quicksand*, or *The Pillars of Society*. "Oskar H.," "'Samfundets Støtter' paa Engelsk Grund: Korrespondance fra London til *Illustreret Tidende*," *Illustreret Tidende* (December 26, 1880), 179.
19. Asbjørn Aarseth, *Ibsens Samtidsskuespill: En Studie i Glasskapets Dramaturgi* (Oslo: Universitetsforlaget, 1999), p. 61.
20. Herman Bang, *Stuk* (Copenhagen: J. H. Schubothe, 1887).
21. *HIS*, vol. 7.1, p. 167.
22. Aarseth, *Ibsens Samtidsskuespill*, pp. 48–50.
23. Moi, *Birth of Modernism*, pp. 218–22. Moi makes ample use of Fried, as does Erik Østerud in *Theatrical and Narrative Space: Studies in Ibsen, Strindberg, and J. P. Jacobsen* (Aarhus, Denmark: Aarhus University Press, 1998).
24. Moi, *Birth of Modernism*, p. 221.
25. *HIS*, vol. 7.1, p. 200.
26. See, for example, Carl Thrane, "Det Kongelige Theater: *Samfundets Støtter*, Skuespil i Fire Akter af Henrik Ibsen," *Illustreret Tidende* (November 25, 1877), 81.
27. *HIS*, vol. 7.1, p. 208. Original emphasis.
28. Thrane, "*Samfundets Støtter*," p. 81.
29. Garborg, "Samfundets Støtter."
30. *HIS*, vol. 7.1, p. 200.
31. Ibid., p. 206.
32. Berthold Litzmann, *Das Deutsche Drama* (Hamburg: Verlag von Leopold Voss, 1894), p. 145. This retrospective account takes a distinctly ethnographic tone, distancing itself from the "Norwegianness" of both character and plot in *A Doll House*.

Notes to pages 69–70

33. For a Lacanian-inflected reading that treats the play specifically as a con tation with partriarchal family structure, see Ross Shideler, *Questionir Father: From Darwin to Zola, Ibsen, Strindberg, and Hardy* (Stanford, CA: Stanford University Press, 1999), pp. 74–82. For the best treatment of the persistence of patriarchal attitudes in later critical reception of the play, see Templeton, *Ibsen's Women*, pp. 110–28.
34. Vagn Kieler and Otto Westengaard-Hildinge, *Fra Aalsgaard: Om Ibsens Nora og en Drengs Erindringer*, Egnshistoriske beretninger 18 (Aalsgaard, Denmark: Hellebæk-Aalsgaard Egnshistoriske Forening, 1985), 5. My thanks go to Astrid Sæther for finding this reference. The same claim is made by Kieler herself in an interview for a newspaper article on January 11, 1924, in which she recalls, "After that time we continued our friendship, and when I married my husband, headmaster Kieler, Ibsen visited my home, which he christened the 'doll home.'" This Danish interview article, entitled "'Nora' 75 Aar: Modellen til *Et Dukkehjem* Fortæller," is located in the archives at the Ibsen Center in Oslo as "Art. Et Dukkehjem 41," but without newspaper attribution. For a useful summary of Kieler's role as a model for Nora, see B. M. Kinck, "Henrik Ibsen og Laura Keiler," *Edda* 35 (1935), 498–543; Templeton, *Ibsen's Women*, pp. 135–37; and Ivo de Figueiredo, *Henrik Ibsen: Masken* (Oslo: Aschehoug, 2007), pp. 184–86.
35. Henrik Ibsen, Letter to Erik af Edholm, January 3, 1880, *HIS*, vol. 14.1, p. 11.
36. *Norsk Riksmålsordbok*, 2 vols. (Oslo: Aschehoug, 1937), 1 A–L, 750: "et tilsynelatende idyllisk hjem hvor mannen forkjæler konen, men ikke behandler henne som en selvstendig personlighet." One can also find the word used in reviews at the time of publication in exactly that way, as if offering a definition or placing the term in citation markers. An article in *Social-Demokraten* from the time period already includes this reference to the term with a brief definition: "This piece reaches into thousands of families' lives; there are surely thousands of such doll homes [*tusinde af saadanne Dukkehjem*], where the husband treats the wife like a child." Cited in Hansen, *Kampen omkring Nora*, p. 60.
37. *Samlede Verker*, vol. 8, p. 442.
38. *HIS*, vol. 7.1, p. 367. Rolf Fjelde, trans., *Ibsen: The Complete Major Prose Plays* (New York: Plume, 1965), p. 191.
39. *Samlede Verker*, vol. 8, p. 358; *HIS*, vol. 7.1, p. 367.
40. There is apparently one handwritten 1879 translation into English by Ernest L. Oppenheim that retains the neologism of the Norwegian title, but I have not had the opportunity to examine it. It is catalogued at the Library of Congress and does not appear to have been published officially. Accessed at http://lccn.loc.gov/mm80002435 on June 26, 2014.

41. Egil Törnqvist, *Ibsen: A Doll's House* (New York: Cambridge University Press, 1995), pp. 53–54.
42. Moi, *Birth of Modernism*, p. 235.
43. Frode Helland, *Melankoliens Spill: En Studie i Henrik Ibsens Siste Dramaer* (Oslo: Universitetsforlaget, 2000), p. 154.
44. Aarseth, *Ibsens Samtidsskuespill*, p. 133.
45. For information on the *Wessels gate 15* exhibit, along with interior photos of each of the eight apartments, visit the Norwegian Folk Museum website: www.norskfolkemuseum.no/en/Exhibits/The-Apartment-Building/, accessed June 26, 2014.
46. Thank you to Erika Ravne Scott, curator of the toy collection at Norsk Folkmuseum, for information about this piece. She relates that this particular piece was chosen for the *Wessels gate 15* exhibit both because it was period appropriate and because of its high quality. The collection of dollhouses at the museum includes many homemade ones as well, and for obvious reasons these tend to be smaller and less furniture-like than those custom-ordered from carpenters.
47. I visited this exhibit in fall 2007, and it is still current at Nordiska Museet in Stockholm. See www.nordiskamuseet.se/press/dockskap. Accessed June 26, 2014.
48. The accompanying information at this exhibit includes the provenance of dollhouses in the Netherlands in the seventeenth century, when they may have been used more as miniature model homes or curiosity cabinets for the adult bourgeoisie than they were as toys for children. Here, too, most of the examples in the exhibit were heavy, bulky furniture pieces.
49. My thanks go to Ulf Hamilton at Nordiska Museet for this information and for help in obtaining a photograph of the dollhouse.
50. Ulf Hamilton, curator at Nordiska Museet, in private correspondence to the author on April 7, 2008. Erika Ravne Scott writes of a well-known counter-example, a homemade interactive *dukkestue* in the family of the Norwegian writer Ågot Gjems Selmer (see this book's Conclusion for more about Selmer's stake in the dollhouse idea). This dollhouse was clearly a toy for children, so there was a range of practice in Ibsen's day. See Erika Ravne Scott, "En Dukkestue til Tordis – 1890," *Norsk Husflid* 5 (1989), 6–7. Although the text of *A Doll House* has some indications that the Helmer's *dukkestue* was the interactive kind (the Christmas present for Emily is an inexpensive doll bed that will soon get wrecked, according to Nora), the thematic development of the dollhouse motif at the end of the play works much better with the hands-off display function of the more expensive dollhouses.
51. The front of the Norwegian *dukkestue* has four hinges, but the doors are no longer with the piece. One has to surmise from the quality of the piece that these doors were of glass. Correspondence with Erika Ravne Scott, July 1, 2008.

52. Aarseth, *Ibsens Samtidsskuespill*, pp. 65–67.
53. *HIS*, vol. 7.1, p. 238.
54. Ibid., p. 291.
55. Brun, "*Et Dukkehjem.*"
56. *HIS*, vol. 7.1, pp. 374, 378.
57. Ibid., p. 360.
58. Ibid., p. 363.
59. Edvard Brandes, "Henrik Ibsens *Et Dukkehjem* paa Det kgl. Theater," *Ude og Hjemme* 118 (January 1880), cited in Hansen, *Kampen omkring Nora*, p. 64.
60. Ibid.
61. Ibid.
62. Warburg, "Ibsens Nya Stycke."
63. *HIS*, vol. 7.1, p. 375.
64. H. Lassen, *Christiania Intelligenssedler* (Christiania), January 22, 1880.
65. "M-.," "Lykken Bedre end Forstanden: Et Efterspil," *Aalesunds Blad* (Ålesund), April 30–May 21, 1880; M. J. Bugge, *Hvorledes Nora Kom Hjem Igjen: Et Efterspil* (Christiania: Cammermeyer, 1881).
66. Ibid., May 7, 1880.
67. Ibid., May 11, 1880.
68. Ibid., May 21, 1880.
69. Meyer, *Ibsen: A Biography*, p. 459.
70. "Der Schluß von Ibsens Nora: Eine Aufklärung," *Das Litterarische Echo* 2:13 (April 1, 1900), 970.
71. *HIS*, vol. 7.1, p. 379.
72. "G.," "Henrik Ibsen: *Et Dukkehjem*," *Bergens Aftenblad* (Bergen), January 2, 1880.
73. Ibid.
74. Ibid.
75. *HIS*, vol. 7.1, p. 366.
76. Ibid., p. 371.
77. Ibid., p. 369.
78. Ibid., p. 377.
79. Errol Durbach, *A Doll's House: Ibsen's Myth of Transformation* (Boston: Twayne, 1991), p. 28.

3 HOME AND HOUSE

1. *HIS*, vol. 7.1, p. 87.
2. Ibid., pp. 312, 429, 642.
3. *HIS*, vol. 8.1, p. 161.
4. *HIS*, vol. 7.1, p. 423.

5. Ibid., pp. 423–24.
6. Ibid., p. 408.
7. My thanks go to Lisbeth P. Wærp for this information. Correspondence with the author, August 31, 2006.
8. *HIS*, vol. 7.1, pp. 394, 503. (The spelling of *sjømand* is not consistent in the text.)
9. Ibid., pp. 503–4.
10. Ibid., p. 512; Eva Le Gallienne, trans., *Six Plays*, by Henrik Ibsen (New York: The Modern Library, 1957), p. 147. It is interesting to note that this verbal play with the terminology in the unfolding naming of the two building projects seems to have been in place in all its details in the first draft; none of the key terms were adjusted in rewriting for the final version, so the variations are not the result of untracked changes in revision. The textual differences in the one existing draft are listed in *Samlede Verker*, vol. 9, pp. 138–73.
11. *HIS*, vol. 7.1, p. 525.
12. Henrik Jæger, *Henrik Ibsen 1828–1888: Et Literært Livsbillede* (Copenhagen: Gyldendalske Boghandels Forlag, 1888), p. 268.
13. Henrik Jæger, "Henrik Ibsen: *En Folkefiende*," *Aftenposten* (Christiania), December 6, 1882.
14. *HIS*, vol. 7.1, p. 559.
15. Ibid., pp. 679–80.
16. Ibid., p. 581. This is one case in which the distinction between house and home plays out differently in each language: the root word in the Norwegian idiom would make it literally a Houseowners' Association (in English "homeowner" would be more idiomatic), but the interests this group defends are clearly those of "home" in its more ideological sense.
17. *HIS*, vol. 7.1, pp. 700, 707.
18. Ibid., pp. 691–92.
19. Ibid., p. 673; as two examples of critics who find it worthwhile to argue the details of the military metaphor, see Eirik Vullum, "*En Folkefiende*," *Dagbladet* (Christiania), November 30, 1882; and Jæger, "Henrik Ibsen."
20. Johan Irgens Hansen, "Henrik Ibsen: *En Folkefiende*," *Dagbladet* (Christiania), November 29, 1882.
21. Ibid., December 8, 1882.
22. Ibid.
23. Michael Johan Færden, *Luthersk Ugeskrift* (Christiania), December 16, 1882.
24. Ibid., December 23, 1882.
25. *HIS*, vol. 8.1, p. 48.
26. Ibid., p. 137.
27. Ibid.
28. Ibid., p. 163.

29. Templeton, *Ibsen's Women*, pp. 166–80.
30. Ibid., p. 167.
31. *HIS*, vol. 8.1, p. 72. Original emphasis.
32. Ibid., p. 130.
33. Ibid., p. 187.
34. Ibid., p. 161.
35. Templeton, *Ibsen's Women*, pp. 168–73.
36. *HIS*, vol. 11.1, pp. 617–18. Original Norwegian: "De sad der, de to, i så lunt et hus / ved høst og i vinterdage. / Så brændte huset. Alt ligger i grus. / De to får i asken rage. // For nede i den er et smykke gemt, – / et smykke, som aldrig kan brænde. / Og leder de trofast, hænder det nemt, / at det findes af ham eller hende. // Men finder de end, de brandlidte to, / det dyre, ildfaste smykke – / aldrig hun finder sin brændte tro, / han aldrig sin brændte lykke." Ibsen wrote the poem as part of the preparation for writing the play *The Master Builder* but apparently decided not to use it in the text itself. He considered briefly the possibility of including the poem overtly in the following play, *Little Eyolf*, in a scene in the working draft that has Alfred Allmers reading the poem aloud to Rita at the end of the play. The poem is unchanged except for the second to last line, which substitutes "burned-up peace" (*brændte ro*) for "faith." (*Samlede Verker*, vol. 12, p. 314; *HIS*, vol. 11.2, p. 855). The poem was not included in the final version of *Little Eyolf*.
37. *HIS*, vol. 9.1, p. 302.
38. Ibid., p. 305.
39. Ibid., p. 284. Original emphasis.
40. Helland, *Melankoliens Spill*, p. 90. Original emphasis.
41. *HIS*, vol. 9.1, p. 213.
42. Helland, *Melankoliens Spill*, p. 156.
43. *HIS*, vol. 9.1, p. 307. Original emphasis.
44. Helland, *Melankoliens Spill*, p. 111.
45. Jørgen Dines Johansen, "Om Sammenhængen mellem Religiøs, Sexuel og Social Tematik i Ibsens *Bygmester Solness*," in Finn Hauberg Mortensen (ed.), *Tekst/Historie: Bidrag til Historisering af Tekstlæsning i Gymnasiet* (Copenhagen: Samlerens Forlag, 1980), 56; *HIS*, vol. 9.1, p. 343.
46. Helland, *Melankoliens Spill*, p. 146.
47. *HIS*, vol. 9.1, p. 345.
48. *HIS*, vol. 8.1, p. 81.
49. Ibid., p. 89. Original emphasis.
50. Aarseth, *Ibsens Samtidsskuespill*, p. 128.
51. Ibid., p. 216.
52. *HIS*, vol. 8.1, p. 526.
53. Ibid., pp. 526–27.

54. Ibid., p. 551.
55. Aarseth, *Ibsens Samtidsskuespill*, p. 216.
56. Ibid., p. 565.
57. The many figurations of the sea in this play grew directly from the special allure it held for Ibsen personally, as Francis Bull discusses at length in his introduction to the play, *Samlede Verker*, vol. 12, pp. 20–23.
58. Bredo Morgenstierne, "Ibsens *Fruen fra Havet*," *Aftenposten* (Christiania), December 5, 1888.
59. *HIS*, vol. 8.1, p. 565.
60. Aarseth, *Ibsens Samtidsskuespill*, 183.
61. *HIS*, vol. 8.1, p. 591.
62. The definition of *husfisk* listed in the *Riksmålsordok* cites *The Lady from the Sea* as the source and flags the term as "rare," indicating that like *dukkehjem*, this is an Ibsenian neologism.
63. Sinding-Larsen, *Om Henrik Ibsen*, pp. 54–55.
64. Moi, *Birth of Modernism*, p. 315.
65. *HIS*, vol. 9.1, p. 25.
66. Ibid., p. 26.
67. Ibid., p. 90.
68. Ibid., p. 68.
69. Ibid., p. 86.
70. Ibid., p. 87.
71. Ibid. The owner of the villa is identified in the original with the social title *Statsrådinde Falk*, in other words, the widow of Cabinet Minister Falk, but the phrase does not translate easily into English. The point of the name in Norwegian would be to identify the former owner as a member of the well-to-do *embetsstand*, or upper civil servant class, the closest to an aristocracy that Norway offered at the time.
72. Ibid., p. 88.
73. Mark B. Sandberg, "Ibsen and the Mimetic Home of Modernity," *Ibsen Studies* 1.2 (2001): 32–58.
74. *HIS*, vol. 9.1, p. 409.
75. *HIS*, vol. 10.1, p. 124.
76. Ibid., p. 154.
77. Ibid., p. 145.
78. Some of the relevant work that explores the sculpture-in-the-text and its ekphrastic qualities are Jette Lundbo Levy, "Skulptur som Intertekst i *Når Vi Døde Vågner*," *Agora: Journal for Metafysisk Spekulasjon* 2–3 (1993), 26–32; Helland, *Melankoliens Spill*, especially pp. 374–410; and Lisbeth P. Wærp, "Oppstandelsen som Forførerisk Morder," in Lisbeth P. Wærp (ed.), *Livet på*

Likstrå: Henrik Ibsens Når Vi Døde Vågner (Oslo: Landslaget for norskundervisning and Cappelen Akademisk Forlag, 1999), 94–121.
79. This argument is pursued at length in Wærp, "Oppstandelsen som Forførisk Morder," pp. 101–6.
80. Aarseth, *Ibsens Samtidsskuespill*, pp. 342–43, 352–54.
81. *HIS*, vol. 10.1, p. 181. Original emphasis.
82. For a focused discussion of Ibsen's actual contact with Darwinian thought, see Eivind Tjønneland, "Darwin, J. P. Jacobsen og Ibsen," *Arr: Idéhistorisk Tidsskrift* 10.4–11.1 (1998–99), 54–64. For a Lacanian-inflected reading of Ibsen and Darwinism, see Shideler, *Questioning the Father*, pp. 59–96.
83. Freud, "The 'Uncanny,'" p. 222.
84. Helland, *Melankoliens Spill*, pp. 438–56.
85. *HIS*, vol. 10.1, pp. 267, 271.
86. Ibid., p. 277. Original emphasis.
87. Ibid., p. 288.
88. Helland, *Melankoliens Spill*, pp. 473–74.
89. *HIS*, vol. 10.1, p. 173.
90. Ibid., p. 177.
91. Wærp, "Oppstandelsen som Forførerisk Morder," pp. 98–99. Original emphasis.
92. Georg Brandes, "Henrik Ibsen. *Naar Vi Døde Vaagner*," *Verdens Gang* (Christiania), December 28, 1899.
93. *HIS*, vol. 10.1, pp. 175, 234.
94. Ibid., p. 256.
95. Ibid., p. 258.
96. Ibid., p. 275.
97. Ibid., p. 173. Original emphases.
98. *HIS*, vol. 9.1, p. 340. Original emphasis.
99. *HIS*, vol. 10.1, p. 239. Original emphasis.
100. Nicholas Howe, "Introduction," in Nicholas Howe (ed.), *Home and Homelessness in the Medieval and Renaissance World* (Notre Dame, IN: University of Notre Dame Press, 2004), p. 10.
101. Lukács, "Problem of Ideological Decay," p. 98.
102. Templeton, *Ibsen's Women*, p. 313.
103. Helland, *Melankoliens Spill*, pp. 471–74.
104. *HIS*, vol. 7.1, p. 371.
105. *HIS*, vol. 9.1, p. 358. Original emphasis.
106. Ibid., p. 289.
107. *HIS*, vol. 10.1, pp. 185–86.
108. *HIS*, vol. 9.1, p. 322.

109. Faith Ingwersen, "Norwegian Women Writers," in Harald S. Naess (ed.), *A History of Norwegian Literature*, vol. 2 of *A History of Scandinavian Literatures* (Lincoln: University of Nebraska Press, 1993), p. 360.
110. Dickmar, *To Literære Studier*, p. 26.
111. Ibid., pp. 26–27. Original emphasis.
112. Ibid., p. 74. Original emphases.
113. Ibid., pp. 52–53. Original emphases.
114. Jon Sørensen, "Naar vi Døde Vaagner," *Norsk Skoletidende: Tillægshefte* 1 (1900), 52, 58.
115. Ibid., p. 59.
116. Ibid., p. 57. Original emphasis.
117. Theodor Caspari, "*Bygmester Solness*," *Aftenposten* (Christiania), January 4, 1893.
118. Ibid.
119. Ibid.
120. Ibid.
121. Ibid.
122. Ibid.
123. Ibid. Original emphasis.
124. Ibid.
125. E. F. B. Horn, "Unødvendig Bekymring," *Aftenposten* (Christiania), January 8, 1893.

4 THE TENACITY OF ARCHITECTURE

1. Marshall Berman, *All That Is Solid Melts into Air: The Experience of Modernity* (New York: Penguin, 1982), pp. 148–55.
2. Peter Madsen, "The Destruction of Rome," in Astrid Sæther (ed.), *Ibsen and the Arts: Painting–Sculpture–Architecture*, Acta Ibseniana 1 (Oslo: Centre for Ibsen Studies, 2002), pp. 151–58.
3. Philip Rosen, *Change Mummified: Cinema, Historicity, Theory* (Minneapolis: University of Minnesota Press, 2001), pp. 44–58.
4. Ibid., p. 53.
5. Ibid., p. 83.
6. Ibid., pp. 58–66.
7. Sandberg, "Ibsen and the Mimetic Home"; and Mark B. Sandberg, *Living Pictures, Missing Persons: Mannequins, Museums, and Modernity* (Princeton, NJ: Princeton University Press, 2003).
8. Cited in Freud, "The 'Uncanny,'" p. 225.
9. *HIS*, vol. 5.1, p. 107.

10. Ibid., p. 106: "Hvad der er dødt, det lyves ej tillive. / Hvad der er dødt, det maa i Mørket ned. / E̲t̲ Hverv kun har det døde: d̲e̲t̲, at give / sig hen som Næring for en nylagt Sæd."
11. *Samlede Verker*, vol. 9, p. 13.
12. *HIS*, vol. 5.1, p. 109: "Se, derfor har jeg vendt mit Syn og Sind / bort fra vor Fortids sjæledræbte Sage, / bort fra vor Løgndrøm om en Fremtids Dage, / og gaar i Nuets Taageverden ind."
13. Rønning, *Den Umulige Friheten*, pp. 250–53.
14. William Ian Miller, "Home and Homelessness in the Middle of Nowhere," in Nicholas Howe (ed.), *Home and Homelessness in the Medieval and Renaissance World* (Notre Dame, IN: University of Notre Dame Press, 2004), pp. 128–29.
15. "Literatur: *Gengangere*," *Aftenbladet (Christiania)*, December 19, 1881.
16. Ibid.
17. *HIS*, vol. 10.1, p. 57.
18. Ibid., pp. 40–41.
19. Edgar Allan Poe, "The Fall of the House of Usher," in Thomas Ollive Mabbott (ed.), *The Collected Works of Edgar Allan Poe*, 3 vols. (Cambridge, MA: Harvard University Press, 1978), vol. 2, pp. 398, 400.
20. *HIS*, vol. 8.1, pp. 328–29.
21. Ibid., p. 499.
22. Two examples: E. V., "*Rosmersholm*," *Dagbladet* (Christiania), April 13, 1887; Thomas P. Krag, "Den Norske Maaned: *Rosmersholm*," *Urd: Illust. Ugeblad for Kvinden og Hjemmet* 12 (September 19, 1908), 448.
23. "Teater, Kunst og Literatur: Kristiania Theater," *Dagen* (Christiania), April 16, 1887.
24. *HIS*, vol. 8.1, p. 432.
25. Ibid., p. 477.
26. Ibid., p. 334.
27. Ibid., p. 337.
28. Caspari, "*Bygmester Solness*."
29. Freud, "Some Character Types," pp. 326–31; Atle Kittang, *Henrik Ibsens Heroisme: Frå Brand til Når vi Døde Vågner* (Oslo: Gyldendal, 2002), pp. 205–9; Lis Møller, "The Analytical Theater," pp. 112–28.
30. *HIS*, vol. 8.1, p. 420–21.
31. Both Eva Le Gallienne and Rolf Fjelde, for example, translate this line respectively as "Will you be my wife?/Would you be my wife?" in Le Gallienne, *Six Plays*, p. 304; Fjelde, *The Complete Major Prose Plays*, p. 545.
32. Kittang, *Ibsens Heroisme*, p. 207.
33. E. V., "*Rosmersholm*."
34. Poul Levin, "Om *Rosmersholm*," *Tilskueren* (1910), 464. Levin misquotes Brendel here as saying "*det bare ingenting*"; in the published text, Brendel

mentions his homesickness for "the great nothing [*det store ingenting*]," *HIS*, vol. 8.1, p. 485.
35. Caspari, "Bygmester Solness."
36. Henrik Jæger, *Henrik Ibsen og Hans Værker* (Christiania and Copenhagen: Alb. Cammermeyers Forlag, 1892), p. 151.
37. Henrik Ibsen, letter to Lorentz Dietrichson, December 19, 1879, *HIS*, vol. 13.1, pp. 530–31. Original emphasis.
38. *HIS*, vol. 5.1, p. 215.
39. The Norwegian word *fogd* is not easy to translate directly into American English, since the usual translators' alternatives ("sheriff" and "bailiff") have very specific, misleading connotations with the American West and the modern court system that interfere with understanding the social position of a *fogd* in the nineteenth-century Norwegian context. A *fogd* was a civil servant appointed to a rural district with authority to enforce the law and to collect taxes, something closer to a rural bailiff in Britain. For lack of better alternatives, Bailiff will be used to translate the character name for *Fogden* here.
40. *HIS*, vol. 5.1, pp. 344–45.
41. Ibid., p. 346: "Vil Byggeplanen blot ej briste, / saa har vi gratis Daarekiste, / har samlet under fælles Tag, / beskyttet af det samme Flag, / de væsentligste Elementer, / hvorfra vor Byggd sin Farve henter."
42. Ibid, p. 350: "Lad Kirken staa, det vil jeg raade; / den kan jo kaldes paa en Maade / et Stykke ædelt Arveguld. / Den *er* et ædelt Arvestykke; – / den skal ei falde for en Nykke!" Original emphasis.
43. See the annotated commentary on this reference to King Bele in *HIS*, vol 5.2, p. 427.
44. Ibid., pp. 448–49.
45. *Foreningen til Norske Fortidsmindesmerkers Bevaring*, Aarsberetning for 1858 (Christiania: Carl C. Werner & Comp., 1859), p. 9.
46. *HIS*, vol. 5.1, p. 392.
47. Ibid., p. 351: "Se, derfor maa jeg rentud sige, / at Kirkens Rivning er umulig; – / det var en skammelig, en grulig / barbarisk Handling uden Lige!"
48. Ibid.: "naar med en liden Smule Skjøttsel / man *saa*vidt støtte kan det gamle, / at det i *vor* Tid ej vil ramle?" Original emphasis.
49. Ibid., p. 352: "gaa foran De, saa gaar jeg bag. / De er i Skuddet; De kan virke, / og jeg kan skridtvis frem meg lirke. – / Brand, *sammen* vil vi bygge Kirke!" Original emphasis.
50. Ibid., p. 354: "Og hvor er Stil, Architektur, / naar rett man gransker Loft og Mur? / Hvad skal man kalde slige Buer? / En Fagmand vil dem kalde fæle; – / ja, jeg maa samme Mening dele! / Og Tagets mosbeklædte Tuer, – / de er minsæl ej fra Kong Bele. / Nej, Pietet kan gaa for vidt! / Det maa dog

Hvermand se og skjønne, / at denne gamle raadne Rønne / i et og alt er noget Skidt!"
51. Ibid., p. 395: "Herrens Hus skal bygges stort; / saa det var jeg trøstig loved; / rydde, jævne, feie bort, / rive ned jeg glatt nok voved; – / nu star Værket færdiggjort."
52. Ibid., p. 396.
53. Ibid., pp. 393–94.
54. Ibid., pp. 398, 399.
55. Ibid., p. 426: "*Helt* I maa det nye ville, – / *alle* raadne Værkers Rømning, – / før den store Tempelhal / rejses, som den bør og skal!" Original emphasis.
56. Ibid., p. 428: "Væk med Værket, her er gjort! / Kun i Løgnen er det stort; / alt i Aanden faldefærdigt, / eders usle Vilje værdigt."
57. Plot point summary and citation taken from *HIS*, vol. 7.1, pp. 432–35.
58. Ibid., p. 437.
59. Ibid., pp. 437–38. Original emphasis.
60. Ibid., p. 431.
61. Ibid., p. 435.
62. Edvard Brandes, "Lindbergs Opførelse af *Gjengangere*," *Ude og Hjemme* 6 (September 2, 1883), 595.
63. *HIS*, vol. 7.1, p. 385.
64. C. D. W. "Litteratur," *Post och Inrikes-Tidningar* (Stockholm), January 2, 1882.
65. *HIS*, vol. 11.1, pp. 559–60.
66. Warburg, "Ibsens Nya Stycke." Original emphasis.
67. Shideler, *Questioning the Father*, p. 84.
68. *HIS*, vol. 7.1, p. 495.
69. Ibid., pp. 612–13.
70. Ibid., p. 454.
71. *HIS*, vol. 9.1, p. 247.
72. Ibid., p. 375.
73. Ibid., p. 378.
74. Ibid., p. 272.
75. Ibid., pp. 363, 383.
76. Ibid., p. 376.
77. Ibid., pp. 243–44. Original emphasis.
78. Ibid., p. 379. Original emphasis.
79. This style has a historical context in 1890s Christiania, when a flurry of building activity favored a residential architecture style with corner towers and a strong sense of presentational façade, especially in the Frogner area west of the palace. See Rønning, *Den Umulige Friheden*, pp. 253–59.
80. *HIS*, vol. 9.1, p. 302.

81. Dickmar, *To Literære Studier*, pp. 37–38.
82. Helland, *Melankoliens Spill*, pp. 106–7.
83. The reconstruction of a housing history like this inevitably reaches a point of ambiguity; although Ibsen was extraordinarily careful in planting clues about this kind of backstory, one occasionally gets the sense of some soft spots in it.
84. *HIS*, vol. 9.1, p. 251.
85. Helland, *Melankoliens Spill*, p. 106.
86. *HIS*, vol. 9.1, p. 301.
87. Ibid., p. 527.
88. Helland, *Melankoliens Spill*, pp. 288–92.
89. *HIS*, vol. 10.1, pp. 11, 57.
90. "*John Gabriel Borkman* paa Kristiania Teater," *Dagbladet* (Christiania), January 26, 1897.
91. Valdemar Vedel, "Ibsens Nye Skuespil," *Tilskueren* 17 (January 1900), 82.
92. Kurt Eisner, "Professor Rubeks Puppenheim," *Sozialistische Monatshefte* 4 (1900), 24–30.
93. *HIS*, vol. 10.1, p. 256.
94. Ibid., p. 258.
95. Ibid., pp. 258–59. Original emphases.
96. Ibid., p. 175.
97. *HIS*, vol. 5.1, p. 260.
98. Ibid., p. 351: "Af egne Midler vil jeg bygge; – / min Arv, alt mit till sidste Skjærv / skal gives ud till dett Hverv."
99. *HIS*, vol. 7.1, p. 408.
100. Ibid., pp. 438, 441.
101. Ibid., p. 408.
102. Fjelde, *The Complete Major Prose Plays*, p. 260. The other four translations are by Eva Le Gallienne ("The cellar is still in flames," *Six Plays*, p. 139); James MacFarlane ("The basement is still burning," *Four Major Plays*, p. 148); R. Farquharson Sharp ("It is burning still in the basement," *Four Great Plays*, p. 116); Peter Watts ("It's still burning in the basement," *Ghosts and Other Plays*, p. 85); and Rick Davis and Brian Johnston ("The basement's still burning," *Ibsen: Four Major Plays*, p. 114).
103. *HIS*, vol. 7.1, p. 495.
104. Ibid., p. 435.
105. Ibid., p. 501.
106. Ibid., p. 429.
107. *HIS*, vol. 10.1, p. 119.
108. My thanks go to Lisbeth P. Wærp for help in tracking down the Norwegian usage of this word. The definition in the *Norsk Riksmålsordbok* for

"*skamstøtte*" reads as follows: "a pillar of older origin with an inscription condemning a crime, erected especially when the criminal escaped justice [*en, om eldre forh., støtte med innskrift som fordømte en forbrytelse, særl. reist når forbryteren selv var undsloppet straffen*]" and is followed by a reference to Ibsen's play.
109. My analysis here is also indebted to the lively discussions of the pillar of shame at the Wildcat Canyon Advanced Seminar in Folklore and Cultural Studies.
110. For a thorough cultural history of memorials to shame in early modern Europe, see Klaus Graf, "Das Leckt die Kuh Nicht ab: 'Zufällige Gedanken' zu Schriftlichkeit und Errinerungskultur der Strafgerichtsbarkeit," in Andreas Blauert and Gerd Schwerhoff (eds.), *Kriminalitätsgeschichte: Beiträge zur Sozial– und Kulturgeschichte der Vormoderne* (Konstanz: UVK, 2000), pp. 245–88. Alessandro Manzoni, author of *The Betrothed* (1825), included in a later 1840 edition of that novel a historical appendix called "Storia della Colonna Infame" ("The Story of the Pillar of Infamy"). Here too a supposed criminal's house was demolished and a pillar erected in its place, although Manzoni's point in his case is to reveal the miscarriage of justice. It is conceivable that Ibsen encountered the idea of the pillar of shame in Italy via Manzoni, although the Copenhagen monument seems more likely to be the source.
111. *HIS*, vol. 10.1, p. 119. Original emphasis
112. Graf documents this case: a *Schandsäule* in Aachen, Germany, was erected in 1616 to ensure the eternal infamy of a church heretic who had been executed. After the political and social context in the city shifted to Protestantism, however, the monument's original meaning could not be maintained as "eternally" as intended and came to be seen as a testimony of the Catholic Church's despotism. See Graf, "Das Leckt die Kuh nicht ab," pp. 266–67.

CONCLUSION

1. *HIS*, vol. 8.1, p. 485.
2. James Walter McFarlane, "Revaluations of Ibsen," in *Discussions of Henrik Ibsen*, ed. James Walter McFarlane (Boston: D. C. Heath and Company, 1962), pp. 22–23.
3. Ågot Gjems Selmer, *Et Hjem for Mennesker: En Menneskeskildring i Tre Handlinger* (Christiania: Aschehoug, 1901), pp. 174–75.
4. Ibid., pp. 185–86.
5. Provensal's painting was less well known until the Musée D'Orsay featured his work in the 2012 exhibition "Architectures de l'Étrange," which included this painting. It can be seen online at www.musee-orsay.fr/fr/collections/catalogue-des-oeuvres/notice.html?nnumid=163591.

6. Henry Provensal, *L'Art de Demain: Vers l'Harmonie Intégrale* (Paris: Perrin, 1904).
7. *HIS*, vol. 8.1, p. 358.
8. Henry Provensal, *L'Habitation Salubre et à Bon Marché* (Paris: Librairie Générale de l'Architecture et des Arts Décoratifs, 1908).
9. Edvard Heiberg, "Hvordan Har De Det?" *Kritisk Revy* 1 (1927), 34.
10. *HIS*, vol. 8.1, p. 449.
11. Heiberg, "Hvordan Har De Det?" p. 34.

Bibliography

NOTES

Alphabetization of the Scandinavian characters (Æ/Ä, Ø/Ö, and Å) will follow Norwegian convention and come at the end of the alphabet.

The city name for Oslo used before 1925, Kristiania, will be used when historically appropriate and with the anglicized spelling "Christiania."

Titles punctuated with single quotation marks in originals have here been italicized instead.

American maximal capitalization has been used for all titles as well, regardless of the original.

"A.," "Henrik Ibsens Drama *Rosmersholm*," *Aftenposten* (Christiania), November 24, 1886

Aarseth, Asbjørn, *Ibsens Samtidsskuespill: En Studie i Glasskapets Dramaturgi* (Oslo: Universitetsforlaget, 1999)

Adlersparre, Sophie, *Gengangere ur Etisk Synpunkt: Föredrag Hållet i Stockholm Våren 1882* (Stockholm: Jos. Seligmann & Comp., 1882)

Aftenposten (Christiania), December 22, 1879, accessed at http://ibsen.nb.no/id/ 11112796.0

Alnæs, Nina S., *Varulv om Natten: Folketro og Folkediktning hos Ibsen* (Oslo: Gyldendal Norsk Forlag, 2003)

Andersen, H. C., "Studenten," *Andersens Samlede Værker*, Klaus P. Mortensen (ed.), 15 vols. (Copenhagen: Det Danske Sprog- og Litteraturselskab/Gyldendal, 2003–), vol. 7, p. 101

Bang, Herman, "*Gengangere*," *Vor Tid* (Copenhagen), August 26, 1883

Bang, Herman, *Stuk* (Copenhagen: J. H. Schubothe, 1887)

Banks, William, "Ibsen and Kierkegaard Revisited: The Dialectics of Despair in *Brand*," *Ibsen Studies* 4:2 (2004), 176–90

Bendixson, Arthur, "Några Ord om Ibsens *Gengangere*," *Ny Svensk Tidskrift* (1881), 455

Benjamin, Walter, *Charles Baudelaire: A Lyric Poet in the Era of High Capitalism*, Harry Zohn (trans.) (London: NLB, 1973)

Berman, Marshall, *All That Is Solid Melts into Air: The Experience of Modernity* (New York: Penguin, 1982)

Borg, Mette, "Her Tales ikke Dukkehjem: Omkring Urpremieren på Ibsens *Et Dukkehjem*," *Norsk Dramatisk Årbok* (1997), 10–17
Brandes, Edvard, "Henrik Ibsens *Et Dukkehjem* paa Det kgl. Theater," *Ude og Hjemme* 118 (January 1880), 148–53
Brandes, Edvard, "Lindbergs Opførelse af *Gjengangere*," *Ude og Hjemme* 6 (September 2, 1883), 594–95
Brandes, Georg, "Henrik Ibsens *Digte*," *Illustreret Tidende* (October 22, 1871), 32–33
Brandes, Georg, "Henrik Ibsen: *Gengangere*," *Morgenbladet* (Copenhagen), December 28, 1881
Brandes, Georg, "Henrik Ibsen. *Naar vi Døde Vaagner*," *Verdens Gang* (Christiania), December 28, 1899
Brochmann, Odd, "Fra Kolde Hvide Vægge til Tegl og Træ," in *Om Hygge: Ti Kroniker* (Copenhagen: Politikens Forlag, 1965), pp. 67–74
Brun, M. V. "*Et Dukkehjem*, Skuespil i 3 Akter af Henrik Ibsen," *Folkets Avis* (Copenhagen), December 24, 1879
Bugge, M. J., *Hvorledes Nora Kom Hjem Igjen: Et Efterspil* (Christiania: Cammermeyer, 1881)
Bull, Francis, "Indledning," *Samlede Verker* (Hundreårsutgave), Francis Bull, Halvdan Koht, and Didrik Seip (eds.), vol. 9 (Oslo: Gyldendal Norsk Forlag, 1932), pp. 9–48
"*Bygmester Solness* i Kjøbenhavn," *Bergens Tidende* (Bergen), March 13, 1893
Bøgh, Erik, "Dit og Dat," *Dagens Nyheder* (Copenhagen), December 24, 1879
"c.," "Kristiania Theater," *Aftenposten* (Christiania), January 13, 1885
C. D. W. "Litteratur," *Post och Inrikes-Tidningar* (Stockholm), January 2, 1882
Cameron, Rebecca, "Ibsen and British Women's Drama," *Ibsen Studies* 4.1 (2004), 92–102
Caspari, Theodor, "*Bygmester Solness*," *Aftenposten* (Christiania), January 4, 1893
Collins, Jo and John Jervis (eds.), *Uncanny Modernity: Cultural Theories, Modern Anxieties* (New York: Palgrave Macmillan, 2008)
Dagbladet (Christiania), January 21, 1880, accessed at http://ibsen.nb.no/id/11157764.0
Dahl, Herleiv, *Bergmannen og Byggmesteren: Henrik Ibsen som Lyriker* (Oslo: Gyldendal, 1958)
Davis, Rick and Brian Johnston (trans.), *Ibsen: Four Major Plays*, vol. 1 (Lyme, NH: Smith and Kraus, 1995)
"Der Schluß von Ibsens Nora: Eine Aufklärung," *Das Litterarische Echo* 2:13 (April 1, 1900), 969–70
Dickmar, Helene, "Henrik Ibsen: Bygmester Solness," *To Litterære Studier* (Christiania: H. Aschehoug & Co., 1895), 24–75
"Din gamle Ven," "Fra Tilskuerbænken (Brev til en Udenbys)," *Aftenbladet* (Christiania), January 28, 1880
Durbach, Errol, *A Doll's House: Ibsen's Myth of Transformation* (Boston: Twayne, 1991)
E. V., "*Rosmersholm*," *Dagbladet* (Christiania), April 13, 1887

Egge, Peter, "Ibsen i Italia," *Minner fra Nord og Syd* (Oslo: Gyldendal Norsk Forlag, 1952), pp. 58–63
Eisner, Kurt, "Professor Rubeks Puppenheim," *Sozialistische Monatshefte* 4 (1900), 24–30
Eriksen, Ludvig and Henrik Jæger, "Et Tilsvar," *Christiania Intelligenssedler* (Christiania), November 18, 1884
Eriksen, Ludvig and Henrik Jæger, "Journalistik og Søndagskritik," *Christiania Intelligenssedler* (Christiania), November 20, 1884
Eriksen, Ludvig and Henrik Jæger, "Seneste Efterretniger," *Christiania Intelligenssedler* (Christiania), November 12, 1884
Eyre, Sarah and Ra Page (eds.), *The New Uncanny: Tales of Unease* ([Manchester]: Comma Press, 2008)
F., "Opførelsen af Et Dukkehjem," *Aftenbladet* (Christiania), January 26, 1880
F–n, "Henrik Ibsens *Gengangere* paa Scenen," *Aftenposten* (Christiania), August 25, 1883
Falkman, Adolf, "Henrik Ibsens *Gengangere* paa Scenen," *Aftenposten* (Christiania), August 25, 1883
Figueiredo, Ivo de, *Henrik Ibsen: Masken* (Oslo: Aschehoug, 2007)
Fjelde, Rolf (trans.), *Ibsen: The Complete Major Prose Plays* (New York: Plume, 1965)
Foreningen til Norske Fortidsmindesmerkers Bevaring, Aarsberetning for 1858 (Christiania: Carl C. Werner & Comp., 1859)
Freud, Sigmund, "Some Character-Types Met with in Psychoanalytic Work (1916)," in James Strachey (ed.), *The Standard Edition of the Complete Psychological Works of Sigmund Freud*, 24 vols. (London: Hogarth Press, 1953–74), vol. 14, pp. 309–36
Freud, Sigmund, "The 'Uncanny' (1919)," in James Strachey (ed.), *The Standard Edition of the Complete Psychological Works of Sigmund Freud*, 24 vols. (London: Hogarth Press, 1953–74), vol. 17, pp. 217–56
Freud, Sigmund, *Det Uhyggelige*, Hans Christian Fink (trans.), afterword by Nils Otto Steen and Steen Visholm, Rævens Sort Bibliotek 43 (Copenhagen: Forlaget Politisk Revy, 1998)
Fried, Michael, *Absorption and Theatricality: Painting and Beholder in the Age of Diderot* (Chicago: University of Chicago Press, 1980)
Fulsås, Narve (ed.), *Biografisk Leksikon til Ibsens Brev – Med Tidstavle* (Oslo: Senter for Ibsen-Studier, 2013)
Fædrelandet (Copenhagen), December 22, 1879, accessed at http://ibsen.nb.no/id/19567.0
Færden, Michael Johan, "*En Folkefiende* af Henrik Ibsen: I–II," *Luthersk Ugeskrift* (Christiania), December 16 and 23, 1882
"G.," "Henrik Ibsen: *Et Dukkehjem*," *Bergens Aftenblad* (Bergen), January 2, 1880
Garborg, Arne, "Henrik Ibsen: *Gengangere*," *Dagbladet* (Christiania), December 14, 1881
Garborg, Arne, "*Samfundets Støtter*," *Fedraheimen* (Christiania), November 3, 1877
"*Gengangere*," *Aftenposten* (Christiania), December 14, 1881

"*Gengangere*," *Morgenbladet* (Christiania), December 18, 1881
"*Gengangere*," *Throndhjems Stiftsavis* (Trondheim), February 6, 1882
Gosse, Edmund, "Ibsen's New Drama," *The Fortnightly Review* 49 (new series) (January-June, 1891), 4–13
Graf, Klaus, "Das Leckt die Kuh Nicht ab: 'Zufällige Gedanken' zu Schriftlichkeit und Errinerungskultur der Strafgerichtsbarkeit," in Andreas Blauert and Gerd Schwerhoff (eds.), *Kriminalitätsgeschichte: Beiträge zur Sozial- und Kulturgeschichte der Vormoderne* (Konstanz: UVK, 2000), pp. 245–88
Halvorsen, Jens Bragge, *Bibliografiske Oplysninger til Henrik Ibsens Samlede Værker* (Copenhagen: Gyldendal, 1901)
Hamilton, Ulf, private correspondence to the author, April 7, 2008
Hansen, P., "*Et Dukkehjem* og Recensenterne: Kritiske Betragtninger," *Kristiansands Stiftsavis* (Kristiansand), February 12, 1880
Hansen, Tom Lerdrup, *Kampen omkring Nora: Et Dukkehjems Tilblivelse og dets Modtagelse 1879–80* (Copenhagen: Gyldendal, 1988)
Heiberg, Edvard, "Hvordan Har De Det?" *Kritisk Revy* 1 (1927), 31–34
Helland, Frode, *Melankoliens Spill: En Studie i Henrik Ibsens Siste Dramaer* (Oslo: Universitetsforlaget, 2000)
"Henrik Ibsen og Kristiania Theater," *Dagbladet* (Christiania), December 22, 1881
"H. H.," "Kristiania Theater," *Dagbladet* (Christiania), January 20, 1885
Holmberg, Hans, "August Lindberg, Herman Bang, och en Historisk Teaterpremiäre i Helsingborg," *Kring Kärnan* 16 (1986), 147–60
Horn, E. F. B., "Unødvendig Bekymring," *Aftenposten* (Christiania), January 8, 1893
Howe, Nicholas, "Introduction," in Nicholas Howe (ed.), *Home and Homelessness in the Medieval and Renaissance World* (Notre Dame, IN: University of Notre Dame Press, 2004), pp. 1–12
Ibsen, Henrik, "Paa Vidderne," *Illustreret Nyhedsblads Nytaarsgave for 1860*, pp. 57–70
Ibsen, Henrik, *Digte* (Copenhagen: Gyldendal, 1871)
Ibsen, Henrik, *Henrik Ibsens Skrifter*, Vigdis Ystad and Narve Fulsås (eds.), 17 vols. (Oslo: Aschehoug, 2005–10)
Ibsen, Henrik, Letter to Erik af Edholm, January 3, 1880, *HIS*, vol. 14.1, pp. 11–12
Ibsen, Henrik, Letter to Lorentz Dietrichson, December 19, 1879, *HIS*, vol. 13.1, pp. 530–32
Ibsen, Henrik, Letter to Sophie Adlersparre, June 24, 1882, *HIS*, vol. 14.1, p. 136
Ibsen, Henrik, *Samlede Verker* (Hundreårsutgave), Francis Bull, Halvdan Koht, and Didrik Seip (eds.), 21 vols. (Oslo: Gyldendal Norsk Forlag, 1928–57)
Ingwersen, Faith, "Norwegian Women Writers," in Harald S. Naess (ed.), *A History of Norwegian Literature*, vol. 2 of *A History of Scandinavian Literatures* (Lincoln: University of Nebraska Press, 1993), pp. 349–71
Irgens-Hansen, Johan, "Literaturtidende," *Dagbladet* (Christiania), November 16, 1884
Jay, Martin, *Cultural Semantics: Keywords of Our Time* (Amherst: University of Massachusetts Press, 1998)

Johansen, Jørgen Dines, "Om Sammenhængen mellem Religiøs, Sexuel og Social Tematik i Ibsens *Bygmester Solness*," in Finn Hauberg Mortensen (ed.), *Tekst/ Historie: Bidrag til Historisering af Tekstlæsning i Gymnasiet* (Copenhagen: Samlerens Forlag, 1980), pp. 39–60

"*John Gabriel Borkman* paa Kristiania Teater," *Dagbladet* (Christiania), January 26, 1897

Jæger, Henrik, "Henrik Ibsen: *En Folkefiende*," *Aftenposten* (Christiania), November 29–December 6, 1882

Jæger, Henrik, "Kristiania Theater," *Christiania Intelligenssedler* (Christiania), January 13, 1885

Jæger, Henrik, *Henrik Ibsen 1828–1888: Et Literært Livsbillede* (Copenhagen: Gyldendalske Boghandels Forlag, 1888)

Jæger, Henrik, *Henrik Ibsen og Hans Værker* (Christiania and Copenhagen: Alb. Cammermeyers Forlag, 1892)

Kieler, Vagn and Otto Westengaard-Hildinge, *Fra Aalsgaard: Om Ibsens Nora og en Drengs Erindringer*, Egnshistoriske Beretninger 18 (Aalsgaard, Denmark: Hellebæk-Aalsgaard Egnshistoriske Forening, 1985)

Kinck, B. M., "Henrik Ibsen og Laura Keiler," *Edda* 35 (1935), 498–543

Kittang, Atle, *Henrik Ibsens Heroisme: Frå* Brand *til* Når Vi Døde Vågner (Oslo: Gyldendal, 2002)

Kjær, Nils, "Ibsens Bog," *Dagbladet* (Christiania), December 12, 1894

Kleist, Heinrich von, "The Puppet Theater," *Selected Writings*, David Constantine (ed. and trans.) (Indianapolis, IN: Hackett Publishing Co., 1997), pp. 411–16

Kleist, Heinrich von, "Über das Marionettentheater," *Berliner Abendblätter* (Berlin), December 12–15, 1810

Knudsen, Trygve and Alf Sommerfelt (eds.), *Norsk Riksmålsordbok* (Oslo: Aschehoug, 1937)

Koht, Halvdan, *The Life of Ibsen*, 2 vols. (New York: W. W. Norton & Co., 1931)

"Korrespondance til *Aftenposten*," *Aftenposten* (Christiania), December 24, 1879

Krag, Thomas P., "Den Norske Maaned: *Rosmersholm*," *Urd: Illust. Ugeblad for Kvinden og Hjemmet* 12 (September 19, 1908), 448–49

Kristensen, Evald Tang, *Danske Sagn som De har Lydt i Folkemunde*, 7 vols. (Copenhagen: Woels Forlag, 1928–39)

"Kristiania Theater. *Vildanden*," *Aftenposten* (Christiania), September 24, 1893

Kövecses, Zoltán, *Metaphor: A Practical Introduction*, 2nd ed. (New York: Oxford University Press, 2010)

Lakoff, George and Mark Johnson, *Metaphors We Live By* (Chicago: University of Chicago Press, 1980)

Langås, Unni, "Fascinasjon og Uhygge: Kunsten og Døden som Kvinne i Ibsens Drama *Når Vi Døde Vågner*," *Tidskrift för Litteraturvetenskap* 31.1 (2002), 28–50

Lassen, H., "Kristiania Teater: *Et Dukkehjem*," *Christiania Intelligenssedler* (Christiania), January 22, 1880

Le Gallienne, Eva (trans.), *Six Plays by Henrik Ibsen* (New York: Modern Library, 1951)

Levin, Poul, "Om *Rosmersholm*," *Tilskueren* (1910), 453–65

Levy, Jette Lundbo, "Skulptur som intertekst i *Når Vi Døde Vågner*," *Agora: Journal for Metafysisk Spekulasjon* 2–3 (1993), 26–32

"Literatur: *Gjengangere* [sic]," *Aftenbladet* (Christiania), December 19, 1881

Litzmann, Berthold, *Das Deutsche Drama* (Hamburg: Verlag von Leopold Voss, 1894)

Lukács, George, "Marx and the Problem of Ideological Decay," excerpted in Charles Lyons (ed.), *Critical Essays on Henrik Ibsen* (Boston: G. K. Hall & Co., 1987), pp. 95–99

"M-.," "Lykken Bedre end Forstanden: Et Efterspil," *Aalesunds Blad* (Ålesund, Norway), April 30–May 21, 1880

Madsen, Peter, "The Destruction of Rome," in Astrid Sæther (ed.), *Ibsen and the Arts: Painting–Sculpture–Architecture, Acta Ibseniana* 1 (Oslo: Centre for Ibsen Studies, 2002), pp. 151–58

Mamroth, Fedor, *Aus der Frankfurter Theaterchronik (1889–1907)*, vol. 2 (Berlin: Egon Fleischel & Co., 1908)

Manzoni, Alessandro, "Storia della Colonna Infama," in *I Promessi Sposi* (Milano: Tip. Guglielmini e Radaelli, 1840), pp. 747–864

McFarlane, James Walter (trans.), *Four Major Plays* (New York: Oxford University Press, 1981)

McFarlane, James Walter, "Revaluations of Ibsen," in James Walter McFarlane (ed.), *Discussions of Henrik Ibsen* (Boston: D. C. Heath and Company, 1962), pp. 19–27

Meyer, Michael, *Ibsen: A Biography* (Garden City, NY: Doubleday & Co., Inc., 1971)

Miller, William Ian, "Home and Homelessness in the Middle of Nowhere," in Nicholas Howe (ed.), *Home and Homelessness in the Medieval and Renaissance World* (Notre Dame, IN: University of Notre Dame Press, 2004), pp. 125–42

Moi, Toril, *Henrik Ibsen and the Birth of Modernism: Art, Theater, Philosophy* (New York: Oxford University Press, 2006)

Morgenstierne, Bredo, "Ibsens *Fruen fra Havet*," *Aftenposten* (Christiania), December 5, 1888

Møller, Lis, "The Analytic Theater: Freud and Ibsen," *The Scandinavian Psychoanalytic Review* 13 (1990), 112–28

Nansen, Peter, "Den Første Opførelse," *Vor Tid* (Copenhagen), August 26, 1883

Norsk Riksmålsordbok, 2 vols. (Oslo: Aschehoug, 1937)

"Oskar H.," "*Samfundets Støtter* paa Engelsk Grund: Korrespondance fra London til *Illustreret Tidende*," *Illustreret Tidende* (December 26, 1880), 178–79

Poe, Edgar Allan, "The Fall of the House of Usher," in Thomas Ollive Mabbott (ed.), *The Collected Works of Edgar Allan Poe*, 3 vols. (Cambridge, MA: Harvard University Press, 1978), vol. 2, pp. 392–421

Provensal, Henry, *L'Art de Demain: Vers l'Harmonie Intégrale* (Paris: Perrin, 1904)

Provensal, Henry, *L'Habitation Salubre et à Bon Marché* (Paris: Librairie Générale de l'Architecture et des Arts Décoratifs, 1908)

Rem, Tore, *Henry Gibson/Henrik Ibsen: Den Provinsielle Verdensdikteren* (Oslo: J. W. Cappelens Forlag, 2006)

Rokem, Freddie, *Theatrical Space in Ibsen, Chekhov, and Strindberg: Public Forms of Privacy, Theater and Dramatic Studies* 32 (Ann Arbor, MI: UMI Research Press, 1986)
Rosen, Philip, *Change Mummified: Cinema, Historicity, Theory* (Minneapolis: University of Minnesota Press, 2001)
Rothenburg-Mens, Arthur, "En Dansk Ibsenopførelse," *Kunst og Dilettantisme paa det Nordiske Teater: Nogle Bemærkninger om Drama og Skuespilkunst* (Copenhagen: Holger Ferlovs Forlag, 1906)
Royle, Nicholas, *The Uncanny* (Manchester: Manchester University Press, 2003)
Rønning, Helge, *Den Umulige Friheten* (Oslo: Gyldendal, 2006)
S–e., "Hvad är Ibsens Mening i *Rosmersholm*? Ett Tolkningsförsök," *Aftonbladet* (Stockholm), January 11, 1887
Sandberg, Mark B. "Ibsen and the Mimetic Home of Modernity," *Ibsen Studies* 1.2 (2001), 32–58
Sandberg, Mark B., *Living Pictures, Missing Persons: Mannequins, Museums, and Modernity* (Princeton, NJ: Princeton University Press, 2003)
Scott, Erika Ravne, "En Dukkestue til Tordis – 1890," *Norsk Husflid* 5 (1989), 6–7
Scott, Erika Ravne, private correspondence to the author, July 1, 2008
Sehmsdorff, Henning, "Two Legends about St. Olaf, The Master Builder: A Clue to the Dramatic Structure of Henrik Ibsen's *Bygmester Solness*," *Edda* 54.4 (1967), 263–71
Selmer, Ågot Gjems, *Et Hjem for Mennesker: En Menneskeskildring i Tre Handlinger* (Christiania: Aschehoug, 1901)
Sharp, R. Farquharson (trans.), *Four Great Plays* (New York: Bantam Books, 1971)
Shideler, Ross, *Questioning the Father: From Darwin to Zola, Ibsen, Strindberg, and Hardy* (Stanford, CA: Stanford University Press, 1999)
Sinding-Larsen, Alfred, *Om Henrik Ibsen: Fruen fra Havet og Personerne deri* (Kristiania: Albert Cammermeyer, 1889)
Skram, Amalie, "En Betragtning over *Et Dukkehjem*," *Dagbladet* (Christiania), January 19, 1880
Skram, Amalie, "Mere om *Gengangere*," *Dagbladet* (Christiania), April 27, 1882
Skram, Erik, "Henrik Ibsens *Vildanden*," *Illustreret Tidende* 26 (March 1, 1885), 285–86
States, Bert O., *Great Reckonings in Little Rooms: On the Phenomenology of Theater* (Berkeley: University of California Press, 1992)
Sæther, Astrid, *Suzannah: Fru Ibsen* (Oslo: Gyldendal Norsk Forlag, 2008)
Sødal, Helje Kringlebotn, "Henrik Ibsens *Brand*: Illustrasjon på en Teologisk Suspensjon av det Etiske?" *Edda* (1999), 63–70
Sørensen, Jon, "*Naar Vi Døde Vaagner*," *Norsk Skoletidende: Tillægshefte* 1 (1900), 51–60
"Teater, Kunst og Literatur: Kristiania Theater," *Dagen* (Christiania), April 16, 1887
Templeton, Joan, *Ibsen's Women* (New York: Cambridge University Press, 1997)
"Theatret: *Rosmersholm*," *Bergens Tidende* (Bergen), January 20, 1887
Thrane, Carl, "Det Kongelige Theater: *Et Dukkehjem*, Skuespil i Tre Acter af Henrik Ibsen," *Illustreret Tidende* 21:1057 (December 28, 1879), 145, 148

Thrane, Carl, "Det Kongelige Theater: *Samfundets Støtter*, Skuespil i Fire Akter af Henrik Ibsen," *Illustreret Tidende* (November 25, 1877), 81–82

Tjønneland, Eivind, "Darwin, J. P. Jacobsen og Ibsen," *Arr: Idéhistorisk Tidsskrift* 10.4–11.1 (1998–99), 54–64

Törnqvist, Egil, *Ibsen: A Doll's House* (Cambridge: Cambridge University Press, 1995)

Vedel, Valdemar, "Ibsens Nye Skuespil," *Tilskueren* 17 (January 1900), 81–86

Vidler, Anthony, *The Architectural Uncanny: Essays in the Modern Unhomely* (Cambridge, MA: The MIT Press, 1992)

Vogt, Nils, "*John Gabriel Borkman*," *Morgenbladet* (Christiania), December 24, 1896

Vullum, Eirik, "*En Folkefiende*," *Dagbladet* (Christiania), November 30, 1882

Vullum, Erik, "Literatur-Tidende," *Dagbladet* (Christiania), December 6, 1879

Warburg, Karl, "Ibsens Nya Stycke," *Göteborgs handels- och sjöfartstidning* (Gothenburg), December 15, 1881

Watt, Peter (trans.), *Ghosts and Other Plays* (Baltimore: Penguin Books, Inc., 1973)

Wirmark, Margareta, *Noras Systrar: Nordisk Dramatik och Teater 1879–99* (Stockholm: Carlssons Bokförlag, 2000)

Wærp, Lisbeth P., "Oppstandelsen som Forførerisk Morder," in Lisbeth P. Wærp (ed.), *Livet på Likstrå: Henrik Ibsens Når vi døde vågner* (Oslo: Landslaget for Norskundervisning and Cappelen Akademisk Forlag, 1999), pp. 94–121

Østerud, Erik, *Theatrical and Narrative Space: Studies in Ibsen, Strindberg, and J. P. Jacobsen* (Aarhus, Denmark: Aarhus University Press, 1998)

Index

Aarseth, Asbjørn, 62–64, 74, 104–105, 108, 112, 113
  doll metaphor and, 71
  façades unmasked, 62
  glasskab, 63
  The Lady from the Sea, 105
Adlersparre, Sophie, 37
Alnæs, Nina, 6
Archer, William, 61
"architectonic masterpiece (*arkitektonisk mesterverk*)", 125
architectural metaphors, 8–17, 23–24, 58, 61–62, 66–69, 79–81, 129, 135–137, 176–179, 189
  in culture and literature, 4
  "foundational," 14
  "Ibsenian house" and, 10
  and *The Lady from the Sea*, 105
  language of, 2
  and McFarlane's views, 179
  of *Pillars of Society*, 2, 79
  theatrical and, 67
  and unmasking the home, 58
The Architectural Uncanny: Essays in the Modern Unhomely (Vidler), 20
"architectural unease," 11
architecture
  architectural discourse, 14–17
  domestic, 181
  façade, 62, 89
  of forgetting, 168–175
  Ibsen's sense of, 182
  metaphors (*See* architectural metaphors)
  modernization metaphor, 8, 178
  persistence, duration, 11–12
  preservation, 131–133
  renovation, razing, 130–131, 153–168
  restoration, 131–133
  tenacity of, 130–175
  theatrical critiques of, 3

bachelor home, 88
Bang, Herman, 47, 62
Benjamin, Walter, 25
Bjørnson, Bjørnstjerne, 123, 157
Brandes, Edvard, 78–79, 87, 155–156
Brandes, Georg, 4, 27, 39
Brand (Ibsen), 41–44, 134, 159, 168–169, 180, 182–183
  church, 146–153
  "To the Accomplices," 133–134
Brun, M. V., 45, 76
"Building Plans" (Ibsen), 3
Bull, Francis, 36, 133
Butenschøn, Helene, 123–125, 162, 184

Cameron, Rebecca, 17
"Captain Alving's Home," 89–90
Caspari, Theodor, 126–129, 146
Change Mummified (Rosen), 131–133
Christiania Theater production of *A Doll House*, 32
Christmas *hygge*, 35–44
"A Church" (Ibsen), 4–6, 146
Clean and Affordable Housing (*L'Habitation Salubre et à Bon Marché*), 188
Collins, Jo, 22

Dahl, Herleiv, 56
"*Das Unheimliche*" (Freud), 18–20
The Day of Resurrection (Rubek's sculpture), 112
det Rentheimske hus (the Rentheim house), 139
"*Det Uhyggelige*" (Freud), 26
Dickmar, Helen, 123
Dietrichson, Lorentz, 147, 157
dockskåp ("doll cabinet"), 74
"A Doll Home," translation as, 72
doll house as physical object, 72–75
dollhouse existence, 86

223

A Doll House (Ibsen), 12, 14–17, 29–37, 45–47, 57–58, 68–84, 87, 95, 120, 123–124, 181, 184
   Brandes's review in 1879, 78–79
   critiques of, 2
   Doll housing, 68–84
   Façades unmasked, 57–58
   Helmer's household, 29
   hide-and-seek game, 57
   hyggelig Christmas, 33, 35–44
   hyggelig effect in, 32–33
   Moi's ethical question, 70–71
   Scandinavian theatre expectations, 46
   sequels to, 79–81
   transparent home, ideas of, 75
   true homes, 87
dukkehjem as neologism, 69–70
dukkestue, meaning of, 70, 73–74
Durbach, Errol, 83

Egge, Peter, 34
Emperor and Galilean (Ibsen), 134
An Enemy of the People (Ibsen), 49, 86, 91–96, 157–158
"Epic Brand," 56, 133, 138

façades unmasked, 58–60
family home, 88
Færden, Johan Michael, 95–96
Fjelde, Rolf, 70, 170
"foundational" architectural metaphors, 14
Freud, Sigmund, 18–19, 21, 26–27, 45, 113, 133–134, 143
Fried, Michael, 58
"From My Domestic Life" (Ibsen), 56, 181

Garborg, Arne, 1–2, 27, 66–68
A Gauntlet (Bjørnson), 123
gengangere and the living dead, 136–140
Ghosts (Ibsen), 2–3, 21–23, 27, 30, 147, 158, 169–171, 182, 185
   Adlersparre's 1882 lecture on, 15
   burning of orphanage complex, 157
   cozy impressions in, 23
   Helene Alving as master builder, 154–155
   Lindberg's traveling production, 155–156
   productions of, 33–35
   reported pain of audience for, 47–49
   Rosenvold villa, 2
   sinkhole metaphors in, 88–91
   spøgelse vs. *gengangere*, 136–138
   tellability of painful reactions to, 47–49
glasskab metaphor, 63–65
Gosse, Edmund, 36
Gråbrødretorv, 172

hængedynd, 78, 91
Hansen, Irgens, 95
"The Happiness that Surpasses Understanding – A Sequel" (*Alesunds Blad*), 80
Hedda Gabler (Ibsen), 2, 38, 109–111, 119, 139, 183
Heiberg, Edvard, 189–190
Helland, Frode, 71, 101, 114–115, 162
Hennings, Betty, 55, 119–121
home and house
   bachelor home, 88
   cleaning, 93
   domestic metaphor, 85
   family home, 88
   homelessness, 20, 59–60, 116–122, 135, 161, 177
   linguistic distinctions, 85–87
   marginal occupants, 115–122
   model home, 60–68
   Osvald's definition, 88
   resilience of home, 122–129
   unmasking of, 58–59, 223
A Home for People (Selmer), 184–185
"homes for people" metaphor, 186
Horn, E. F. B., 129
Howe, Nicholas, 118
hygge, uhygge, 25–35, 181
   Christmas *hygge*, 35–44
   Ibsen as master of, 44–55, 181
   physical effects, 50
   uncanny, usage of term, 50

Ibsen, autobiography attempt, 3
"Ibsenian house," 10
Ibsen's Women (Templeton), 97–100, 118–119, 122

jagtslot (hunting castle), 114
Jay, Martin, 22
Jervis, John, 22
Johansen, Jørgen Dines, 102
John Gabriel Borkman, 7, 38, 106–107, 111, 119, 139–140, 164–166, 171–175
Johnson, Mark, 9
Jæger, Henrik, 49–55, 91–92, 146–148, 189

Kieler, Laura, 69
Kittang, Atle, 144
Kritisk Revy, 189
Kövecses, Zoltán, 9

The Lady from the Sea (Ibsen), 23, 29, 38, 104–109, 113, 139, 164
Lakoff, George, 9
La Maison de Solness le Constructeur (Provensal), 186
Langås, Unni, 21
L'Art de Demain: Vers l'Harmonie Intégrale (Provensal), 186

Le Gallienne, Eva, 90
Levin, Poul, 145
L'Habitation Salubre et à Bon Marché (Provensal), 188
Lindberg's production of *Ghosts,* 33–34, 47–49
Little Eyolf (Ibsen), 7, 105–106, 111, 163–164
løvhytte (arbor), 105
Lukács, George, 23, 118
lysthus (garden pavilion), 105

Manzoni, Alessandro, 172
The Master Builder, 21, 23, 58, 71, 100–102, 111, 117, 119, 136, 146, 158–163
  audience familiarity with text of play, 13–14
  doll motif in, 71
  "homes for people" theme in, 114
  idealist readings of, 123–126
  poem linked to the play, 100
  radical reading of, 126–129
  reviews, 13–14
  as source for critical metaphor, 2, 6–7, 122–123
  true homes, Ibsen's thinking about, 101
Maurice, Chéri, 80–81
McFarlane, James, 179–180
metaphoric entailment, 9–10
metaphoric relationships, 9–10
metaphoric source domain, 9–11
Metaphors We Live By (Lakoff, Johnson), 9
Meyer, Michael, 80–81
Miller, William Ian, 136
mindesmærke (memorial), 169
mirror and the uncanny, 56–58, 181
Moi, Toril, 39, 41, 60, 64–65, 70–71, 82, 109
Morgenstierne, Bredo, 107

Niemann-Raabe, Hedwig, 80–81
"Nordic nihilism" (Ibsen), 2
Norwegian Folk Museum, 72–74

"On the Heights" (Ibsen), 38–41, 44, 55, 56, 59, 128–129, 160
"On the Marionette Theatre" (von Kleist), 57–58

partial metaphorical utilization, 9
Peer Gynt (Ibsen), 3, 5, 128, 133–134
The Pillar of Shame (*skamstøtten*), 173
Pillars of Society (Ibsen), 23, 25, 30, 60–68, 74–75, 78–82, 86, 95, 139, 181
  Aarseth analysis, 62–64
  architectural metaphor of, 2
  Garborg critique, 1–2, 66–67
  pillar of society as metaphor, 65–67, 79, 95
  theater as *glasskab,* 62–63
  title in English translation, 61
Poe, Edgar Allan, 4, 21, 142

The Pretenders (Ibsen), 133
Provensal, Henry, 186–188, 186–189

Rentheim house (*det Rentheimske hus*), 139
resilience of home, 122–129
Rosen, Philip, 131–133, 164–165
Rosmersholm (Ibsen), 2, 14, 21, 31, 38, 50, 127–128, 138–146, 164, 177, 183, 189–190
Rothenburg-Mens, Arthur, 55
Royle, Nicholas, 18–19
Rønning, Helge, 24–25, 136

"The School House" (Ibsen), 3
Selmer, Ågot, 184–185
sexually transmitted diseases, 89
Shideler, Ross, 157
Sinding-Larsen, Alfred, 38, 108–109
sinkhole metaphor, 91, 93
skamstøtten (The Pillar of Shame), 173
Skien (Ibsen's birthplace), 3
Skram, Amalie, 16
society-as-building, 9–10
States, Bert O., 7
Stucco (Bang), 62
"The Student" (Andersen), 35
Swedish *dockskåp,* Nordic Museum, 74–75
syphilis, 89, 91
Sæther, Astrid, 11
Sørensen, Jon, 125–126

Templeton, Joan, 97–100, 118–119, 122
theatrical and architectural metaphors, 67
"They Sat There, Those Two" (Ibsen), 100
Thrane, Carl, 35, 66
"To my Friend the Revolutionary Speaker" (Ibsen), 156
"To the Accomplices" (Ibsen), 133–134, 136, 146, 148–149

uhygge. See *hygge, uhygge*
Ulfeldts Plads, 172
the uncanny
  architecture as uncanny, 23–24
  critical thinking on, 18–20
  doll motif as uncanny, 71
  Freud's essay on, 18–19, 26, 113
  Gothic motifs, imagery in Ibsen's plays, 21–22
  Ibsens's reputation for, 18, 20–21
  mirror and, 56–58, 181
  modern, 21–23, 166
  ownership as aspect of, 134–146
  "the unhomely," 20–25
  translation as *det uhyggelige,* 26–27
  wildness as aspect of, 113–114
unmasking the home, 58–61

Vedel, Valdemar, 166
Vidler, Anthony, 20–21, 27
The Vikings at Helgeland (Ibsen), 133

Werenskiold, Erik, 4, 180
Wessels gate, 15
When We Dead Awaken (Ibsen), 112–118, 125–126, 166–168, 183

The Wild Duck (Ibsen), 6–7, 12, 16, 30–31, 34–35, 38, 49–50, 57, 71, 86, 96–100, 103
   hygge's role in, 30–31, 49–55
   idealism's depiction in, 96
   illustration of set, 52
   "lightning journalism and," 12, 50–55
   Wilse's photograph of set, 53
Wirmark, Margareta, 17
Wærp, Lisbeth, 116